LORD HAWKE

A Cricketing Legend

JAMES P. COLDHAM

TAURISPARKE
PAPERBACKS

James P. Coldham, member of the Cricket Society and the Association of Cricket Statisticians, has long been an ardent follower of Northamptonshire. His fascination for the Golden Age of English cricket was inherited from his father and cricket historian, James D. Coldham.

To Tina With Love

Published in 2003 by Tauris Parke Paperbacks
an imprint of I.B.Tauris & Co Ltd
6 Salem Road, London W2 4BU
175 Fifth Avenue, New York NY 10010
www.ibtauris.com

In the United States of America and in Canada distributed by
Palgrave Macmillan, a division of St Martin's Press
175 Fifth Avenue, New York NY 10010

First published in 1990 by The Crowood Press

ISBN 1 86064 823 1

A full CIP record for this book is available from the British Library
A full CIP record for this book is available from the Library of Congress

Library of Congress catalog card: available

Printed and bound in Malaysia by SRM Production Services Sdn. Bhd.

Contents

Preface

It was while researching a book about F.S.Jackson that I first began to wonder whether or not posterity had given Lord Hawke a fair crack of the whip. Since there had been no biography of his lordship in the fifty years following his death, I came to the conclusion that it was a question I might attempt to answer myself. This book is the result; it is for the reader to judge whether history has treated our subject justly, or otherwise.

To assist the flow of the narrative I have adopted two conventions throughout: firstly, in those chapters in which I quote directly from Hawke's own *Recollections and Reminiscences,* published in 1924, I fully attribute only the first such quotation. Subsequent quotations of at least two lines or more which are not so attributed may be assumed to have been drawn from this same source. Secondly, I have retained the spelling of place names as they were in Hawke's time (for example, modern day *Pune,* in India, appears as *Poona*).

I recall with gratitude the generosity of those who have offered me support in this endeavour. However, to paraphrase Lord Hawke, a writer's life 'is not all beer and skittles', and with due deference to my friends, I shall name just one person whose patience and understanding has been quietly constant – and without whom I should have been quite at sea – my wife, Tina.

James P. Coldham
1990

Prologue

Bobby Peel was at the height of his powers in 1897. With the possible exception of Lancashire's Johnny Briggs he was the foremost slow left-arm bowler of his day, a remorseless opponent. Peel was a taciturn man who rarely betrayed his emotions on the field; his expression remained the same whether he was being flogged into the deep or he was running through a side. No man was steadier under fire, no bowler less liable to flinch under punishment than Bobby Peel. Over after over he simply went on bowling with the same wicked loop which had the best batsmen playing forward into the unknown, and the rest groping at thin air, thoroughly bamboozled. On a good wicket he was the master of line and length; on a bad one he was a holy terror, virtually unplayable.

Peel had donned the mantle of Edmund Peate, the first of Yorkshire's great left-arm bowlers, a decade before. Unlike his predecessor, in whose shadow he had waited for so long, Peel had, over the years, developed into an all-rounder of the first rank. In his day he was worth his place in any side in the land for his batting alone. Twice in his career he had hit unbeaten double-centuries, 226 against Leicestershire in 1892 in a second-class match, and 210 against Warwickshire in 1896. In the course of the latter innings he had participated in a stand of some 292 runs for the eighth Yorkshire wicket and in so doing created a record in English cricket that endures to this day.

Since the retirement of George Ulyett at the end of the 1893 season Bobby Peel had been the senior professional in the Yorkshire dressing-room. On the field he was the epitome of steely professionalism. Off it he had an Achilles' heel, which was to cause his sudden and irremedial fall from grace; Bobby Peel was more than somewhat partial to ale.

In an era when even in Yorkshire a professional either brought his own fare to a match or took his chances with the public in the nearest beer tent, Peel's failing was one shared with many of his contemporaries. In Yorkshire there was hardly a man alive who would have turned down the opportunity to buy the great Bobby Peel a pint, or two or five.

Bobby Peel collided head-on with his destiny – in the tall, patrician shape of his county captain, Lord Hawke – on the morning of Thursday 19 August, 1897; the day Yorkshire commenced their penultimate Championship match of the season, against Derbyshire at Bradford.

Earlier that day George Hirst had done his level best to save his friend from himself, but to no avail. Peel had staggered down to breakfast at the professionals' modest hotel while Hirst was eating. Few kindlier men than George Hirst have ever played cricket for either Yorkshire or England. He knew that if Bobby reported for duty in a 'proper state' it would probably be the end of his career with Yorkshire, so he had coaxed, threatened and – when all else failed – manhandled his team-mate back to bed. When Hirst arrived at the Horton Park Avenue Ground he sought out his captain, Lord Hawke, and reported: 'I'm sorry, my lord, Peel's apologies and he's been taken very queer in the night and won't be able to turn out this morning.'

Lord Hawke was most concerned to hear that Peel was unwell and promised to visit him at the close of play. Hirst had anticipated just this response. While many of Hawke's fellow county captains treated their professionals like servants – the redoubtable Joe Darling who captained the Australians in England in 1899,1902 and 1905 said 'like dogs' – his lordship accorded his men both dignity and respect and, what was more, insisted that others should do likewise. However, whilst it was true to say that no other county captain was as interested in the welfare of his professionals as Lord Hawke, the reverse of the coin was that no captain expected so much from them in return. Hirst knew that when Lord Hawke was solicitous on account of Peel's health he was being entirely sincere. But he knew, too, how displeased his captain would have been to have known the true reason for Peel's indisposition.

Derbyshire won the toss and duly took first use of the wicket. It was as Lord Hawke led Yorkshire on to the field that Bobby Peel shambled, red-faced, dishevelled and in as 'properer' a condition as ever, on to the scene. A horrified George Hirst did not dare meet his captain's eye. The situation was then compounded when Peel got his hands on the ball. Lord Hawke approached him. His first thought was probably that the bowler had turned out despite his ailment, in which event the fact that Yorkshire now had twelve men in the field, since Peel had not been named in the eleven, was simply an unfortunate misunderstanding arising out of the player's laudable, if misplaced, devotion to duty. When he discovered Peel was drunk, Hawke's mood swung from mild vexation to simmering, tight-lipped rage.

'Leave the field at once, Peel,' he commanded grimly. The professional stood his ground.

'Not at all, my lord,' he replied, cheerfully. 'I'm in fine form this morning.' Whereupon, legend has it, Peel ran up and bowled a ball to the sightscreen. Another story maintains that the bowler urinated on the wicket. In a sense it hardly matters which tale one believes, for history is in no doubt as to what followed. Lord Hawke took Bobby Peel by the arm and gently guided him off the field and out of Yorkshire cricket. Later the Yorkshire Committee announced that Peel had been suspended. In reality there could be no return for Bobby Peel. Yorkshire's senior professional had publicly disgraced himself, his team and his profession. Like Edmund Peate before him he had transgressed Hawke's law and he had to go. It mattered not one jot that he was the best all-round professional cricketer of his day, nor that he was an automatic choice for any England side, nor even that Yorkshire had no ready replacement for him.

Peel himself was not immediately aware of his predicament. That evening Hirst went looking for him and found him sleeping the sleep of the just, apparently oblivious of the morning's débâcle. The next day Peel was doggedly unrepentent.

'You must write an apology to his lordship at once,' Hirst told him. It was good advice, perhaps the only course of action that might have stayed his friend's execution.

'That I niver will,' Peel declared.

Hirst was appalled: 'Then you're finished, Bobby.'

'Niver i' this world,' Peel said, defiantly. 'They'll have to send for me; they can't do without me.'

Peel was right about the club sending for him. Lord Hawke did ask Peel to come and see him, to be officially dismissed. It was the end of the old Yorkshire Hawke had inherited from Tom Emmett. Peel was the last survivor of the rumbustious band of cricketing buccaneers that Hawke always remembered – with a mixture of pride and sadness – as 'the boys of my old brigade'.

The new Yorkshire that emerged was to dominate English cricket. Hawke's legacy is with us still.

1
Lord Hawke

Lord Hawke was captain of Cambridge University, Yorkshire and England in a time when, as A.A.Thomson has observed, 'there were giants in the land'. His era is now lost to us, shrouded by the fog of war and by economic and social revolutions that would beggar the Victorian imagination. For this reason it is as well to place our subject in the context of his time from the outset.

English cricket has enjoyed many 'golden ages'. The merits of one age can easily and pleasurably be set against those of another; such a debate is intrinsic to the joy of cricket; it wards off despair when the rain falls during the Roses match at Manchester, and it sustains one's soul through the cricketless months of winter. To the true cricket lover every age is a golden age, yet if ever there was a golden age among golden ages it was surely the quarter-century leading up to the Great War; the age of the amateur batsman *par excellence,* that halcyon era in which cricket blossomed not just as the foremost national game, but as the expression of the age.

In those years before the holocaust the batsmanship of W.G. Grace, K.S. Ranjitsinhji, F.S. Jackson, A.C. MacLaren, R.E. Foster, L.C.H. Palairet, C.B. Fry, G.L. Jessop, R.H. Spooner and a host of others stamped itself not simply on the sporting pysche of the nation but upon that of the whole Empire. It is no accident that clichés like 'play up', 'play the game', and 'it's not cricket' became common currency in this period.

Although the game has been through several periods of adaptation and adjustment since 1914 cricket remains the quintessential pastime of the English. The resilience and vitality of the game in the face of what, periodically, have seemed to be unthinkable sea changes, has astonished both its administrators and its practitioners. The abandonment of the distinction between amateurs and professionals meant the loss of the Gentlemen versus Players fixture as recently as 1962.

Since then the advent of limited overs cricket has been a mixed blessing: it has filled grounds, been the financial salvation of first-class counties, and put fielding skills at a premium; but in batting it has put improvisation before technical accomplishment and in bowling changed the emphasis from wicket-taking to containment.

Test matches and the latter stages of the one-day competitions are now the focal points of the modern season, Eton versus Harrow and the Varsity match have declined in importance so that they represent no more than sideshows. Yet English cricket is still recognisably the game it was at the turn of the century. The County Championship survives at the heart of the first-class programme, even if it is the crowds who flock to Test matches and limited-over contests who pay the bills. The Championship remains the cricketing bread and butter of every professional player. If sponsorship and commercialism are the uglier faces of the contemporary game, it is too easy to forget that every age has its darker side and that perhaps the real and imagined evils of the present might be no more or less malign than those of former times.

That despite everything English cricket not only survives in its traditional form, but thrives, is in no small measure the enduring achievement of three men, three eminent Victorians who devoted the greater part of their lives to cricket, and who largely determined the form in which it has come down to later generations: W.G. Grace, Lord Harris, and Lord Hawke.

Tradition has it that W.G. Grace was the ultimate exponent of the game, that Lord Harris was its foremost administrator and that Lord Hawke was its great exporter. W.G. Grace towered over English cricket in those years before and after the turn of the century like a colossus. 'The Champion' was captain of England until he stepped down in 1899 when he was in his fifty-first year. To all intents and purposes W.G. was cricket, the living symbol of every-thing for which Britain and the British stood. In an era before radio or television his face was known the length and breadth of the English-speaking world.

Lord Harris, bulwark of Kent and great man of Lord's and the MCC, ruled English cricket as if it was his personal fiefdom to do with as he pleased. If W.G. was the face of cricket, Harris was its first minister; as others deferred to W.G. on the field, so they bowed to Harris in the Long Room as Lord's.

Of Martin Bladen Hawke, seventh Baron Hawke of Towton, Sir Pelham 'Plum' Warner was to say 'he was the Odysseus of cricket' and that 'he was the first to preach the gospel of cricket throughout the Empire'. Hawke was an indefatigable organiser and leader of tours to Australasia, North and South America, India and Ceylon, South Africa and the West Indies. But the exportation of cricket to the dominions was the beginning, rather than the end of his unique contribution to English cricket. The true object of his life's work was the construction and consolidation of an indestructible cricketing institution; the Yorkshire County Cricket Club.

Of the three men, W.G., Harris and Hawke, Hawke has received by far the worst press. History tends to portray Hawke as an unsympathetic figure, a narrow, inflexible man unable or unwilling to change with the times, a man who put the good of Yorkshire cricket before the good of the wider game. However, in many ways Hawke was his own worst enemy. His detractors were never short of ammunition; indeed most of it was deflected into his critics' hands from the edge of his own bat. His most famous *faux pas* occurred in 1925 when at the Yorkshire Annual General Meeting he departed from his prepared text to speak out spontaneously in defence of A.E.R. Gilligan's captaincy of the England Team in Australia, and concluded:

> Pray God, no professional shall ever captain England. I love and admire them all but we have always had an amateur skipper and when the day comes when we shall have no more amateurs captaining England it will be a thousand pities.

The furore that enveloped Hawke in the following days may be recalled by an anecdote told years later by his friend and confidant, Sir Home Gordon, in his *Background of Cricket* concerning the publication of the fourth edition of Hawke's autobiographical *Recollections and Reminiscences:*

> In the evening paper brought to me just before leaving my office, I read that in acknowledging the vote of thanks, Martin had gratuitously said: 'Pray God, no professional shall ever captain England'. Instantly seizing the telephone, I cancelled the new edition. My common sense was justified, because afterwards only thirty-seven copies in all were sold, and therefore no subsequent cheaper issue could be contemplated. In twenty years of practical experience as a publisher, I never heard of another book being murdered by a single observation.

Plum Warner and Lord Harris were soon in print in their friend's defence, commenting sagely on what they thought Hawke had actually intended to say. It was too late, the damage had been done. The cricketing world suffered a bout of selective amnesia and conveniently forgot that the English professional cricketer had few more influential friends than the Baron.

Hawke was god-fearing, decent to the core, but sometimes very naive. Personally, he was a man of no little charm and diplomacy, but somehow when he got into print, or found himself confronted by an audience he was suddenly fallible. Amongst friends, in the company of his professionals, or in the Committee Room at Lord's he was a model of diplomacy. In the stark light of the public arena where his pronouncements were dissected word by word, his every idiosyncrasy was seized upon and the autocratic iron man of Yorkshire cricket was rarely given the benefit of the doubt. The problem was that to Hawke cricket was never merely a game. In his vision cricket was the embodiment of everything that was best in the British way of life, something above politics, a bridge across cultural, social and racial divides, an immense power for good in the world. Cricket was not therefore a matter about which a gentleman, and by definition an honest man, minced his words. He believed it was his duty to speak his mind about the issues of his day and often it was his undoing. Frankness can be an unsettling thing in private life; in the public eye it is a crippling liability. Hawke never really came to terms with the fact that leadership, whether in sport or any other walk of life, is an essentially political business and so requires a certain sleight of hand and intellectual dexterity. And for this his reputation has been unjustly diminished in the fifty years since his death.

That wise observer of Yorkshire cricket, A.A. Thomson, summed up Hawke's contribution to the shire of the broad acres in his book, *Rhodes and Hirst*:

> The picture of him painted by some modern journalists as an arrogant peer, spurning with his cane a mob of ragged, trembling serfs labelled cricket professionals, is as false as it is ludicrous. When he took over the captaincy, he found himself in charge of a body of talented, hearty and unruly buccaneers; when he retired he left as splendidly welded a county side as ever took the field, and, throughout that time he was more benevolent and less autocratic than Brian Sellars, Yorkshire's other great captain, could begin to be.

In so doing Thomson was echoing the valedictory thoughts of that other doyen of the affairs Yorkshire cricket, J.M. Kilburn, writing in his *History of Yorkshire County Cricket 1924–1949* on the subject of Hawke's leadership of the club:

> He gave to professional cricket a status of dignity and pride, and by his insistence upon an attractive standard of payment and living conditions he could ask for a correspondingly high standard of conduct, so drawing to professional cricket men of admirable character. It was one of life's ironies that he who had devoted so much time and endeavour to the welfare of the professional cricketer should bring a world-wide storm upon himself by a misunderstood reference to professional cricket.

As a player Hawke suffers from any comparison with W.G. Grace or Lord Harris. W.G. had no equal, while Harris was a batsman worthy of inclusion in any representative side of the 1880s. However, Hawke was no makeweight. In his *Cricket Scores and Biographies, Volume XIV*, Arthur Haygarth paid him the following compliment:

> A first-rate batsman, steady and sure, combined with hard hitting. He possesses an excellent style, and has obtained many long scores in the best matches of the day. Is also a capital field, generally taking long leg, or long off.

High scoring was the exception, rather than the rule, in first-class cricket when Hawke came into the game in the 1880s. Pitch preparation was then in its infancy and the ball generally held sway over the bat. Of the batsmen of the period W.G. Grace alone was the master of his art. An average in the mid-twenties was often sufficient to top a county's list for a season. In 1890 Hawke was second in the Yorkshire batting averages behind G.P. Harrison – a tail-ender who owed his elevated position to having only been dismissed twice that year – with the modest average of 23.17. In later years when higher scoring, particularly by Yorkshiremen, became customary, there were those who claimed Hawke did not warrant his place in the side. It was an argument that the captain wrestled with for many years, and there can be little doubt that had a suitable candidate for the captaincy come forward at almost any time after the 1902 season Hawke would certainly have stepped down in his favour. As it was, he showed from time to time, invariably when his side most needed runs, that he was more than equal to the task of putting together a handy score. He was in his forty-fourth year when he scored his last Championship century in 1904, and was good enough to hit fifties in each of the seasons of 1905, 1907 and 1908.

He was the most unselfish of batsmen. At the outset he was an opener, but in the 1890s when Yorkshire could boast an order built around the professional core of Jack Brown, John Tunnicliffe, David Denton, George Hirst, Bobby Peel and Ted Wainwright, augmented by amateurs of the calibre of Stanley Jackson, Frank Mitchell and Ernest Smith, Hawke dropped down to eighth or ninth, even tenth in the batting list. In the second half of his career he rarely had the opportunity to play the long innings he was capable of playing. In an age when declarations were not permitted until the third day of the match, it was frequently his lot to go out to bat and deliberately throw away his wicket in order to let his bowlers get at the opposition. He had no time for batsmen who fawned on their average or for gifted individuals who could not or would not give their all for the good of the team.

Hawke's career in the first-class game spanned the years 1881 to 1912. His first match was for Yorkshire against MCC at Scarborough, his last, for the premier club against the Argentine Republic in Buenos Aires. He appeared in 633 matches, scoring 16,749 runs at the respectable average of 20.15. In the course of 936 innings he hit thirteen centuries and sixty-nine fifties. He was a bad starter, never very secure when he first came in, but once he began to see the ball he was a powerful driver and a beautiful late cutter. It is a measure of his ability that he notched no less than seven scores of fifty or more against the old enemy, Lancashire, and at least one half-century against each of the first-class counties he played against. His highest score, 166 against Warwickshire at Edgbaston in 1896, was compiled in the course of a partnership of 292 for the Yorkshire eighth wicket with Bobby Peel and remains to this day the English record stand for that wicket. If Hawke was not a great batsman, then neither was he a bad batsman.

However, it was as captain of the White Rose County that Hawke broke the mould of English cricket. Under his captaincy Yorkshire achieved periods of dominance and near invincibility that only later Yorkshire teams have ever really matched; and yet even among his friends there were those who begrudged him the accolades that were his due. C.B. Fry spoke for the doubters in his *Life Worth Living*:

Lord Hawke may or may not have been a good captain. The
authorities differ on this; personally, I think he was a very
good captain off the field. He was certainly a superfine manager
of a cricket tour ... Martin Hawke was a lovable man,
although the story of his being a great captain was a myth.

J.M. Kilburn, in *A History of Yorkshire cricket* articulated the view
of the uncommitted in noting:

Lord Hawke alone could not have created his chosen form of
Yorkshire cricket. He conceived his ideal of a county team, he
shaped it and he directed it in operation, but he was dependent
on discovery of the appropriate constituents.

A.A. Thomson had no time for the doubters. He was a man who
knew considerably more than a thing or two about Yorkshire
cricket and did not baulk at throwing down the gauntlet to the
detractors, maintaining that Hawke 'was not merely his professionals'
mentor', but also 'a skilful strategist'.

Hawke first captained Yorkshire in the Championship in 1883.
Although he nominally retained the captaincy until he formally
resigned in favour of E.J. Radcliffe in November 1910, he played his
last county match at the end of the 1909 season. The profit and loss
account of the Yorkshire captaincy in the serious business of county
cricket between 1883 and 1909 tells its own story. Yorkshire won
the Championship eight times under Hawke's stewardship. His
theory of captaincy was simple; attack. Attack became ingrained
into the psyche of Yorkshire cricket. Under Hawke Yorkshiremen
were brought up to believe that it was their birthright to rule English
cricket.

The Yorkshire teams that conquered English cricket in those
years were heart and soul *his* teams; they were the product of *his*
system, playing cricket the way *he* thought it should be played. For
his critics to turn around and say that any man could have led those
incomparable Yorkshire XIs of the golden age is to miss the point
completely.

Yorkshire always has had and, one suspects, probably always will
have a pool of cricketing talent far deeper than that of most of the
other counties. Hawke's achievement was to unite the disparate
strands of Yorkshire cricket and thus unleash the latent potential
which had previously been hamstrung by a want of discipline and

leadership on the field and faction fighting off it. Hawke gave Yorkshire cricket a common cause and defended it to the end of his days and in so doing changed the face of English cricket.

This is his story and inevitably, the story of the first great flowering of Yorkshire cricket.

2
The Early Years
(1860–1874)

Martin Bladen Hawke was born on Thursday 16 August 1860 at Willingham Rectory, near Gainsborough in Lincolnshire. He was the second son of Jane and The Reverend Edward Henry Julius Hawke. By birth Martin Hawke was neither a member of the nobility, nor Yorkshire-born. His father was a country parson at one remove from the Hawke blood line and two removes from the peerage. Although the family was hardly impoverished by the standards of the day, the Hawkes of Willingham Rectory were listed among the poor relations of the Hawke clan.

Martin Hawke's infancy was spent in the Rectory at Willingham in the bosom of his growing family. From his earliest years he relished the whole range of country pursuits; riding, hunting and fishing. He had a natural flair for the rough and tumble of country life and an appetite for good company and competitive sport. As a boy he was blooded by the famous huntsman Will Dale and was never happier than when he was out riding to hounds.

The family was not without its share of tragedy. Hawke's elder brother, Edward, died a lingering death in childhood following an operation on his hip after an accident at school. His final illness lasted a year. Even in an era when sickness commonly decimated families, Edward's suffering cast a dark shadow over his brother's formative years. Often in later life Hawke would seem preoccupied with morbid reflections on pain and death. Edward had been a bright, strong boy and in many ways Hawke spent much of his life trying to live up to what he might have achieved had he lived.

Hawke's uncle, Bladen, also lived at the Rectory. He had been the first Hawke since the great Admiral to go into the Navy. Whilst serving on the China station he had fallen from the rigging. His back broken, he was invalided home a cripple. For the rest of his life he lived in his brothers's household. In his *Recollections and Reminiscences* Hawke said of Bladen's fortitude in the face of such cruel adversity:

> So for seven-and-thirty years he lay on his couch on his back, and if he went out it was only after being lifted on to his donkey carriage. I think we all owed him much for instructing us in our boyhood. Never once did I hear him complain, and if ever youngsters had a splendid example of patience and brave-heartedness to follow, his was one which could not be surpassed.

Hawke's father, the Reverend Edward Henry Julius Hawke, was a wise, somewhat contemplative man who was devoted to his young family. Born in 1815 he was a cousin of the fourth Baron Hawke. Hawke described him as 'a perfect sahib'. Educated at Tours and St Catherine's College, Cambridge he was an unrepentent Francophile. He spoke French perfectly, mourned the Prussian victory of 1870 and passed on his enduring admiration for France and its culture to his children. He was a placid man, religious without being overly self-righteous, and despite his age closer to his sons than many fathers of the period. He had broken his leg as a boy and in Hawke's words 'the doctors made a mess of setting it, so it was permanently stiff'. Unable to participate in team games he became an expert fisherman and a fine shot, whether mounted or on foot. It was said that his sermons tended towards longevity but were nevertheless well received; he was also a prize-winning cultivator of hollyhocks and gladioli, a magistrate, and a pillar of the village community. Cricket was the great unfulfilled passion of his life. The village team was his XI, and it was from his father that Hawke inherited his love of the game.

Hawke's mother, Jane, was the third daughter of Henry Dowker, of Laysthorpe. Her family was steeped in ecclesiastical life and three of her ancestors had been vicars of Salton. An austere, formidable woman she dominated the family. She met her future husband when he was curate at Stonegrave, near Helmsley in Yorkshire; he had baptised her when she was a girl and by coincidence they shared the same birthday, Christmas Eve. When they married in 1857 he was 42 and she was 17. Despite having had ten children Hawke later records that 'she carried her good looks to her grave'. He doted on his mother, freely admitting that 'with her, Martin could do no wrong, so no wonder I remained a bachelor until a year after her death'.

In reflecting upon his childhood Hawke was always struck by the dignity with which his father had carried off the family's straightened circumstances. It was part and parcel of being a Hawke, of being a descendent of the great Admiral. Hawke was raised in an atmosphere redolent with the traditions of the family. The history of the Hawkes was inseparable from the history of England, and the poor relations of Willingham Rectory were no more immune to the call of the past than their rich cousins. The Hawke children knew that they were different, that they were not like others.

The legend of the Hawkes was the legend of Admiral Lord Hawke. In the long history of England few men can claim to have saved their nation in its hour of direst peril: the first Lord Hawke ranks among such a brotherhood. If after the Battle of Trafalgar Horatio Nelson's fame came to exemplify the Royal Navy and the battle itself came to be seen as the crowning glory of Georgian naval supremacy, then it should never be forgotten that the architect of that supremacy, the man who was 'the Father of the Navy' was Admiral Lord Hawke, the victor of Quiberon Bay.

In 1717 at the age of twelve the first Lord Hawke went to sea. He rose slowly through the ranks and by the age of 22 was a 3rd Lieutenant. Like many a promising naval officer his career was blighted by periods ashore on half-pay and was revived only by war. In 1743 the War of the Austrian Succession rescued him from the land and saw him in command of HMS *Berwick*, a new 74-gun ship-of-the-line. A year later in 1744 off Toulon the *Berwick* was one of the few English ships that was handled with any spirit in an inconclusive clash with the combined French and Spanish fleet. The battle was a humiliating débâcle for the Royal Navy. The two senior officers present had been at cross purposes, more concerned with their own professional rivalry and personal enmity than with getting to grips with the enemy. Although the butcher's bill had not been heavy, the reputation of the Navy had sunk to a low ebb.

Promoted Rear-Admiral of the White, Hawke was instrumental in repairing the damage when his squadron – ignoring 'fighting instructions' – won a crushing victory at the second Battle of Cape Finisterre, a service for which he was swiftly knighted.

During the Seven Years War, now a full Admiral, he was sent out to replace the wretched John Byng, whose fate for losing a battle – or to be precise, for letting the enemy get away – prompted Voltaire to comment 'In this country it is thought well to kill an admiral from time to time to encourage the others'. Constrained by restrictive orders and his own blind obedience to the sacred 'fighting instructions', Byng was thwarted at the Battle of Minorca as much by ill-luck as by the French. He returned home to face trial on trumped-up charges, was convicted of failing to do his utmost to engage the enemy, and was shot.

Admiral Lord Hawke's appointment with destiny arrived in November 1759 when the French were gathering an invasion fleet at Brest and Rochefort. A storm had forced Hawke off station, and driven his fleet north-east until he was forced to take shelter off Torbay. As the storm subsided Admiral Hubert de Conflans put out to sea from Brest with twenty-three French sail-of-the-line under his flag, ostensibly to join forces with the rest of the armada assembling at Rochefort. The rumour that de Conflans had broken the blockade and had put to sea brought the mob out on to the streets of Portsmouth. Hawke's effigy was being burned in his hour of glory.

Hawke, with twenty-five sail-of-the-line under his command, crammed on every square inch of canvas and steered to intercept de Conflans. Off Quiberon Bay on the Breton coast the French fell in with Hawke's frigates. Unlike the big two- and three-deckers-of-the-line, the frigates had held station and continued to report the movements of the French. As Hawke's frigates skirmished at the fringes of the enemy fleet, the rest of his battle fleet hove into view over the grey horizon.

French ships tended to be larger than their English counterparts and, ship for ship, fire a significantly heavier weight of shot. However, de Conflans had no intention of joining battle on the high seas. Whilst on paper his twenty-three sail-of-the-line were a match for Hawke's twenty-five, Hawke had a dozen other men-of-war under flag, mainly frigates, but including four 50-gunners. In any general fleet engagement in these 'fourth-raters' and Hawke's marauding frigates would swoop on any French ship that fell out of the line. Such were the tactical considerations. A British admiral in de Conflans' place would surely have been court-martialled had he failed to join battle at the earliest moment, but de Conflans was, of course, not a British admiral and indeed the grand strategy of the French and Spanish fleets hinged upon the successful concentration of the combined invasion armada gathering at Rochefort. So the

French ran for the protection of Quiberon. By the afternoon of 20 November 1759 de Conflans had anchored in the bay, little suspecting that Hawke would risk his ships – all that stood between Britain and invasion – to the reefs, sandbanks and artillery that now guarded his fleet.

Hawke's sailing master warned him of the perils of pursuing the French into the bay without charts or pilotage and with dusk approaching. Hawke thanked him for his warning and directed him to 'Lay us alongside the French Commander-in-Chief'.

The sea was rough, the wind gusting on to the shore and the rain came and went in savage squalls. The English ships were rolling so heavily that no captain would risk opening his lower gun ports. It made no difference. One by one Hawke's storm-tossed ships-of-the-line sounded their way through the narrow, reef-flanked entrance to the enemy's anchorage. Two ships were wrecked on the rocks, but the others with the flagship in the vanguard wreaked havoc in the crowded bay. What ensued is commemorated in Sir Henry Newbolt's ballad *Admiral's All*:

'Twas long past noon of a wild November day
When Hawke came swooping from the west;
He heard the breakers thundering in Quiberon Bay,
But he flew the flag for battle, line abreast,
Down from the quicksands, waving out of sight,
Fiercely blew the storm-wind, darkly fell the night;
But they took the foe for pilot and the cannon's glare for light,
When Hawke came swooping from the west.
The guns that should have conquered us, they rusted on the shore,
The men that should have mastered us, they drummed and marched no more,
For England was England and a mighty brood she bore,
When Hawke came swooping from the west.

Seven French ships were destroyed or captured, the rest variously mauled and scattered as the survivors put to sea and hoped for sanctuary. Nightfall saved de Conflans from complete disaster, but not before Hawke had broken the spine of French seapower. His tactics at Quiberon Bay flew in the face of 'fighting instructions' and were Nelson's blueprint four decades later at Aboukir and Copenhagen. When Nelson declared 'No captain can do more than lay his ship alongside the enemy', he was reiterating the doctrine of the man acknowledged in his day as being 'the Father of the Navy'. What post-Trafalgar generations have deemed Nelsonian deeds were, in Nelson's time, deeds that owed much of their inspiration to the Hawke tradition. Had Nelson obeyed fighting instructions the Battles of the Nile, Copenhagen and Trafalgar might never have been fought, let alone won. It was Hawke who observed that 'a single ship may struggle with a hard gale of wind when a squadron cannot' and he who framed his tactics on the implicit assumption that the seamanship and the gunnery of the Royal Navy was inherently superior to that of any enemy and therefore the most effective manner of fighting was to pit ship against ship, rather than attempt to manoeuvre the fleet as a single unit.

Hawke's philosophy changed the Navy for ever. The ethos of excellence, of virtual invincibility that lasted from Quiberon to the outbreak of the Great War, the very idea that Britannia ruled the waves dates from his time. Central to his philosophy was a new concern for the welfare of the men who manned Britain's ships, iron discipline and the primacy of seamanship. In the words of the naval historian Afred T. Mahan 'the spirit of Hawke became the spirit of the Navy'.

In the young life of our subject, the legend of the great Admiral was still imbued with a reality and an immediacy that has long since been lost to modern generations. The young Martin Hawke was rightly proud of his indomitable ancestor; to him the great Admiral was 'Nelson's prototype', a leader of men whose triumphs were born out of his tenacity in the face of the enemy, his sense of personal honour, the discipline he imposed on his subordinates, and his determined efforts to improve the desperate lives of the men who manned the ships of the King's Navy. These were history lessons that imprinted themselves indelibly on not just the mind, but the personality of the future seventh Baron Hawke during his most formative years.

There was no forgetting history in the Hawke household. As a boy he was told the story of how his grandmother rode close to the Battle of Quatre Bras 'out of curiosity' and how proud she had been to dance at the ball in Brussels before Waterloo had been won. Hawke's great uncle, Nisbet, had been with the 13th Light Dragoons at the battle, was wounded and then left for dead on the field. In the chaos looters roamed the battleground, robbing the dead and murdering the wounded if they resisted. Nisbet was shot in the arm where he lay yet survived to tell the tale. As a child Hawke was shown his great uncle's medals, memorised the names on the bars: Nive and Nivelle, Toulouse, Orthez and Waterloo.

From childhood Hawke felt himself to be part of the unbroken chain of British history, a new link forged to carry forward the family name. It would have been strange if he had thought otherwise; the world was a canvas upon which to paint great deeds and it was now awaiting the exploits of the next generation of the Hawke family. But until he was ten, Martin Hawke was no more than the son of a country parson.

The Hawke line progressed from father to son from the great Admiral to the fourth Baron. Thereafter, the blood line altered and the title and family estates parted company. The fourth Lord Hawke was twice married but left only a daughter, Cassandra. On his death he was succeeded by his younger brother, Stanhope, 'a confirmed old bachelor'.

In 1862 Stanhope's horse, The Marquis, had won the St Leger and the Two Thousand Guineas and come second to Caractacus in the Derby. However, he was not a wealthy man. He never gambled and had to live carefully. Upon the reading of the fourth Baron's will, he was mortified to discover that he was to receive not one penny. Everything had been left to Cassandra, who later married Lord Rosse. The Towton estate, which had come into the family from the great Admiral's wife, Catherine Brooke, and the Admiral's papers and log books were thus lost to the family. His brother's widow rubbed salt into the wound by asking poor Stanhope why he thought that he should have been left money 'to gamble away on the turf'.

Hawke's father, the sixth Baron, succeeded to the title when his cousin Stanhope died in 1870. His position was invidious – Stanhope had had no property to leave and little cash – and he actually contemplated allowing the title to lie dormant. In the end he decided to take up the peerage on the grounds that in the long run it seemed less expensive than attempting to revive the title at some later date. The measure of the family's impoverishment can be gauged by the fact that they resided at the Rectory in Willingham until 1874 when the sixth Lord Hawke retired. Had it not been for the munificence of friends the plight of the family would indeed have been dire. One such friend was The Reverend Walter Brooke, a distant descendant of the Admiral's wife, who bequeathed monies to Hawke's father by way of compensation for the injustice that had been done to

Stanhope, and The Reverend, by the fourth Baron's will. Another was the millionaire Andrew Montague who furnished a fifty-year lease on Wighill Park, a Georgian mansion at Tadcaster, at a price that was commensurate with the family's means.

Hawke's father became a 'city man' in the last years of his life. At one time or another he sat on the boards of the Buenos Aires Great Southern Railway, the Direct United States Cable and the Taital Railway, but he was too set in his ways to adjust fully to his new role. To his dying day he was at heart a country cleric.

Hawke's first school was at Newark and the headmaster was The Reverend Herbert Plater, cruelly nicknamed 'Peggy' because he had a stiff leg. This was the gentleman who did incalculable damage to the embryonic batsmanship of the infant Hawke, whose natural inclination was to bat left-handed. To this day many pundits maintain that a left-hander can never be as elegant at the crease as a right-hander. One only has to think of David Gower or Sir Garfield Sobers among contempory batsmen to recognise that some left-handers are better-looking than others, just as there are both graceful and ugly-looking right-handers. In the Victorian era a gentleman batted right-handed and that was that. Then as now, the root of the prejudice was that left-handedness was somehow 'cack-handedness'.

The Reverend Plater noted that Martin Hawke was batting the wrong way round and so he made him bat right-handed. Without wishing to compare Hawke's batsmanship with that of Bradman, one wonders how many hundreds the Don would have scored if somebody had turned him around at the very moment when his skills were developing. Later when he took up billiards and shooting he played billiards left-handed and put his gun to his left shoulder.

At the age of ten Hawke was sent to St. Michael's, Aldin House, at Slough, a well-known school that existed mainly to prepare boys for their time at Eton. Under the headmastership of The Reverend J.W. Hawtrey, the regime at Aldin House was markedly more liberal than in many such institutions. Each boy had his own cubicle, classes were small and swimming was included among the many sports on the curriculum. The Reverend Hawtrey had been a master at Eton and by common consent his headmastership was benign and, to a degree, enlightened for his time. By present standards the regime would seem spartan, the curriculum narrow and the discipline barbaric. The young Hawke enjoyed his four years at the school for he was a broad, strong lad for his age and at Aldin House his athletic prowess began to blossom.

Cricket at Aldin House was played under idyllic conditions. Flat wickets were provided for matches and net practices and the coaching was in the patient and capable hands of Edward and George Hawtrey. Their coaching concentrated on bringing the best out of a boy, however that might be achieved. The young Hawke had an appetite for putting bat to ball with as much vigour as possible whenever the opportunity presented itself. It was a trait that was heartily commended and encouraged at Aldin House for such qualities were welcomed with open arms at Eton.

3
Eton Days
(1874–1880)

Martin Hawke entered Eton College in September 1874. At Eton a new boy quickly learned that there was one way of doing things, the Eton way. The Iron Duke had remarked that 'the Battle of Waterloo was won on the playing fields of Eton' and in many respects the school had been content to rest on its laurels ever since 1815. Although Eton was now beginning to take in the sons of the new northern aristocracy the education it offered remained essentially classical; Eton existed to turn boys into gentlemen. The Industrial Revolution might never have happened. Hawke later described the headmaster of his day, Dr Hornby, as a 'man who drifted along the flowing tide of Eton traditions'. Complacency ruled. The school was not interested in broadening young minds, only in toughening its boys for the struggles it envisaged they would face in the future. That Latin and Greek were of limited value to a man in business or destined for high government office, whereas a solid grounding in mathematics and a passing acquaintance with elementary science and modern history might prove invaluable, was never discussed or thought necessary to be discussed. Boys marked out for military careers would sometimes seek coaching in practical subjects, but otherwise the old ways continued unchallenged until long after Hawke's Eton days.

A boy's education was, in any event, a secondary matter; a boy came to Eton to be prepared for membership of the ruling class, and so his formal education was entirely incidental. In his *Recollections and Reminiscences* Hawke recounts a telling exchange between his father and F.W. Cornish, his housemaster, on Hawke's first day at Eton:

I still remember my father's somewhat evident surprise at being asked if I was to be made to work. Needless to specify what the answer was.

Floreat Etona more accurately expressed the sporting, rather than the educational, ethos of Eton College. As the Victorian age lengthened and the years went by without a general European War – the Crimea seemed like a very distant place in the 1850s and the various wars between Germany, France and Austria hardly ruffled the calm waters of the *Pax Britannica* – endeavour on the field of play became a metaphor for life's struggles. In the absence of war, or even the fear of war, the British turned to sport as an outlet for passions that previous generations had exhausted in campaigns of an altogether bloodier kind. The great public schools were in the vanguard and by the latter decades of the nineteenth century, prowess in sport had assumed a mystical significance that has dominated the perception of public schools and public school life down the years.

Scholastic excellence was the *bête noire* of a boy's time at Eton. The school was happy to reward mediocrity in the classroom, but scholastic rewards were as nothing compared to the prizes that were to be won in the hurly-burly of games. Intellect was scorned, pause for contemplation interpreted as weakness. Scholars were 'saps' or 'swots', tolerated by the majority, despised by some, respected by few. Sportsmen were 'characters', 'fine fellows' and 'leaders of men', heroes lionised in *Eton Songs*. If a boy was good at games the world was his oyster; if he had no aptitude for games or lacked the appetite for the rough and tumble, then he was stigmatised to the end of his days by his peers. Scholarship was an intrinsically personal exercise; by definition an outstanding scholar was an individual ploughing his own furrow and individualism was anathema to the Eton ethos. The team was everything, even when an individual competed as an individual, it was always under the banner of his team, his house, his college. The system stressed a man's responsibility to his fellows, never let him forget that others relied on him as he relied on them, enforced conformity of thought and action and ruthlessly stamped out innovation. Such was the atmosphere in which the nation's budding men of affairs spent their last years of childhood. It was a jungle, the fittest survived and the rest went to the wall; indeed at Eton the weakest quite literally went to the wall, hacked and trampled in the mêlée of the wall game.

At Eton all *honourables* were called plain 'Mister' and Mister

Martin Hawke revelled in Eton life. He had no pretensions to scholarship, was blessed with natural athleticism and in the heat of battle frequently displayed a reckless disregard for personal injury; with gifts such as these Eton took him to its ancient heart.

In Hawke's day cricket at Eton was not, strange as it may seem, the be all and end all. The wall game, fives, football, athletics, shooting, beagling and, of course, rowing were pursued with a fervour that was positively religious and, in a sense, cricket was – at least until the 1890s – just one among several College games. At Harrow and Winchester cricket was king; at Eton it was perhaps cast in the role of pretender. The triumphs of Etonian cricket were all the sweeter for being achieved in the face of adversity. The Reverend Edward Lyttelton, one of seven brothers to play for Eton and who succeeded the reforming Edmund Warre as headmaster in 1905, described the disadvantages under which, in 1894, Eton cricket laboured in *The Cricket Field:*

> What with confined spaces, floods, bad pitches, which are due to the football played on them, and the fact that although the eleven is looked after wonderfully well there is scarcely any attention given to the rest, it is astonishing that . . . results have been obtained. It only shows that talent will come to the front under almost any circumstances . . . the success of Eton is simply a proof that coaching has less influence than is generally supposed.

It was only in 1867 when R.A.H. 'Mike' Mitchell returned to Eton as an assistant master and cricket coach, that Etonian cricket began to blossom. Mitchell was acknowledged as one of the finest amateur batsmen of his era and his elegant forward style was to become the hallmark of Eton batsmanship. For thirty years 'Mike' was the ruling spirit of Etonian cricket.

C.I. Thornton, a notable old Etonian and redoubtable hitter of a cricket ball who in later years became the organiser of the Scarborough Festival, reflected on his own experiences at Eton in the last days before Mitchell's arrival, in *Cricket:*

> I should have been in the eleven in 1865 but I knocked the bowling of the professional about, and he did not like it at all. The usual way of coming to the front at Eton, at any rate in my time, was to keep on getting runs in the lower games until you

attracted the attention of someone in authority who would place you in the Upper Club, where you could get some practice. If you happened to come off in one of the first-class games you might be put into the eleven.

In the years after Mitchell's return to Eton cricket flourished. However, it was a fragile renaissance that was always threatened by other competing sports. 'Mike' was as much a prisoner of Eton tradition as generations of headmasters had been. His coaching concentrated on developing a man's strengths and he never claimed that he could turn a moderate player into a great performer. When Etonian cricket was in the doldrums in the 1880s and early 1890s he told *The Cricket Field*:

> Eton cricket has certainly gone down in the last ten years from various causes. A vast amount of attention is given to boating, and the school does not take the same interest as is shown at Harrow and Winchester in what is to them the one event of the season – their match with us. There are many other causes, some of a nature which could hardly be understood by anyone not living on the spot; and our ground is not at all adapted to the game. Then there have been no players who are so good that they could make a name for themselves in spite of all drawbacks – no such players, for instance, as the Lytteltons, C.J. Ottaway, C.T. and G.B. Studd, C.I. Thornton, Lord Harris, F.M. Buckland, Ivo Bligh, H. Whitfield, P.J. de Paravicini, A.S. Tabor, A.W. Ridley, H. Philipson, Lord G. Scott, F. Marchant, and one of the best of all, G.H. Longman. You can't *make* players like these. I am inclined to think, too, that boys are now coached when they are too young, and are made cramped and artificial by this.

At Eton it was common for a boy to participate in a wide range of seemingly incompatible sports requiring entirely different and non-complementary skills. Hawke enthusiastically and successfully competed in fives, Eton football, running, beagling, shooting and cricket, with pride of place in his affections shifting continually from one pursuit to another during his five years at the school. At Eton, in those days, boys were encouraged to be all-rounders, specialism smacked of individualism. Besides, sport was an integral part of the disciplinary system of the school, they had found it to be the single most effective way of keeping its young gentlemen out of mischief.

Although posterity remembers Hawke for his services to cricket, it is as well to record that he never captained the XI, nor was he ever its leading light. Among his contemporaries were the likes of C.T. Studd, Ivo Bligh and H. 'Babe' Whitfield, men who would adorn any school side in any age.

Nothing in Hawke's schooldays gave him as much satisfaction as being keeper of the Field, or in the non-Etonian idiom, captain of the Field game. Football as it was practised in the great public schools before the turn of the century bore very little resemblance either to the Union or Association codes. To the outsider the Field game was a reckless mix of Rugby and soccer, quite incomprehensible. To the devotee it was compulsive sport and unlike Rugby or football, it had the advantage of being exclusive. To appreciate the finer points of the Field game properly one had to be an insider, one of the chaps, gone to the right school. Hawke was in no doubt as to the prestige attached to the game:

> I would never play the Wall game, for I feared I might be hacked and so prevented playing what I dearly loved, the Field game. To be Captain of the Boats or Captain of the Eleven are no doubt the blue ribands of Eton, and not because I did not succeed to be the latter do I assert that to be Keeper of the Field is on a just equality. I would sooner, for one reason, be the last-named, simply because it is a more responsible position. The Eight is practically chosen by the coach, so also the selection of the Eleven is assisted by the counsel of the master in charge of the cricket, but the Field is selected by the Keeper and Co-Keeper, thus giving scope for more observation and an opportunity of gaining experience by judging for oneself.
>
> I just loved the Eton game – it is my ideal of football. It may possibly handicap either for Rugger or Soccer, but it is the truest football imaginable and I hope the day will never come when it is superseded.

It was at Eton that Hawke discovered his flair for running. He was tall and strong for his years, but lacked the mobility to make the best of these advantages in the Field game. As a runner his natural sprinting speed and developing athleticism quickly brought him to the fore. At Aldin House he had been discouraged by his apparent lack of stamina on cross-country runs and paper-chases, yet in only his second term at Eton he suddenly realised that he had new and unsuspected reserves to call upon. He made the discovery in the course of a paper-chase in the spring of 1875. The flavour of such chases can be gleaned from the recollections of A.C. Ainger in his *Memories of Eton Sixty Years Ago* (published in 1917):

> Paper-chases, as is their wont, involved a good many wettings
> . . . the ditches in the neighbourhood were often ripe with the
> deposits of the villages of Bucks, and undesirable not only
> because of the depth of water. The ditch which runs along the
> road from Agar's Plough to Upton was known as the 'Black
> Ditch', and was enriched with the drainage of Slough, as was
> evident both to the eye and the nose. This did not prevent it
> forming part of the 'course' for the College steeple-chase.

On this occasion Hawke, much to his surprise, actually caught the *hound*, a boy called Ramus. While basking in the glory of this strange new triumph he found out that Ramus intended to run in the junior mile race. Spurred into action, Hawke went off and timed himself over a mile along the Dorney Road, a distance he covered in some seven minutes. He promptly ordered running shoes and shorts and began to train in earnest; he won the junior mile in a time of five minutes and thirty-two seconds. Three years later he was winning the senior race with the highly respectable time of four minutes and forty-nine seconds. In that year of 1878 he swept the board, winning both the sprint over hurdles and the main distance event, the steeple-chase. The previous year he had won the quarter-mile. In 1877 and 1878 he took second place in the school walking race, a discipline for which he never trained.

Although the Field game, and to a lesser extent his running, were winter pursuits Hawke's devotion to them must be held, at least in part, responsible for the erratic progress of his cricket at Eton. He was awarded his 'sixpenny colours' in the summer of 1875. The next season he scored 171 out of 191 in the first innings of the 'lower boy cup match', and following it with 91 out of 121 in the second. W.F. Forbes, the Eton captain, noted Hawke's promise and took him under his wing, picking him for the match against Maidenhead and two other fixtures in 1876. However, his batting disappointed in higher company and did not justify his inclusion in the sides that faced Harrow and Winchester. The following season his form completely deserted him, confounding the promise of his early summons to the ranks of the first XI.

So it was that Hawke had to wait until his eighteenth year before he won his first XI colours against Harrow and Winchester. He established himself high in the batting order and scored useful runs in both matches. Eton lost to Winchester by six wickets at the end of June, an inauspicious preparation for the ordeal of facing Harrow at Lord's two weeks later.

Before crowds of between fifteen and twenty thousand on both days, Eton lost a closely contested match by 20 runs. Hawke was out for a single in the second innings, but on the first day of the game he had hit 32 of his side's total of 117 runs. As Hawke himself said later, the massive crowds made 'batting a pretty good test for young cricketers'. His 32 at Lord's was his highest score of the season and *John Lillywhite's Cricketers' Companion* noted him as a 'good general player, hits well all round him; a very good field at times'.

Hawke retained his place in the XI in 1879 even though his form was erratic. *Lillywhite's* verdict was that he had not been 'as successful as anticipated', and that he was 'slow in the field'. Injuries and illness has disrupted his running and his suspect fitness told on him that season. Hawke was not one to complain, such problems were simply to be overcome and he enjoyed his cricket that year. The matches against Winchester at Eton and Harrow at Lord's were both low-scoring affairs. Hawke registered 4 and 1 against the Wykehamists and 4 and 12 against the Harrovians. Winchester were bowled out for 34 on the first day of the match at Eton, the Etonians eventually triumphing by 45 runs. The Lord's match was drawn, a victim of rain when the bowling of C.T. Studd, the Eton captain, was threatening to rout the old enemy.

On the second afternoon of the Winchester match the band of the Life Guards, stationed in nearby Windsor, came down to Eton and struck up as Charles Studd was bowling. Winchester had fought back from the disasters of the previous day and the contest was evenly balanced. The musical accompaniment was an unwelcome distraction to the Eton captain. Calling Hawke over, he declared that he could not bowl in time to the music, and told him to ask the band to stop playing. At first the bandmaster acquiesced but later the Life Guards struck up anew. Again, Hawke was despatched to the boundary. This time the Life Guards marched off the ground. Their Colonel awaited Studd in the pavilion in high dudgeon: 'That's all the thanks we get for sending you our band!' he complained angrily. To which Studd retorted: 'We never asked for it', which, as it happened, was perfectly true. On the first day of the match a lady had apparently commented to the Colonel in passing that all the occasion lacked was a band – and he had taken it upon himself to play the knight errant.

Charles Thomas Studd was the outstanding schoolboy cricketer of his day, an Eton Legend. In 1879 he was captain of cricket, opening batsman and opening bowler. While still at Cambridge he was acknowledged as the finest all-rounder in the land. He was top of the first-class batting averages in 1882 and second in 1883, taking well over one hundred wickets in both seasons. Then in 1884 at the age of 24 he and his elder brother, G.B. Studd, gave up the game and went to China as missionaries.

To latter-day eyes Studd's decision to abandon the sport he loved and cast himself into the unknown seems incomprehensible. But in Victorian Britain few would have thought it even remotely odd. Muscular Christianity was the bedrock of the Empire, a colonial force every bit as potent as the Navy that commanded the seas and the Army that policed the margins. In an age when the Queen Empress really was the Protector of the Faith, every Englishman abroad was a missionary; Charles Studd, gentleman cricketer supreme, was simply carrying the idea to its logical conclusion.

Hawke's own profound Christianity came upon him as a boy in the Rectory at Willingham and stayed with him until the day he died. Wherever he was in the world he never missed church on Sunday and always encouraged his players and friends to attend with him. The very fact that he was so earnestly God-fearing made a deep impression on everybody he met, regardless of their own backgrounds. As lord of the manor in Tadcaster in later life he was a pillar of the church and wherever Yorkshire were playing he would return home every Sunday to read the lesson. To Hawke and his Eton fellows church and state were, to all intents and purposes, inseparable. They believed that they were members of the ruling elite of an Empire that stood for all that was just and right in the world, an Empire founded on what they believed was the moral superiority of the Anglican tradition and the inalienable right of their class to rule. When Charles Studd chose to give his life to God, he was also giving his life over to the service of his country, not perhaps in the same sense as if he had joined the Army, the diplomatic corps or the Indian Civil Service, but he was nevertheless dedicating himself to the service of the self-same imperial ideals which schools like Eton have always willingly drummed into its young men.

Hawke's schoolboy cricket never emerged from Studd's shadow. Throughout his career he would have to defer to others whose natural talents far exceeded his own. At Eton, as in the years to come, Hawke was a good player whose aspirations to greatness came to naught. If sometimes he stumbled across inspiration it tended to be a flash in the pan, soon offset by failure. Already in his Etonian cricket the strengths and weaknesses of his batting were apparent; he was a bad, nervous starter. His courage was often a liability, he would stand up and hit out, take the knocks and try to keep the scoring going regardless of the quality of the bowling or the condition of the wicket. On the variable Eton pitches of the 1870s his best strokes were often frustrated and his adventurous hitting was frequently his downfall. He was very much an eye player, technically competent without ever being defensively secure. His style was free, suited to hitting good bowling rather than attempting to survive it. The young Hawke never conceded that the same virtues of application and tenacity which had made him a champion athlete might have transformed his schoolboy batsmanship. He entertained the fanciful notion that batting was something that came naturally; his style was instinctive and he relied upon the speed of his reflexes and the power in his broad shoulders.

He was never less than a good-looking batsman, and many admired his positive approach. Hawke's philosophy of batting was simple; a cricket ball existed to be hit, and hit hard. At Eton his failures with the bat were painful, made all the worse for him and other mere mortals in the XI by the triumphs of the incomparable Charles Studd, whose star was soon to ascend over Cambridge cricket.

Hawke bore his cricketing disappointments manfully and with a cheerful air. Cricket was but one string to his bow at Eton. In the holidays he turned out for the Gentlemen of Yorkshire, scoring creditably. He was a very mature youth in his last year at Eton; tall, strong-featured with mutton-chop whiskers and a moustache that was the rage among the elder boys at the school, he was easily taken for a man in his mid-twenties, though still in his teens.

His father had come into the peerage late in life, set in his ways and unable ever to come to terms with his new role; his son, however, showed every sign of taking to the peerage like a duck to water when the time came for him to bid his farewell to Eton

College. His father was doing his best to groom him for the future even though the worst of the family's financial straits had yet to be negotiated safely. Hawke was a young man mindful of the traditions of his family, a devout Christian, an equally devout disciple of the hunting, shooting and fishing fraternity, a sportsman to his soul and a cricketer of promise. If he was hardly yet a spoiled son of the aristocracy, he enjoyed his privileged life to the full, throwing himself into his sport and into the social fray while he waited, like every Hawke, for the call of duty.

His father had envisaged a military career, yet somehow Hawke never settled on it. Of his younger brothers, Stanhope went into the Navy and Henry into the Army, but Cambridge lay between Martin Hawke and the Army when he came down from Eton and by the time his University days ended, he would have stumbled upon the great cause that would sustain him thereafter.

4

Cambridge and Yorkshire
(1881–1885)

Hawke was a moderate scholar. His father had decided he should go up to Magdalene College, Cambridge, but not directly he left Eton; first, his son's scholastic shortcomings would be addressed by private tuition. It was a decision which recommended itself on both educational and financial grounds. The prospect of deferring the considerable expense of keeping his son at Cambridge for a year or two was not unattractive. As a result, Hawke did not go up to University until October 1881, a full two years after the majority of his Etonian contemporaries. Charles Studd, who was three months younger than Hawke, had already played in two Varsity matches by the time his old schoolfellow joined him at Cambridge.

In the interim Hawke occupied himself hunting, socialising and in making appearances on the cricket field for the Yorkshire Gentlemen. When he was out hunting Hawke was in seventh heaven. He loved riding and the working of hounds, the kill was incidental; indeed in one respect a kill spoiled a good day's hunting because it brought it to an end. He had become an expert shot and during the season he was inundated with invitations to shooting weekends. When he was 21 his father made him a member of the Carlton Club.

Since his latter days at Eton Hawke had been his father's frequent companion. The old man was proud of his sportsman son and wise enough to know that he was a doer, not a thinker, and that no amount of coercion was going to alter the fact.

Hawke's enforced interregnum between Eton and Cambridge was to have an unforeseen, almost accidental consequence that was progressively to take over his life. During the summers of 1880 and 1881 he became closely involved with the Yorkshire Gentlemen's

Cricket Club. The club drew its membership from the districts around York, where it had its ground. It was an amateur club whose ideals were essentially Corinthian. In keeping with those ideals its playing members found their own out-of-pocket expenses. Founded in 1863, shortly after the modern Yorkshire County Cricket Club had come into existence in Sheffield, it had never seriously impinged upon the Sheffield monopoly.

According to the Reverend R.S. Holmes, writing in *The History of Yorkshire County Cricket: 1833–1903*, the club had been born out of 'the desire for several years of many gentlemen in Yorkshire to have the County well and thoroughly represented in the cricket field in what might be termed county matches and also in gentlemen's matches'. This ambitious plan expressed itself in the creation of two separate teams; one, the county club, which would have no permanent home and the other, the Yorkshire Gentlemen's Cricket Club, which would play at a new ground of its own, at York. The rival county club never materialised, but the Gentlemen's Club was a going concern from the outset and in the fullness of time even the Sheffield monopoly buckled before the wind of change that was to blow from the Yorkist camp. However, when Hawke first turned out for the Yorkshire Gentlemen Sheffield's hold on Yorkshire cricket was absolute.

The life and soul of the Yorkshire Gentlemen's Cricket Club was The Reverend Edmund Sardinson Carter. He had been a double blue at Cambridge, representing his university in the two most prestigious sports, cricket and rowing. Whilst in Australia recovering from pleurisy he had appeared for Victoria and on his return to England in 1869 had been asked to take a touring side back to the Antipodes. Holmes described him as 'a first-class performer with bat and ball, a thorough sportsman, and a delightful companion'. He played in the club's first season, 1864, and continued to appear until sciatica in his fifty-sixth year finally induced him to lay down his bat in 1900. Carter was an influential figure in the early days of Yorkshire cricket: he had discovered Edmund Peate; in league with Lord Londsborough he had founded the Scarborough Festival; he had invited the then Honourable M.B. Hawke to play for the Yorkshire Gentlemen; and two years later introduced his protégé into the county side at Scarborough, an event he always said was 'the best day's work I ever did'.

By the early 1880s the 'gentlemen' of Yorkshire had long been disaffected with the dominance of Sheffield. Sheffield was the seat of the President and Treasurer of the county club, M.J. Ellison, the master of Yorkshire cricket. Ellison was the Duke of Norfolk's agent, a rich and powerful man in his own right who had poured his own money into the county club in the years since its formation. All fourteen members of the County Committee were elected by the Sheffield districts; all fourteen were Ellison's men – and the County Secretary, J.B. Wostinholm, was Ellison's first lieutenant. The rest of Yorkshire was – to all intents and purposes – disenfranchised. In the two decades in which the county club had been in existence, opposition to the Sheffield plutocracy had been widespread and often vociferous. Historically, because the resistance was fragmented, it had achieved nothing. At this remove it is impossible to know with any degree of certainty precisely what Carter's motives were when he brought Hawke into the Yorkshire fold; but he had triggered a chain reaction that would tear down the Sheffield monopoly and carry Yorkshire to as yet undreamed-of triumphs.

The politics of Yorkshire cricket have always been a tangled web of vested interests and deeply rooted passions. Cricket is not simply cricket in Yorkshire. Cricket is to a Yorkshireman what soccer is to a Liverpudlian, or, as the one and only Bill Shankly said of football: 'It's not a matter of life and death, it's more important than that!' The reason Yorkshire cricket seems to an outsider to be in a state of perpetual turmoil is quite simply that nowhere else in England, perhaps in the world, is cricket taken to heart as it is in Yorkshire. Under Ellison's iron rule Sheffield's grip on Yorkshire cricket gave an appearance of calm in the shire of the broad acres, but beneath the surface the discontent rumbled. The gentlemen of York were a thorn in Sheffield's flank, but hardly a threat. York was isolated and awaited its champion.

Meanwhile, Hawke enjoyed his cricket with the Yorkshire Gentlemen. In 1879 he averaged 23.00, with a highest score of 48, while the following season he scored 164 runs to average 20.50, his top score being 61. He finished high in the season's lists both years.

It was at the end of the 1881 season that Hawke was invited to join the Yorkshire XI in Scarborough Week for the matches against MCC and I Zingari. Festival cricket was organised not so much by the Yorkshire Committee as by C.I. Thornton, the old Etonian, with Carter acting as the agent of Lord Londsborough who was the patron of Scarborough Week and a vice-president of the Yorkshire Gentlemen. The first Yorkshire XI to include Hawke was not therefore, selected by the Yorkshire Committee. However, for reasons of its own, the Sheffield lobby regarded Hawke's appearance in the side as something of a coup. Yorkshire cricket was essentially professional cricket and the professional cricketers of the day were a breed quite beyond the ken of Ellison and his Committee. The captain of the side, Tom Emmett, was the idol of the Yorkshire crowds and a law unto himself. The introduction of a young amateur – and, what was more, the heir to the Hawke peerage – into the side offered the county both prestige and the prospect of obtaining a captain through whom the Committee might confidently expect to exert a modicum of control over its professionals. The fact that Hawke was, so far as Sheffield was concerned, an outsider was not considered a serious impediment. What mattered was that he was the sort of man with whom Ellison felt he could work and that he was available.

The Yorkshire team comprised of five members of the Yorkshire Gentlemen's Club, including E.S. Carter, the balance of the side being provided by the cream of Yorkshire's professionals: George Ulyett; Ephraim Lockwood; William Bates; Tom Emmett; Joseph Hunter; and Edmund Peate.

Hawke's début in the first-class game against MCC was a sobering experience. Batting seventh in the order he scored 4 and 0, Yorkshire losing in two days by an innings and 35 runs. In the second innings of the match against I Zingari he top-scored with 32 before falling to the bowling of his old captain at Eton, W.F. Forbes. In this contest the Tykes went down to a crushing defeat by 159 runs.

Within a month Hawke had taken up residence at Magdalene College, Cambridge. He was quickly back in training for the freshman's sports, running a close second in the quarter-mile in his first term and thereafter carrying all before him at Magdalene on the track. In 1882 he won all the events he entered, despite the College's cinder track which he hated. Once again his running threatened to put his cricket in the shade. In the winter he played soccer, more for exercise than pleasure, apparently missing the Etonian brand of football.

The Cambridge University freshman's match took place on a rain-ruined wicket on the first two days of May, 1882. Hawke opened for C.T. Studd's side and registered the unremarkable scores of 7 and 2. As a trial the game was a farce, only three batsmen managing scores of over twenty. Thinking that a blue was unlikely that season Hawke departed Cambridge for nearly a month for militia training and was unavailable for selection for any of the

University's matches in May. However, on his return to Cambridge Hawke gave a demonstration of imperious hitting and overnight he found himself contending for a blue. In his *Recollections and Reminiscences* Hawke described the events of the last day of May:

> Playing for Athenaeum *v.* I Zingari, I hit up 171, and, in my second knock, when I had made 91, Alfred Lyttelton went on with lobs on purpose to let me get my double century, but actually bowled me with a grub when my score was 97. He was much more vexed over it than I was.

Inside two weeks Hawke made his début for Cambridge University against Lancashire at Old Trafford. On a glue-pot wicket in between Manchester downpours Cambridge slumped to 9 for 7 in reply to Lancashire's first innings total of 90. Hawke, batting at number three in the order had contributed 4 of the University's 9 runs, a boundary struck of a leg-side full toss before he received the inevitable unplayable ball and departed. The light blues struggled on to make 31 before the rain eventually put both sides out of their misery.

Cambridge travelled down to the Kennington Oval where Surrey gained their first victory over the 'Cantabs' for many years. The University batted poorly, but Hawke's first innings knock of 58 was the highest score of the match and, combined with his 44 against MCC at Lord's the following week, was sufficient to earn him his place against Oxford at the end of the month.

Cambridge proved much too strong for a moderate Oxford XI in the Varsity match at Lord's; the Studd brothers were irresistible, G.B. scoring 120 while C.T. scored 69 and took 9 wickets for 102 runs in the match. F.E. Lacey and P.J.T. Henery contributed useful runs, as did Hawke with innings of 15 and 30, and Cambridge emerged triumphant by a margin of seven wickets.

In July Hawke joined Yorkshire at Sheffield where he made his Championship début against Surrey. On his arrival at the ground Tom Emmett the Yorkshire captain approached him, and offered him the captaincy. Hawke declined: 'No, no, I prefer to play under you for the season and to pick up a few wrinkles'.

It was the start of an association based on an unlikely mutual respect between two men whose characters and backgrounds could not have been more different.

At this point – with Hawke about to make his Championship

entrance – the reader may recall that our subject was not Yorkshire born: a state of affairs that would presently bar him from playing for the county. However, under the rules in force at the time – 1882 – and for many years thereafter, Hawke had an unimpeachable right to play for the county by virtue of his residential qualification, namely, that since 1874 his family home had been Wighill House, near Tadcaster. Indeed Hawke himself always considered that he came from Yorkshire stock: the great Admiral's mother was a Bladen of Hemsworth; the Admiral's wife was a Brooke, the heiress to the estates of Scarthingwell, Towton and Saxton; the wives of the third and fourth Barons both came from old and respected Yorkshire families while his own mother could trace her Yorkshire ancestry back to the seventeenth century.

Over the years the jibes about Hawke's right to play for Yorkshire rankled more, rather than less. From the very beginning whenever it was mentioned that he was not himself Yorkshire-born Hawke's sense of humour was wont to fray a little at the edges. When reminded that the Yorkshire captain was Lincolnshire-born, Ellison would retort: 'Don't tell me then, and let me have a convenient memory.'

In the Surrey match Hawke opened with George Ulyett who plundered 120 on the first day. Hawke managed 20. As the third day drew to a close Yorkshire went out to bat needing 44 to win in thirty minutes. In those thirty minutes the young Hawke learned an early lesson in the realities of the game at the highest level as the Surrey bowlers set about frustrating the batsmen and saving the match. C.E. Horner described the events of that late afternoon in July 1882 in *The Cricket Field:*

> The great thing, of course, was to keep the ball short . . . I was a little too excited at first, and began with two full pitches to leg, which Ulyett hit for four each, and the second one he hit into the seats, and the ball so injured a lady that she was carried out. After that I kept them straight and short, so that the batsmen couldn't get them away, though I have never seen men try much harder . . . Hawke persuasively suggested that there would be much finer cricket if we pitched them up, and we quite agreed with him, though we were unable to adopt his suggestion. When time was up they had made 35 with all their wickets standing.

A glance at the scorecard shows that Ulyett had made 25 to Hawke's 10 off the twenty-one four-ball overs that had been bowled. Before one chastises the Surrey tactics, it is as well to note that in the half-hour available for the Yorkshire innings the bowlers, Horner and Maurice Read, bowled the equivalent of fourteen six-ball overs.

Hawke played out the remainder of the season under Emmett's captaincy, often being the only amateur in the side. This was the year Bobby Peel first turned out for Yorkshire, making his début in a two-day fixture against a Yorkshire Gentlemen's XVI at Sheffield, taking a creditable 9 for 39 in the first innings. Hawke was his first victim, clean bowled. It was a miserable game for Hawke, out for 2 in his first knock and bowled by Bates for 3 in the second.

Hawke fared even worse in his first Roses match, recording a pair, but redeemed his pride a week later with a match-winning innings of 66 against Gloucestershire at Sheffield. At the end of the season the Yorkshire Committee nominated him captain for 1883 and, with reservations, he accepted the honour. The appointment coincided with the first significant reorganisation of the Yorkshire Committee since the creation of the county club; Sheffield retained its fourteen seats and its built-in majority, but seven new members were elected, one each from Leeds, Huddersfield, Dewsbury, Bradford, Hull, Halifax and, of course, York. The member for York was The Reverend E.S. Carter. With the installation of an amateur captain and the reconstruction of the Committee, a fragile peace broke out in Yorkshire.

Hawke had in fact assumed the captaincy during the Scarborough Festival in the last week of August 1882 when Yorkshire won handsome victories over MCC and I Zingari by an innings and 70 runs and by an innings and 91 runs respectively.

Exactly how aware Hawke was of the machinations behind the scenes is not altogether clear. It seems that he was an instrument of change rather than its architect, although in any event his succession to the captaincy represents a watershed in the history of Yorkshire cricket. While the ruling Sheffield clique congratulated itself on having averted a schism, it had, in reality, only put off the inevitable, delayed the final reckoning and in so doing condemned the club to a decade of strife.

However, the first indications were that the representation of other districts on the Committee and the appointment of a young, vigorous amateur to the captaincy had put an end to the internecine squabbles behind the scenes and revitalised the XI on the field.

When in 1883 Yorkshire were demonstrably the equal of any other county practically everybody connected with the club began to believe Hawke has ushered in a brave new era. It was to prove a false dawn; 1883 represented the high-water mark of the tide of Yorkshire cricket in the 1880s.

In 1883 Hawke's time of trial lay ahead of him in a future that must have then seemed full of possibilities. For the first half of the summer the leadership of the Yorkshire XI reverted to the capable hands of Tom Emmett because Cambridge had prior call on Hawke's services. University cricket, however, held no burdens of captaincy for Hawke; at Cambridge C.T. Studd was king. Hawke began the season in fine fettle, stealing a little of his skipper's thunder. On a wet wicket at Fenner's he top-scored in both Cambridge innings in a low-scoring match against MCC, hitting 29 and 20. Then in the next match, against C.I. Thornton's scratch side, he plundered his maiden first-class century off an attack that included Edmund Peate, George Ulyett and perhaps the finest professional all-rounder in England at the time, William Barnes of Nottinghamshire. Hawke's innings lasted 260 minutes and included one five and nine fours. Batting third in the list he had gone out to bat late on the first evening and reached 32 by the close. The next day he carried his score to 141 before Peate induced him to hole out to Ulyett, his dismissal signalling the end of a punishing stand of 160 with C.T. Studd, during which all but one of Thornton's side had been tried with the ball in a vain attempt to break the partnership. Studd departed twenty minutes later, whereupon the Cambridge batting crumbled before Ulyett's onslaught.

The following week against his own county, Yorkshire, Hawke's 37 was the best score of the students' second innings. Thereafter, his batting declined. It was not a happy period:

I seemed to have shot my bolt, for I could not succeed in playing myself in. To add to my misfortune, I injured my knee pretty badly, and it became a question whether I should be fit to turn out against Oxford. However, I took the field, though not of much use. H.V. Page bowled me first ball, and I did not go in again when only some sixty runs were needed.

Cambridge won the Varsity match by seven wickets. Built around the old-Etonian nucleus of C.T. and J.E.K. Studd, P.J. de Paravicini and Hawke, augmented by the talents of C.A. Smith (in latter years

Sir Charles Aubrey Smith of Hollywood fame) and the wicket-keeper batsman, C.W. Wright, the light blues were much the stronger XI even though, in Oxford's defence, it has to be said that they were unfortunate in losing the toss when there was rain in the air.

Hawke rested his twisted knee for a few days and then travelled to Trent Bridge to captain Yorkshire for the first time in the Championship. Injury robbed Yorkshire of the services of the veteran batsman Ephraim Lockwood and his steadying influence was to be sorely missed. Hawke, half-fit and out of form elected to bat at three in the order, registering scores of 2 and 3. Yorkshire were caught on a drying wicket and beaten by a margin of nine wickets inside two days. Bowled out for 61 in reply to the home side's 151, Yorkshire would doubtless have gone down to an innings defeat but for Ulyett's cavalier second innings knock of 61.

Inspired individualism, collective inconsistency and fecklessness in the field characterised the Yorkshire team that Hawke inherited from Tom Emmett. Emmett in his way was as hard a man to follow as Hawke himself was to prove. Make no mistake, Hawke was every bit as much in Emmett's hands, and to a lesser extent in those of his senior professionals, when he took over the captaincy, as his successors were in the hands of Rhodes, David Hunter, Hirst and Denton in the years before the Great War. The day when Hawke could snap his fingers and make Yorkshire cricket dance to his tune lay far ahead in a future no one in the shire of the broad acres could foresee.

Yorkshire cricket mirrored Tom Emmett in those days. Emmett was an erratic, infuriating and ultimately brilliant cricketer and by 1883 he was a Yorkshire institution. He was in his forty-third year yet his left-arm bowling remained unnervingly fast, the violence of his hitting was undimmed and his reckless courage in the field unequalled. Cricket was an all-or-nothing affair to Tom Emmett and after W.G. Grace he was the best known and the best loved cricketer of his day. Hawke had studied captaincy under Emmett throughout the season of 1882 and he continued to do so for as long as Emmett was in the side. Gradually, the balance of power shifted, but while Emmett was in the team Yorkshire could never truly be Hawke's to command.

Fortunately, the old professional took pity on his new captain. The two men could not have been more different: one the son of a peer of the realm, the other an incorrigible, lovable sporting brigand. Against all odds the two men formed an enduring affection and respect for each other, a friendship of a kind. Their friendship was always guarded, but it was nevertheless robust enough to survive Emmett's departure from Yorkshire cricket at a time when it had become apparent that Hawke had embarked upon a campaign to 'de-Emmettise' Yorkshire cricket. Emmett was a great cricketer who led by sheer force of personality and frequently got carried away. One day, legend has it, he opened the bowling and went on bowling until just before the luncheon interval when he was heard to mutter, 'Why doesn't the old fool take me off?' He had entirely forgotten that he was the captain.

When Tom Emmett was around life was rarely dull. Asked why he sometimes packed the off side with fielders and then bowled three or four balls to leg, he would laugh and explain: 'I expect it was bad bowling.'

Batting, bowling and fielding were immense fun to Emmett, indeed cricket was fun. He was the perfect antidote to his young captain's earnestness; nobody was allowed to take the game, or themselves for that matter, too seriously when Emmett was in the neighbourhood. No one was immune, not even Hawke, as witnessed by a story Emmett recounted in *The Cricket Field*:

> I used to try and get the ball as nearly as possible just out of a man's ordinary reach, and yet just within the distance which he could reach if he tried, and, fortunately for me, he often did try. But as men vary ever so much in the distance they can cover, I sometimes used to make mistakes, which the umpires described as wides . . . I remember Lord Hawke saying to me in a match, 'I say, Tom, do you know you have bowled 44 wides this year?' 'Have I, my Lord?' I asked. 'Then just give me the ball and I'll soon bring them up to 50, and earn talent money.

Emmett cut a fine figure on and off the field. A lean, energetic man with a weathered face and a large red nose, he might have been John Bull's nephew. Hawke said of Emmett's nose: 'if not so obtrusive as that of Cyrano de Bergerac, yet was as highly coloured'. Tom was the first to joke about his nose, boasting that after one night of celebration it had 'made the washing water fair fizz' in the morning. For all that he was no drunkard, and in his time as captain drunkenness was by no means as rife in the ranks of the Yorkshire professionals as either Hawke, or his supporters, later claimed. Emmett was very protective of his players, something that speaks volumes of his generosity of spirit in an era when professional cricketers were not so much employees of their county as free agents hired and fired according to the whims of the Committee.

It was under Tom Emmett's knowing eye that Hawke began to learn the trade of captaincy. In return Yorkshire cricket in general, and the Committee in particular, treated its former captain rather shabbily after 1883. Whilst it is important to stress that Hawke was very much the Committee's servant at this time, he was without doubt the prime mover behind the appointment of Louis Hall as vice-captain for the 1884 season. After this, Tom Emmett played out his career as the senior professional. Louis Hall, that supreme stone-waller amongst opening batsmen, became Hawke's trusted lieutenant in Yorkshire. Emmett's humour and advice was always welcomed but in Hawke's absence the side would be entrusted to Hall, the austere, unsmiling, teatotal lay preacher. A lesser man than Emmett would have despaired, but Tom took it in his stride and without complaint.

Change was in the air in 1883. Ironically, the Yorkshire XI Tom Emmett had built went through the season beaten only twice. In the aftermath of the drubbing at Nottingham Hawke rested his knee and came back to lead the county to six wins and two draws in the last two months of the Championship campaign. The outcome of the season seemed to vindicate the Sheffield monopoly and the decision to turn to an amateur captain. R.S. Holmes was to record in *The History of the Yorkshire County Cricket: 1833–1903* that 'at the close of the season the "hon. gentleman's captaincy was highly commended" by the County Committee'.

Not unnaturally, expectations were high for 1884, but it proved to be a torrid year for Hawke. Far from building on the promise of the previous season everything he touched turned to dust; it was the sort of experience that would have tested any man's character:

> The season of 1884 was my least successful. Once more my Militia duties interfered with my University cricket . . . When it came to the University match, I stood down for the Old Harrovian, D.G. Spiro, on the express understanding that this in no way affected my captaincy in the following year.

It was an *understanding* that put C.W. Wright's nose out of joint. By dint of seniority and cricketing flair he was every inch Hawke's equal in the Cambridge side, and, if anything, had the prior claim to the captaincy. Hawke emerged from that dismal season of 1884 a wiser man. His best effort from a year in which his sixteen first-class innings grossed a miserable 108 runs was a score of 22 made against Lancashire at Manchester. Hawke was only available for four of Yorkshire's Championship fixtures; Louis Hall had by default become the real captain of Yorkshire.

The year of 1885 was an altogether better year for the new Cambridge captain. He turned his back on Yorkshire – failing to turn out in a single county match – and concentrated on leading the light blues and enjoying country life. Cambridge won just one match in 1885, but it was the one that mattered, at Lord's against Oxford.

The week before the Varsity game Hawke hit 73 against MCC, the first time he had passed fifty in an important match for almost two years. His batting had recovered a little of its former poise and it was a happy period, Cambridge seeing off the dark blues by seven wickets. After Oxford had been rattled out for 136, Charles Wright (78) and H.W. Bainbridge (101) put on 152 for the first wicket. Oxford fought a valiant rearguard action only to be struck down by Aubrey Smith's fast bowling when it seemed as if they might set Cambridge an awkward last innings target.

Hawke was a surprisingly pragmatic student captain and his selection policy at Cambridge was one more often found in the professional arena:

> In my view preference, when skill is about equal, should be given to freshmen rather than seniors, because the newcomer is gaining experience which will be of increased value in the subsequent summers. Also, given nearly similar cricketing prowess, there is not the slightest doubt that an Etonian or Harrovian should have the greater chance, because he has already had his *baptême de feu* in facing a big crowd at Lord's and is therefore less likely to be nervous. . . I have no patience with the sentimentality of giving a Blue to a man because he is in his last year. To my mind it is absolutely childish unless he has made a remarkable advance in the current season. Places in the University Eleven should not go by favouritism, but absolutely to the best, with, however, an eye to the composition of the side in the following summer.

He was a popular captain at Cambridge. He led from the front and his side respected his shrewd cricketing brain. *Lillywhite's Cricketers'*

Annual said of him: 'captain, and a right good one; dangerous bat when set, and a sure catch'. Yorkshire again saw little of him; he took the University up to Sheffield in early June, later he brought a scratch side to Horsforth Hall Park near Leeds to meet, and defeat, a Yorkshire XI under Hall's captaincy. At the end of the season he turned out for Yorkshire against MCC at Scarborough during festival week. Curiously, Louis Hall led the team.

Hawke had grown into the Cambridge captaincy. Almost without knowing it the lessons he had learned under Tom Emmett's tutelage in Yorkshire had begun to sink in and he had come of age as a cricketer. Of his Cambridge cricket he was to recall:

> . . . except for an occasional punishing innings, I was not much good in those days. I had yet to learn by laborious application to be useful at a pinch, which was how I was to prove of chief use in the years ahead.

When Hawke returned to reclaim the Yorkshire captaincy in 1886 the Committee discovered that he was a man with a mission.

5

The Old Guard
(1886–1887)

Hawke had first taken the field as captain elect of Yorkshire on the last day of August 1882. Between then and the beginning of June 1886, he had appeared in only nineteen of the sixty-seven first XI matches played by the county. In his absence the captaincy had passed initially to Emmett and latterly to Louis Hall who had led Yorkshire on thirty-seven occasions in 1884 and 1885. There were those who mistakenly suspected that Hawke had turned his back on Yorkshire cricket. However, he returned to the fold with new energy and optimism. In his own words his 'consistent association with the county began in 1886'.

In earlier years he had been the figurehead, the man who tossed the coin on the first morning and subsequently exerted little or no control over the activities of his band of brigands. Now he was the captain of Yorkshire and whilst he was always ready to listen to unsolicited advice from his senior professionals – Hall, Emmett, Ulyett, Joseph Hunter and Bates – there was never again in his time as captain any doubt about who was in charge.

So it was that when Hawke took his men down to Lord's to play Middlesex in the first week of June 1886 that a new broom swept into Yorkshire cricket. Hawke's obvious commitment to the county club and his support for change within it marked a turning point in the history of English cricket. Hawke regarded his team as the equal of any other side in the land and, having reached this conclusion, he tried to understand how it was that its Championship showing had hardly reflected its underlying strength. He identified the problems and then set about systematically resolving them. There were two long-standing obstacles, the structure of the first-class game and his players. In 1886 his influence in the English game was more or less limited to the bounds of his own county and so, being an essentially pragmatic man, he turned his mind to matters closer to home; his professionals.

The Yorkshire XI of 1886 was a remarkable amalgam of extraordinary cricketing talents. Hawke was proud of his team, they were forever 'the boys of my old brigade'. On paper, the side Hawke inherited from Tom Emmett was every inch the equal of the Yorkshire teams that he was to lead to so many triumphs in the coming decades. Hawke began with high hopes for his old guard, convinced that firm leadership and a sense of common purpose would mend all its ills. What Hawke did not realise was that his 'old brigade' was already in decline; a decline that his captaincy tended to accelerate.

The seasons of 1886 and 1887 were to be the last flowerings of the old guard Hawke inherited from Tom Emmett; afterwards Yorkshire cricket floundered in the wilderness until its renaissance in the 1890s. These were Hawke's years of trial; his Yorkshire side at this time were never the champion county, indeed they were rarely second or third – more often than not they were simply also-rans. Many men in his position would have wearied of the turmoil, picked up a career in the city, indulged their love of country living; not Martin Hawke.

One can not understand Hawke or the traumas that Yorkshire cricket underwent in those dark days before its revival without understanding something of the nature and mood of the 'old brigade'. The side that Hawke led at Lord's against Middlesex on his return to the captaincy in June 1886 was – with one notable exception – the strongest XI Yorkshire were able to put in the field. In batting order (with the age of each man in parentheses) it was:

Louis Hall (33), George Ulyett (34), William Bates (30), Martin Hawke (25), Frederick Lee (29), Bobby Peel (28), Joseph Ambler (26), John Preston (21), Tom Emmett (45), Joseph Hunter (30) and Edmund Peate (31).

Hawke said of Louis Hall that he was 'a strict teetotaller, the first who ever played for Yorkshire'. With his successor in the Yorkshire side, John Tunnicliffe, Hall shares three distinctions; he was abstemious, a lay preacher and perhaps one of the most effective opening batsmen never to have played for England. By reputation he was the prince of stonewallers, but he was more than just a dour, defensive batsman. W.G. Grace was astounded on one occasion when Hall suddenly broke out of his shell and hit him out of the ground – and others were similarly disconcerted by Hall's block-and-hit style. On his day he was a notable leg-side hitter and he carried his bat through no less than fifteen first-class innings, scoring a thousand runs in a season on four occasions, in an era when to achieve the feat once was an unusual event.

He was known as the 'Batley Giant', for although he was only 5 feet 10 inches tall, he was a brilliant close fielder, whose presence loomed huge in most batsmen's minds. His whole approach to the game was determined by the principle of calculated risk: after a narrow escape fielding at very silly mid-on, he decided that he had tempted fate once too often and subsequently never again fielded in a position that was truly silly mid-on. R.G. Barlow – a batsman who was not normally renowned for his hitting – recounts the story:

> Before long Bates gave me one that I let go at, and the ball hit
> Hall full on the head. Louis spun round like a top and dropped;
> I thought I had killed him.

Fortunately, the injury was superficial.

Of angular build, painfully thin and severe of expression, Hall stood apart from his fellows. As captain in Hawke's absence Hall was respected as a man who practised as he preached. When Billy Bates was forced out of cricket by injury, Hall deferred his own benefit in Bates' favour.

George Ulyett had first played for the county in 1873, the same year as Louis Hall. Hall and Ulyett were cricketing opposites. At the time of his death in 1898 (at the age of 46 after contracting pneumonia when watching Yorkshire play Kent at Bramall Lane) Ulyett was universally regarded as the greatest professional batsman Yorkshire had ever produced. While Hall blocked, deflected and worked the ball away, Ulyett plundered the bowling. Together they registered ten century opening partnerships, and they were the first openers ever to strike up a hundred in both innings of a first-class match.

In his *Recollections and Reminiscences* Hawke said of Ulyett: 'To him every match was simply a jolly game, and he did not care if he made a duck or a century.' 'Happy Jack' Ulyett broke bowlers' hearts with the same abandon that he sank pints of beer. Built like a heavyweight boxer, few men have matched his capacity for sustained, controlled hitting. As a fast round-arm bowler Ulyett took hundreds of wickets and in the field his big hands pouched all manner of unlikely catches. An irrepressible man who had the crowd roaring with approval one moment, laughing or baying for blood the next, George Ulyett hit a thousand runs in season no less than ten times. Time and again on the rough, dangerous wickets of the 1870s and the invariably wet, ruined pitches of the 1880s Ulyett's bat alone stood between Yorkshire and defeat. Ulyett also scored the first English century in a Test match in Australia; his innings of 149 at Melbourne in 1882 standing as the record score by an Englishman on the opening day of a Test in Australia for eighty-four years.

Cricket history is replete with Ulyett tales. Hawke tells of the occasion when Happy Jack was the breakfast guest of the Studds at Cambridge, Ulyett having come down to turn out for C.I. Thornton's scratch side against the University: 'Whilst he was eating a chop, Devonshire cream was handed round to him by mistake. He looked at it, wondered, took it, and ate the lot.' Ulyett was pleasantly surprised by Cambridge. Following one match against the light blues he observed:

That's the best spot of eddication as ever I set eyes on, for them decent young fellers get taught to drink beer from morning till night with baccy thrown in, just as school children learn reading and writing.

In the match against New South Wales at Sydney in 1879 during Lord Harris's tour there was a riot when an Australian batsman was run out. In defending the umpire concerned Harris was struck by one of the mob, whereupon Ulyett and Tom Emmett, the two professionals in the side, ripped up stumps and had to be restrained by their captain from seeking physical redress for the affront. In the same match, in an atmosphere that was decidedly charged, Harris had joined Ulyett in the middle at a time when two English wickets had fallen in quick succession. Harris instructed Happy Jack to 'play steady'. The burly Yorkshireman promptly laid about the bowling to the tune of two fours and a three off the next four balls. When his captain asked him what he thought he was doing, he laughed and declared, 'My Lord, I rather felt like hitting them!' He continued to hit them until, with 55 against his name, he tried to hit once too often. That was how George Ulyett played his cricket.

Like Emmett, Happy Jack was a folk hero in Yorkshire and far beyond. Like Emmett it did not matter how many friends he had, how much he drank, what he said or did or whom he offended, for Ulyett was a cricketing institution. It would be quite wrong to say Ulyett was the sort of man one loved or hated; nobody could hate Happy Jack. Ulyett played on serenely through the upheavals of the coming years, eventually succeeding Louis Hall as Hawke's right-hand man.

If Ulyett was a larger than life character, then William 'Billy' Bates, was no less. W.G. Grace said of Bates that had his fielding been of a higher order he would have been classed 'the greatest all-round player of his time'. Born in Lascelles Hall, that famous nursery of cricketing excellence near Huddersfield, he was a stylish right-handed batsman and off-spin bowler. Hawke said of him:

> Billy Bates was always so dressy and smart that he was known as 'The Duke' ... I do not think Yorkshire had a more attractive bat than Billy Bates. Indeed, until Hobbs came, I think he was the most engaging of all professional run-getters. He never let a ball go by, but was always after it ...

Peter Thomas in his exhaustive work, *Yorkshire Cricketers: 1839–1939*, attempts to encapsulate the magic of 'The Duke':

> Everything that Billy Bates did was in the grand and splendid style. He dressed superbly in days when cricket professionals were not renowned for sartorial elegance, he bowled at times brilliantly, medium to slow off-breaks, and batted like a techni-coloured dream. On fast wickets his batting was superb and his on-drives broke more than one bowler's heart ...

Billy Bates was the first English bowler to achieve a hat-trick in Test cricket, against the old enemy at Melbourne in January 1883, dismissing P.S. McDonnell, George Giffen and the giant George Bonner. Bates took fourteen wickets in the match and scored 55 batting ninth in the order, England winning the contest by an innings, the first instance of a Test being decided by such a wide margin. The record book shows that Bates was also the first player in Tests to score fifty and take ten or more wickets in a match.

In all, Bates went on no less than five tours to the Antipodes. In February 1884 he scored the first 46 runs on the board for Shaw's side against New South Wales. Indeed all his big scores were struck in cavalier fashion, his batsmanship the epitome of elegance and an arrogant disdain for the bowling. At home he scored a thousand runs in a season five times and, with Edmund Peate, tormented Yorkshire's foes on the wickets of the rain-cursed 1880s. When a tragic accident ended his career at the age of 32 the cause of Yorkshire cricket suffered a blow from which it took many years to recover; whilst practising in the nets at Melbourne in 1887 he was struck in the face by a cricket ball. At one time it was feared he might lose his sight, but although he regained partial vision he was never again able to play cricket at the highest level. On the boat home he attempted to commit suicide. In all of cricket there have been few more tragic figures than Billy Bates. The dashing young Yorkshireman who had been a hero wherever he went died, at the age of 45, in 1900, ten days after attending the funeral of his old friend and cricketing colleague John Thewlis. He had caught a chill. He was later buried alongside his friend.

Frederick Lee was an infuriating batsman. He was inconsistent, selfish, occasionally inspired. In 1885 he had hit a faultless century against Nottinghamshire and made a string of useful scores. In 1886 he was dropped half-way through the season due to a loss of form. The following year he hit 119 against Kent and 165 against Lancashire, to add to innings of 206 and 144 taken off the Cheshire attack in two second-class matches.

Hawke was never especially impressed with Lee. In 1887, against Nottinghamshire at Sheffield, the county was set 119 to win in ninety-five minutes. Billy Bates hit 63 in fifty-seven minutes, leaving 28 to get in even time with six wickets in hand. Lee, who was in while Bates was getting after the bowling, scored just 14 and Yorkshire ended the match three runs short. Hawke had a long memory: 'Fred Lee would not play the game for our side, but stuck in without forcing.'

It was during this match against Middlesex at Lord's in 1886 that Hawke first 'realised that Bobby Peel was going to be almost as good a bat as he promised to be a bowler'. He hit 43 and 75 in the match. However, that season Peel remained in Edmund Peate's shadow. He was a different breed of bowler to Peate, a bowler more in the modern image. Whereas Peate was a round-arm bowler Peel's action was higher and his loop more deceptive as a result. Match after match Peel would stand in the outfield watching Peate and Bates wreak havoc amongst the batsman on wickets that were taylor-made for him. He hid his frustration, sometimes with the aid of copious quantities of ale. A third spinner in a side that already had two supreme practitioners of the slow-bowler's art understood the necessity to cultivate patience or perish; in any case all the while Bobby Peel was learning his trade. Indeed there were many who believed Peate's powers were on the wane; Bobby Peel's time was to be sooner rather than later.

When his day came to hold centre stage, he was a formidable adversary. Archie MacLaren paid him this tribute:

> Probably the cleverest bowler in my time . . . He was never worried by a perfect wicket and always appeared to have some conjuring trick up his sleeve with which to outwit his opponents, no matter how good the wicket was. He would vary his pace and the height of the ball most cleverly, with an occasional one coming quickly into the batsman with his arm. No one ever had a better knowledge of the game and he was the quickest I have ever played with or against at spotting the weak point of the batsman against whom he was bowling. It was this combination of qualities that made him the England bowler that he was on a run-getting wicket. When the ground was sticky his accuracy of length and spin made him practically unplayable. I place Peel first on my list of great left-handed bowlers that I have seen on account of his wonderful judgement, his diabolical cleverness and his great natural ability.

Joseph Ambler was a stranger in the Yorkshire XI. He appeared in only a handful of matches before relinquishing his place in the side to Irwin Grimshaw, a free-hitting batsman who had notched several good scores in the previous two seasons and from time to time would compile other notable innings without ever really becoming a fixture in the team.

Joseph Merrett Preston was, by his captain's admission, something of a character, but one who never realised his potential:

> An irresponsible individual, who, had he possessed the least self-restraint, might have become one of the finest cricketers Yorkshire ever produced. He was as brilliant as Billy Bates, but he had too many friends.

An aggressive bat, lively fast-medium bowler and exceptional fielder, Preston was endowed with all the natural gifts most cricketers are denied. Peter Thomas offers his considered view that Preston 'was one of the great imponderables in cricket history; one of the might-have-beens'. Drink was to be his downfall.

Tom Emmett's bowling had lost something of its nip and bounce over the years, yet wickets fell to him whenever he bowled. In the field his energy seemed boundless and both off and on the pitch he remained the heart and soul of Yorkshire cricket.

Joseph Hunter had succeeded the seemingly immortal George Pinder – wicket-keepers of the 1870s and 1880s kept going until their hands failed them. On the poor wickets of the day a stumper's life was less than idyllic. Joseph Hunter was among the best in the land and if not as famous as his younger brother David, who stepped into his shoes when he retired, he did achieve the one honour that was to elude his brother; he played five times for England in Australia. At a pinch he was a better than moderate batsman, capable of either blocking or hitting.

Edmund Peate hit more than one useful score in his relatively short Yorkshire career. However, it is for his bowling that Peate will always be remembered in cricket's hall of fame. He was the first of Yorkshire's great slow left-armers, although he had started out as a fast bowler. (Legend has it that Peate turned himself into a slow bowler after a winter spent perfecting his action in the shed of the Yeadon factory where he was employed as a warp-twister.) In 1875, when he was 19, he joined 'Treloar's Cricket Clowns', a circus that comprised eight acrobats, eight clowns and eight cricketers. The Cricket Clowns were not well received at Sheffield where a crowd of cricket enthusiasts reportedly 'mobbed' and 'sodded' the performers. The so-called booby cricket never caught on in Yorkshire.

It was none other than The Reverend E.S. Carter (who subsequently introduced Hawke to the Yorkshire XI) that recommended Peate to the county club after coming up against him in a match between Scarborough and Manningham in 1878. Initially, Yorkshire were uninterested, but eventually Carter's persistence gave Peate a match for Yorkshire Colts. Needless to say Peate took a hatful of wickets and never looked back. Ever since the authorities have been divided about just how good a bowler Peate really was. Hawke had his opinion:

> Peate was blessed with the most perfect action of any man I have ever seen deliver the ball . . . he had no theories. Nobody ever bowled more with his head . . . his only principle, with all

his variations, was always to bowl with a length – a golden rule he acquired from watching Alfred Shaw.

David Hunter, who only kept wicket to Peate at the end of his Yorkshire days when some thought he was past his best, nevertheless maintained that:

Peate was the finest left-arm bowler I ever saw. He had a beautiful action and was extraordinarily accurate, seldom, if ever losing his length.

R.H. Lyttelton called Peate 'the last of the genuine slow bowlers who relied upon length and natural break and whose bowling arm never raised above his shoulder'. He was accused of being a wet-wicket bowler, but he took his wickets on wet and dry pitches and was always impassive, in control and impossible to hit off a length, qualities his apprentice, Bobby Peel, was to mirror in the decade after Peate's departure. Peate himself explained his method by saying, 'I used to beat the batsmen by length bowling, by studying his weak points, deceiving him with pace and flight and so on.' He mocked the suggestion that he could pitch on a sixpence if he chose; 'it will take a man all his time to pitch on a square yard, not to mention a sixpence'.

At the Holbeck ground in Leeds he once had figures of 8 for 5 against Surrey. For Yorkshire he took nearly nine hundred wickets at an average of less than thirteen runs apiece. He was also involved in the dramatic closing stages of the famous Test at the Oval in 1882 when England lost to Australia by just 7 runs. Peate had gone out to bat with C.T. Studd with ten runs to score. Peate managed two, but was then out playing a forcing shot. Taken to task for failing to keep his end up while Studd tried to hit the runs, he retorted, 'I couldn't trust Mr Studd.'

What most people did not know was that Charles Studd and two other England men were unwell. Before he had gone out to bat Studd had spent most of the day shivering with a fever. In the aftermath the *Sporting Times* published the mock obituary penned by Shirley Brooks, the son of the editor of *Punch*, in 'affectionate remembrance of English cricket which died at the Oval', an event 'deeply lamented by a large circle of sorrowing friends and acquaintances'. Brooks concluded; 'the body will be cremated and the Ashes taken to Australia', little knowing what he had started.

Peate's life outside cricket was chaotic and if drink was partly to blame, his notoriety and the hero-worship that attended it was his undoing. He was another of Yorkshire's professionals who died early in life – at the age of 44 in 1900. Although his death was from pneumonia, *Wisden* commented that 'for some time as a result of his way of life he had been in a poor condition'. As long as he remained the premier bowler of his kind in the land Hawke tolerated his disruptiveness – and his 'friends' – but when he slipped from his pedestal Bobby Peel was ready and waiting to take his place and Hawke dismissed Peate from Yorkshire cricket.

Indeed Edmund Peate's playing days were numbered in June 1886, as were those of others. Tom Emmett was coming to the close of his illustrious career; Bates and Hunter would soon have been forced out of the game by injury while Preston, Lee, Grimshaw and Saul Wade – a promising all-rounder who first appeared for the county that year – never managed to come to terms with the wind of change blowing through Yorkshire cricket and one by one they found themselves swept aside by Hawke's new broom. The season of 1886 was the lull before the storm, a tempest of such ferocity that Yorkshire cricket came perilously close to foundering. At the height of the storm Hawke contemplated abandoning ship, but was thwarted by a quirk of fate.

Yorkshire had been beaten only twice in the Championship in 1885, but the campaign of 1886 began with a narrow defeat at the Oval, followed by draws against Sussex at Huddersfield, Middlesex in the Lord's match and Kent at Bramall Lane. Victory in a close run contest with Derbyshire at Derby was followed by a convincing 7-wicket win over Cambridge University in Sheffield. By the last week of June Yorkshire had seemed to have overcome their indifferent start to the season, but successive defeats at the hands of Surrey, Nottinghamshire, Lancashire and the touring Australians in the space of a little more than a fortnight left the Tykes' season in ruins.

Despite these setbacks Hawke's batting visibly matured. In twenty-five innings in county matches he recorded Yorkshire's highest score on five occasions. Against Kent at Sheffield, he hit 76 and 56 not out, outscoring his team-mates in both innings. The match was not entirely successful, however, since 'on Whit Monday there was a nasty row, the big holiday crowd breaking onto the ground, trampling on the pitch and tearing up the stumps when the wet condition would not let us play after lunch'. His form fell away a little in mid-season before picking up again in August when he registered several telling innings, including his second first-class century, a hard-hit 144 in 195 minutes against Sussex at Hove, the longest score made by any Yorkshireman that year. His 831 first-class runs were collected at the very respectable – at least for the mid-1880s – average of 23.74. In Yorkshire only Louis Hall stood above his captain in the batting lists.

There were few big scores in 1886, it was very much a bowler's year and Yorkshire's bowlers ought to have carried all before them. That Emmett, Peate, Bates, Ulyett, Peel and Preston failed to do so was less a reflection on their bowling than a statement about the fallibility of Yorkshire's catching. The Reverend R.S. Holmes in *The History of Yorkshire County Cricket: 1833–1903* commented:

> The team was terribly slack in the field: indeed their weakness
> in this respect became so notorious that it was said that
> Yorkshiremen were far too polite to run a man out.

The 'old brigade' were well aware of their reputation in the field, it was something they often joked about almost as if they were, in a strange sort of way, proud of their Achilles' heel. Individually, many of the professionals were brilliant fields, but others, notably Bates, were at best ordinary and sometimes very ordinary catchers and ground fielders. The side gave away too many runs and dropped too many catches. The reason why what, by any standard, was a remarkable Yorkshire XI never fulfilled its potential in the eighties was self-evident as Hawke was to remark:

> I have never known a side do well that could not hold catches,
> but I remember several teams that owed more to smart reliable
> fielding than to definite skill in batting or bowling.

A decade later Yorkshire supremacy would be built upon the bedrock of the near-infallible combination of John Tunnicliffe and Edward Wainwright standing at first and second slip; in 1886 Hawke would have paid a king's ransom for a safe pair of hands in the slips. The situation was exacerbated by the fact that Hawke himself was neither the nimblest of fielders nor the safest of catchers and so he was hardly in a position to lead from the front. In terms of dropped catches he was as culpable as any man and he knew it. On one occasion against Surrey at Bramall Lane he got under a lofted top-edge from Walter Read's bat off a Tom Emmett long-hop and spilled the catch before a typically large and raucous Sheffield crowd:

> I felt like disappearing into the earth. Tom was not worried. All that was on his mind was to give Read the same sort of ball and let him try the same stroke again – namely, what was then known as the 'Walter Read pull'. So says Tom to me:
> 'A little more west, please, sir.'
> The bait succeeded. Walter Read had an almighty smack, and it looked all the world over I should miss him again, as I never saw the ball against the pavilion. Luckily, at the last moment, up went one hand and there the ball stuck. Shall I ever forget the delight of the crowd? For a long time after that I could do no wrong at Sheffield.

Such happy sequels were rare events. In 1886 Yorkshire won five and lost eight of their first-class fixtures; the following year the county was harder to beat, but victories were elusive. In 1887 Edmund Peate departed, playing in only three games before he was banished. His bowling powers were little diminished, but he was a disruptive influence, a trouble-maker and Hawke made an example of him. Bobby Peel was waiting to step into the breach, potentially as fine a left-arm spinner as ever there had been, a more modern bowler than Peate, even if by upbringing and inclination essentially the same manner of man as his predecessor. The very idea of a Yorkshire side without Tom Emmett in it was alien, unthinkable, yet that year it was apparent that the great man's powers were, at last, failing. Although the wickets still fell to the wiles of the old master, most batsmen had clearly lost their awe of him.

The summer of 1887 was relatively dry, at least by comparison with the procession of damp, dismal summers that had preceded it. Batsmen's pitches were encountered in the most unexpected places. In August Yorkshire hit scores of 559 against Kent at Canterbury and 590 against the old enemy at the Horton Park Avenue ground, Bradford. At Canterbury the first three batsmen Hall, Ulyett and Lee all registered centuries. At Manchester in the return fixture against Lancashire Hawke scored 125 out of his side's 414. At this time a total of over three hundred was thought to be very heavy scoring and that seen in 1887 was to many a disturbing eye-opener. It showed conclusively that, given dry weather and flat wickets, the bat need not be the servant of the ball. It was an omen of what was to come in the golden years ahead. Yorkshire's batsmen revelled in the sunshine, Yorkshire's bowlers toiled – and Yorkshire's fielders spilled countless catches.

Hawke had scored 967 runs at an average of 24.79 and in county matches he had averaged 28.90. His form had been considered good enough to warrant his inclusion for the Gentlemen against the Players for both the Oval and Lord's matches. Unfortunately, he was unable to cover himself in glory in either contest, both of which were dominated by the professionals. However, he had made his mark as county captain. His authority was now the firmer for having withstood the outcry that followed Peate's departure and he had taken over Canon Carter's seat on the Committee.

The dismissal of Peate had split the Bramall Lane crowd and displayed to one and all who was captain of Yorkshire. The county President, M.J. Ellison, and the Secretary, J.B. Wostinholm, had given Hawke their unqualified support throughout and the three men now enjoyed an excellent working relationship. Far from being considered an interloper from the Yorkist camp, Hawke was taken to Sheffield's heart. Hawke, for his part, liked and respected Ellison and Wostinholm yet inevitably, as he settled into the captaincy and grew in assurance, the influence of Ellison and Wostinholm and the perpetuation of the Sheffield monopoly became an irritant and later a dragon to be slain.

By the end of the 1887 season it was obvious that Yorkshire faced a protracted period of rebuilding. What was not apparent at this stage was that the problems of rebuilding the team would be as nothing compared to the reconstruction of the club itself, which was to dominate proceedings off the field.

6

New Horizons
(1887–1890)

On Saturday 17 September 1887 the Orient Line steamer *Iberia* weighed anchor in Plymouth Sound and set sail for Australia. On board were twenty-six cricketers – eleven amateurs including the then Honourable M.B. Hawke, and fifteen professionals – members of the tenth and eleventh English teams despatched to the Antipodes. It was the first and, history records, the last time two representative English sides toured Australia in a single season. That such a thing could happen owed as much to the rivalry of Melbourne and Sydney as it did to the chaotic administration of the English domestic game.

In Australia the Melbourne club – thwarted the previous winter in its attempts to bring out a party of English amateurs by the New South Wales Association's invitation to Shaw, Shrewsbury and Lillywhite to bring out a professional side – had commissioned G.F Vernon to raise a team for the coming winter. Meanwhile, the New South Wales camp in Sydney had – without consulting the Victorian lobby – issued a new invitation to the English professionals, motivated primarily in this endeavour by the financial success of the previous tour. In England Vernon had gone about his business in good faith, assuming that the Australian authorities had matters in hand; only relatively late in the day did he realise that the Australian authorities were in fact divided and that a potentially ruinous clash of tours was unavoidable. *Wisden*'s verdict on the affair was scathing:

> Two English teams visited Australia in the season of 1887–88, but it is certain that such a piece of folly will never be perpetrated again . . . The Melbourne Club authorities averred that it was well known their intention of bringing out an

English team had only been postponed from the previous year, while the Sydney people, who supported Shaw and Shrewsbury, declared that for all they knew, when they asked Shrewsbury and his friends to get up an eleven for the centenary celebration in New South Wales, the Melbourne Club's project had been abandoned. Wherever the blame lay, the effect was to throw a complete damper on the visits of English cricketers to the Colonies.

However, to lay all the blame at the door of the Australians does seem a little unfair and one is left to wonder at the obduracy of both Vernon and the professional triumvirate of Shaw, Shrewsbury and Lillywhite in putting together their competing parties. Appeals were made by several notables in England to avert the impending fiasco, but it soon became clear that the MCC was not in a position to dictate to the principal protagonists. The evident impotence of the MCC in the affair was to be instrumental in leading to major changes in the administration and structure of English cricket in the coming decade.

In 1887 the plain fact was that if English cricketers chose to embark upon a venture that was obviously going to be a financial débâcle from the outset – and in so doing drive a wedge between the game's ruling bodies both at home and abroad, offending all concerned and so retarding the global expansion of the game itself – there was very little that the MCC or anybody else could do about it. If amateurs were a rule unto themselves professionals were quite beyond the pale. In the winter the professional was a free agent, compelled to go wherever work was offered. During the summer individual counties had a modicum of influence, out of season they had none whatsoever. MCC had not yet considered sponsoring overseas tours, preferring to allow private ventures. By remaining aloof it had surrendered the field.

Hawke had been asked to captain Vernon's Team. Initially, he hesitated. He had good reason to pause and in any event his father had been very ill that year and Hawke was rightly reluctant to leave the country. In the end his father told him to go and so, when the *Iberia* nosed slowly out in the English Channel on that September afternoon in 1887, Hawke had much to contemplate. If his worries centred upon his father's health, he could not help but be aware that as the *Iberia* set sail for Australia, disquiet was spreading across the cricketing world. His position was, in many ways, invidious; his invitation to captain the side had arisen only when W.G. Grace had declined to tour and whereas the champion's mere presence would have been the financial salvation of the venture Hawke was now being asked to make the best of a rather bad deal.

It was Hawke's first long sea voyage and he had been advised to kit himself out in white ducks for the journey. Crossing the Bay of Biscay he cursed the tight, constrictive clothes and determined that in future comfort would be the order of the day aboard ship.

At sea the two separate touring parties ceased to exist as such. The amateurs and the professionals from each side formed their own societies and shipboard life settled into its routine. The cream of English cricket was gathered together on the ship. An eleven drawn from the combined strength of the two sides – granted the exception of W.G. – would have graced any representative arena. On paper Shaw, Shrewsbury and Lillywhite's side under the captaincy of Hawke's fellow Cambridge graduate, C. Aubrey Smith, the Sussex captain, was marginally stronger, but in the heat of battle Vernon's Team would steal most of the honours. The teams were:

G.F. Vernon's Team

Amateurs: M.B. Hawke (Yorkshire), G.F. Vernon, A.E. Stoddart, T.C. O'Brien (Middlesex), W.W. Read, M.P. Bowden (Surrey), A.E. Newton (Somerset)
Professionals: R. Abel, J. Beaumont (Surrey), J.T. Rawlin (MCC), R. Peel, W. Bates (Yorkshire), W. Attewell (Nottinghamshire).

A. Shrewsbury's Team

Amateurs: C.A. Smith, W. Newham, G. Brann (Sussex), L.C. Docker (Derbyshire)
Professionals: A. Shrewsbury (Nottinghamshire), J.M. Read, G.A. Lohmann (Surrey), J. Briggs, R. Pilling (Lancashire), G. Ulyett, J.M. Preston (Yorkshire), A.D. Pougher (Leicestershire), James Lillywhite (jun.) (Sussex).

At Naples Hawke received his last letter from his father. In it the old man apologised for not coming to see him off at Paddington owing to his heart condition and ended the missive with the words 'be kind to your mother and sisters'.

The *Iberia* passed through the Red Sea in late September. Sharing a three-berth cabin with Walter Read and Monty Bowden in the stifling heat Hawke later commented that there was not 'much elbow-room'. There was a coaling stop at Aden and then the steamer cast off for Western Australia. Deck sports, amateur theatricals – with Aubrey Smith as the leading light – and cricket talk from morning to night filled the long days. Landfall was Fremantle, but the *Iberia* steamed on south to Albany, a former penal settlement established in 1826 some two hundred miles south of Perth, where she anchored in King George's Sound for eight hours to take on coal. After several weeks cooped up aboard ship the English cricketers eagerly took the opportunity for a run ashore and it was at Albany the trials of G.F. Vernon's Team began in earnest.

Vernon himself was the first victim of the ill-fortune that was to dog the tourists that Australian summer when he contrived to fall down a companion-way; within hours Walter Read had sustained a badly sprained ankle. Initially, Vernon's injuries gave his fellows grave cause for concern. It was an inauspicious beginning; neither Read nor Vernon took the field in the opening match of the tour a week later.

On Wednesday 25 October the *Iberia* at last steamed into the anchorage of the Orient Line off Adelaide. It was the parting of the ways for the two rival touring parties, but Vernon was not well enough to disembark with the rest of the team who boarded the train for the eight-mile journey to the city, where a civic reception awaited them.

Hawke was never comfortable speaking in public. He loathed making speeches. In later life his blunders on numerous public forums were to blight his declining years. Talking to individuals or small groups Hawke's personal charm, tact, and not least, his 'straightness', were immense assets; before a large audience a combination of stage fright and too great a reliance on prepared notes tended to negate his strengths and emphasise his limitations. Nevertheless, on formal occasions when all that was required was to smile and respond to the platitudes of a local dignatory, Hawke soon learned the drill, but it was as close as he ever came to mastering the art of public speaking.

At Adelaide Civic Hall he was confronted with a crowd of some four hundred souls when he replied to the warm welcome extended to the team by the mayor. He struck a positive note, stressing that the two English teams hoped to combine in a match against 'All

Australia' and expressing the hope that the tours would strengthen links between the old and the new countries. His views on the receptions given to touring elevens were formed early in his wanderings. In his *Recollections and Reminiscences* he observed:

> They are so well meant. But sometimes when the touring side is tired and feeling dilapidated, also perfectly certain none of them is looking even tolerably presentable, much less at their best, it is in our hearts to wish this cordiality postponed to a more comfortable hour.

After luncheon with the mayor Hawke took his men straight to the nets at the Adelaide Oval where, in the company of Stoddart and O'Brien, he flexed his muscles to good effect, entertaining the crowds with some spectacular hitting before a cloudburst put an end to practice and drove the tourists to their hotels. The rain then returned in the morning to disrupt any further work in the nets.

The opening match of the tour began on Saturday 28 October. Without Walter Read, whom Hawke regarded as the best batsman in the side, G.F. Vernon's team beat South Australia by 71 runs. But for defiant innings of 37 not out and 81 by George Giffen, the opposing captain (who also took 8 for 156 in the match), the tourists would have trounced their hosts. For a side straight off the boat from England and woefully short of practice it was a notable victory. Ten days later, in Melbourne, Victoria were beaten by an innings. Stoddart had hit 94 and then Peel, Beaumont and Bates had harried and teased the Victorian batsmen, with disastrous results for the Australians.

Fortified by these early successes and with Walter Read (whose tour was later blighted by bouts of neuralgia) back in harness, the tourists set off up country. First call was Castlemaine, a large, sprawling shanty town that had grown up during the rush to the Mount Alexander gold strike. Touring XIs were in great demand for matches against 'odds' in the boom towns of the interior; handsome guarantees were to be had and trips up country were often the financial salvation of a tour.

At Castlemaine the local club banqueted and fêted its guests from the old country and a grand time was had by all. On the field twenty-two of Castlemaine's finest found little joy against Hawke's professional bowlers on the first day and even less against Stoddart's deliveries on the second. It was not a match for batsmen. The contest was staged in what was virtually open countryside, manicured for the occasion. The wicket was without malice, but hardly a batsman's paradise, and the home side's inevitable fast bowler, Costello, took the wickets of Abel, Stoddart, Hawke, Read and Newton as the visitors were dismissed for 181. Bobby Peel saved the day, hitting 63, imperturbably punishing the slightest lapse in line and length.

The next day Hawke led his team into the field against XVIII of Sandhurst. Sandhurst, or Bendigo as it was also known, was another gold town. In the late 1880s it was the third town of Victoria, boasting a strong local team. Five English batsmen passed fifty as a hefty total of 417 was amassed by the second morning, the tourists skilfully threading the ball between the eighteen fielders – or simply lofting it over them. In the time remaining eleven local wickets fell as Sandhurst struggled to 135 off 114 four-ball overs.

The matches at Castlemaine and Sandhurst had been poorly attended. However, from Sandhurst Hawke took the tourists on to Ballarat, where a crown of about a thousand turned up for the first day of the match against the local XVIII. Ballarat was the capital of the gold-mining industry in Victoria, a town of some forty thousand inhabitants. The correspondent of the *Sporting Life* said of it 'there is not a prettier town in Victoria'. He was also impressed by the town's cricket ground, noting that it was 'in a delightful situation'. The playing area – by Australian standards – was relatively small and, since the Ballarat wicket was reputed to be fast and true, batsmen often prospered. Hawke won the toss and the tourists plundered 477 runs in a little over six hours. The English captain was missed early in his innings, two fielders colliding as they ran to get under a steepling mishit. Hawke took full advantage of his good fortune and laid into the bowling. His innings ended with a flourish, three successive balls disappearing over the boundary chains before Hawke departed, stumped stepping out to the bowling. His contribution to a stand of 105 with Walter Read had been 70. A crowd of some 1,500 was present to witness the end of the English innings on the second morning. When Ballarat batted Peel, Beaumont and Attewell put them out for 67. Following on the local club had reached 51 for 2 by the close of play leaving the match drawn.

An altogether sterner test awaited the tourists a week later in Sydney when, on 25 November, they went into the field against the formidable New South Wales side that had trounced Shrewsbury's Team by ten wickets in two days earlier in the month. Crowds of between four and five thousand attended on three of the five days and had it not been for the rain which curtailed play early on the afternoon of the second day and returned to dog the final two days of the match, many more people would have come to see what was perhaps the most eagerly awaited fixture of the tour.

The Englishmen, strengthened by the inclusion of the now re-covered Vernon, were fortunate to have first use of a good batting wicket. Against an attack which included C.T.B. Turner, J.J. Ferris and T.W. Garrett the tourists compiled what seemed a respectable total, although in the event it was anything but an impregnable total on that Sydney wicket. Stoddart, Abel and Peel hit fifties and Hawke a cavalier 48 before Turner rifled a ball through his guard. With Hawke's dismissal the tourists had declined from the promise of 198 to 3 to 340 all out.

In reply New South Wales batted with a grim and relentless purpose. A.C. Bannerman, who had scored the first century in Test cricket, stonewalled while his opening partner, P.S. McDonnell, took on the bowlers. Bannerman was eventually bowled by Peel with 62 on the board. Out came Harry Moses to join McDonnell. Moses has a rather unenviable place in Australian cricket history for he was probably the finest Australian batsman never to tour England. To successive English touring XIs Moses was an implacable opponent whom *Cricket* described in the following glowing terms:

> He certainly has a strong claim to the title of 'champion left-hand batsman in the world', and he is perhaps a better man than any left-hander who has been before the public during this decade.

This was the only time Hawke had the opportunity to watch Moses go about his business. He concluded that although Moses was 'without great pretensions to style', his defence was 'virtually invulnerable'. While Percy McDonnell stood firm-footed and crashed the English bowling hither and thither, eventually putting up a catch to Vernon off Attewell, Moses kept up his end. With McDonnell gone for 112 out of the 151 scored while he was at the wicket, Moses took up the challenge. By the time he fell clean bowled to Stoddart for 77, New South Wales had progressed to 245 for 4. In the end the Englishmen were happy to restrict their hosts to 408.

On the fifth day of the match the rain came and Hawke's men found themselves batting in the wet against 'Terror' Turner and his equally ferocious accomplice, Ferris. Turner made the initial inroad, removing Stoddart, and after that Ferris smashed through the English middle order. Only Bobby Peel kept him at bay and averted a complete rout, Vernon's Team stumbling to 106 and leaving New South Wales just 39 for victory. Peel induced an error from McDonnell, but with the wicket easing there was never any hope of retrieving the situation.

The tour itinerary gave G.F. Vernon's Team scant opportunity to collect themselves. The next day the party travelled to Parramatta. Overnight rain had soaked the ground where the tourists were to take on a local XVIII and when play began Attewell and Peel ran through the batting. On the second day the Englishmen were all out for 116 before more interruptions by the elements condemned the match to a draw. From Parramatta the tourists then travelled to Richmond, on the Hawkesbury River north of Sydney. On another sodden wicket Attewell and Peel ran riot against the local XVIII, taking 30 wickets in the match. At Hawke's suggestion the tourists drew lots to decide the batting order, Hawke going in at number nine and scoring 5. In the conditions skill counted for naught.

At Richmond on Tuesday 6 December Hawke received the news that his father had died. Whilst writing to an old-Etonian friend to congratulate him on his recent marriage, Hawke had paused to rise and look out of the window of his hotel room. Outside he had seen Walter Read and George Vernon deep in conversation and he had sensed that it was bad news. When Vernon came up Hawke took one look at his face and said, 'You need not tell me; my father is dead.'

Hawke's tour had ended; his new life had begun. Walter Read assumed the captaincy of the side and Hawke travelled to Sydney to catch the overland express to Melbourne. By morning he was homeward bound aboard the fast steamer, *Ormuz*. Within a fortnight the team he left behind had suffered another, even more traumatic blow. A few days before Christmas a stray ball had struck Billy Bates in the face in the nets at Melbourne. At first it was thought poor Bates would be blinded in the right eye and soon he too was on the boat for England, alone with his despair. His livelihood in ruins, returning home on the *Orizaba* to obscurity and penury, Bates tried to commit suicide.

The accident illustrated the knife-edge upon which professional cricketers lived. Bates's livelihood depended wholly on his cricketing skills; now unable to exercise those skills he was, at the age of 33, unemployed and with no means of support. From being a national hero in command of his own destiny he had suddenly been reduced to a beggar, reliant upon charity. In Victorian Britain he had every reason to despair although in the event he discovered that he had more friends than he knew. In Yorkshire, old players who had been loyal to the county were not knowingly left to fend entirely for themselves. Through Ellison's offices Bates was whisked off the *Orizaba* at Southampton and taken to be examined by Dr Crichett, an eminent eye specialist. Complete rest was recommended and hope expressed that in time Bates would grow accustomed to the impairment of his vision and be able to resume his career. In the meantime, Vernon and Hawke began organising a subscription on his behalf. When some months later it became clear that Bates would never again grace the first-class game, Louis Hall deferred his own benefit in his favour.

Notable performances by Stoddart and Read did much for the reputation of English cricket, but the Melbourne Club recorded a loss of four thousand pounds on the tour. The death of Hawke's father and the injury to Bates had marred the whole enterprise. A sad postscript to the tour was the dismal failure of a benefit match organised by the Melbourne Club to assist Bates; which barely a hundred people attended.

That spring, as the new Lord Hawke ordered his affairs, the mounting problems of Yorkshire cricket were never far from his thoughts. While he had been away in Australia English cricket had awakened to the fact that the county game had outgrown its administrative structure. The ludicrous double tour of Australia that winter had galvanised MCC and the counties into action, or at least the appearance of action. The result was the creation of the first, ill-fated Cricket Council, which held its first meeting at Lord's on the 5 December 1887, coincidentally the day Hawke's father died.

Lord Harris was elected the first Chairman of the Cricket Council, his proposer being none other than Ellison, the Yorkshire President. For Ellison the creation of the Council was a major advance for whilst it did not directly challenge the authority of MCC, the Council provided for the first time a forum in which the counties could discuss and promote change. The first-class game was in crisis, it had developed too fast and was now paying the price. Of all the counties none was as wedded to the professional game as Yorkshire; here change was not just a cricketing matter, it was to do with hard cash. Paradoxically, in an era when the game was expanding across the globe crowds at county matches had been falling and Ellison's primary concern was therefore the financial viability of county cricket. Yorkshire were beginning to feel the pinch.

If Yorkshire were feeling the pinch, other counties were not safe either. The consensus was that something had to be done and done quickly; the game had to be made more attractive to the paying public. W.G. Grace suggested standardising the hours of play in county matches, Ellison offered the opinion that the umpires might be given limited powers to extend play beyond the normal hours if a result was imminent. Other ideas included changing from four-ball overs to five-ball overs and permitting bowlers to change ends at any time during an innings providing they did not bowl consecutive overs. However, it was Ellison who put forward the most radical recommendation with regard to the leg-before-wicket rule, that:

> . . . the striker is out if with any part of his person he stops a ball which, in the opinion of the umpire at the bowler's end, would have hit the wicket, such part of the striker's person, when being hit being in a straight line between wicket and wicket.

The argument was that whereas in former times when cricket had been played on unprepared, rough surfaces, the only way a man could protect his stumps was to stand in front of them; in modern times, when first-class cricket was played on flatter, truer surfaces, batsmen no longer needed the protection of the lbw law to keep up their wickets. The original law had been framed to accommodate underarm or lob-bowling and needed to be revised to take into account the fact that most bowling was now of the round-arm or overarm kind. As the law stood, any fool could play the best bowler in the land with his pads and get away with it and as a result the crowds were being driven away from the game. Spectators wanted to see cricket played with bat and ball, not with the pads.

Lord Harris warned the Council of the dangers of meddling with the laws, but MCC's views on the subject found little favour with Ellison and his supporters and a special meeting was called to deal with the lbw question. When that meeting convened it recommended to MCC that law twenty-four, pertaining to lbw, be amended along the lines suggested by Yorkshire. However, history records that the campaign to get the lbw law changed failed and for decades batsmen were allowed to go on playing cricket with their pads instead of their bats.

Nevertheless, the counties had established that, even if nothing concrete had emerged from the doomed Council, in future they and the MCC would have to work together. The Council itself was largely the creation of Lord Harris and when he went to India as Governor of Bombay it soon withered on the vine. Ellison was in the chair when a motion was put to its last meeting that 'the Council should be suspended *sine die*'. Without Harris the Council had become a talking shop unable, perhaps unwilling, to address the pressing problems of the first-class game. Many counties despaired, none more than Yorkshire; henceforth the county would place the interests of Yorkshire cricket before all else. In later years, when Hawke was condemned for his Yorkshire-first policy, he was doing no more than pursuing the line adopted by Ellison after the failure of the Cricket Council.

Hawke made only a few first-class appearances in 1888. The weather was grim, wet and stormy and his form deserted him. In twenty first-class innings he reached double figures on only seven occasions, his best effort being an unbeaten 21 against Gloucestershire at Clifton. Distracted by the settling of his father's estate, and inconvenienced by minor injuries he was unable to find his touch. In his absence Louis Hall stepped into the breach and held the line. As if losing the services of Peate and Bates within a year was not tragedy enough, Yorkshire were now deprived of Tom Emmett who announced his retirement from the game. The Committee had engaged Emmett for what amounted to a trial period of three matches at the beginning of the season and when this contract expired the old warrior decided – rather than accept an insulting match-by-match engagement – to call it a day. Bobby Peel bowled magnificently, David Hunter, Robert Moorhouse and Edward Wainwright came into the county side and remarkably Yorkshire shared second place in the Championship with Kent.

Hawke had more time for cricket in 1889. In another dull, wet summer he registered an unbeaten 52 against Lancashire at Huddersfield and 69 against Nottinghamshire at Trent Bridge, his twenty-five first-class innings bringing him 426 runs at an average of 17.75.

Bobby Peel headed the Yorkshire batting and bowling averages that season, he scored the county's solitary Championship century and took twice as many wickets as any other man. The 1889 season also saw the débuts of J.T. Brown, George Hirst, Ernest Smith and Lees Whitehead. Nevertheless, this year, in the words of The Reverend R.S. Holmes, was:

> The low-water mark of Yorkshire cricket. For the first two months they were behind all their rivals and their final position was last but one. As a set off to ten defeats they could only claim a couple of victories, over Sussex and Gloucestershire. When they met Sussex at Brighton at the end of August each county had only won one match; so that this encounter should decide who should be the holder of the wooden spoon.

There were many reasons for the sudden decline; one was that the decline was not in fact sudden at all, it had been going on for years and only in 1889 did the full extent of the decline at last become apparent. For years the cracks had been papered over, the genius of individuals had rescued countless lost causes. Holmes pointed the finger at the sympton, rather than the root, of the malaise when he declared: 'Yorkshire's fielding was execrable, a dozen chances being missed off Peel's bowling at Brighton alone.'

The failings of the Yorkshire team came as no surprise to their captain; if anything it underlined the fact that it was high time that Ellison, Wostinholm and the Sheffield lobby gave him the freedom to act as he thought fit in the interests of his county side. Hawke had come to the conclusion that it was pointless to try to rebuild the XI without also changing attitudes. The old problems he had inherited from Tom Emmett in the early 1880s were still prevalent in the ranks of Yorkshire's professionals at the end of the decade. Yorkshire cricket was at a crossroads; drastic action was required and Hawke was prepared to take it. At the end of the 1889 season he acted. In the club's history Holmes states that:

> The curtain fell on the cricketing of four men who seemed at one time certain to take a foremost place; I refer to Fred Lee, Saul Wade, Irwin Grimshaw and Joe Preston – cricketers of whom it may be said in all charity that they had only themselves to blame for the disappointment they proved to all followers of county cricket.

When the young nobleman who captained their county explained himself before the Committee, nobody dissented. Hawke had presented Yorkshire cricket with a *fait accompli* and Ellison and Wostinholm acquiesced. The dismissals of Peate and (later) of Peel are part and parcel of Yorkshire folklore. Neither event strengthened Hawke's position, each in its own way undermined him; the sacking of Peate made him beholden to Ellison and his summary treatment of Peel set the Yorkshire public against him, unjustly casting him in the role of the bully. The dismissals of Lee, Wade, Grimshaw and Preston – essentially for not pulling their weight, although in Preston's case his drinking had long made him a marked man – entrenched Hawke's influence and created openings in the side that allowed his men to come through.

That winter G.F. Vernon invited Hawke to captain a team of English amateurs he was taking out to India and Ceylon. Bitten by the touring bug two years earlier, Hawke gladly accepted. No doubt the thought of a winter spent far away from the hotbed of cricketing passions in Yorkshire was not without its attractions and besides, it offered an ideal opportunity for him to indulge the other great love of his life: hunting and shooting. Hawke recalled that, 'having had a young man's fill of shooting at home, it was only natural that I should sigh for fresh fields to conquer'. India offered a marvellous diversity of big game and the prospect of a tiger shoot. In the late 1880s nobody questioned the casual slaughter of what were then relatively common animals; pangs of conscience, spasms of disgust are more modern responses to a sport which left unchecked would have eradicated countless species. Hawke was a very conventional man and the morality of big-game hunting was unimpeachable in his day. Our modern world of global warming, vanishing tropical forests, acid rain and endangered species is not the world in which Hawke lived. Hawke gloried in his hunting. To him it was an honourable pursuit and throughout his life so it remained. It is in the perspective of his own age that he should be judged.

Landing in Bombay on 4 November, a week before the rest of the party sailed for the subcontinent, he travelled up through Gwalior with his cousin, H.C.V. Hunter, and made camp on the Sardha River near the Nepalese border. His first encounter with a tiger occurred within days. However, his elephant had been attacked by a tiger on a previous shoot and as soon as it laid eyes on the big cat it bolted, preventing Hawke bringing his gun to bear. There was plenty of other game, including sambur, for Hawke to bag, but no more tigers were driven on to his gun that season.

While staying with the Rana of Dholpur, shortly before he was due to join up with Vernon's Team, Hawke was struck down with a severe attack of gastritis. The British resident quickly put him in the hands of Dr Crofts, the personal physician of the Maharajah of Gwalior, who took him into his own house. Hawke was very ill. The crisis came – and went – on Christmas Eve when he startled Crofts, who at the time was holding his hand in an effort to comfort him, by saying, 'I'd give a fiver for a whiskey and soda.'

Hawke always remembered Crofts as 'one of the kindest men I ever met and on leaving Gwalior the kindly doctor would accept nothing for his services. Hawke's illness was one among many misfortunes to befall Vernon's Team both before and during its Indian adventure (H.E. Rhodes, a member of the original party, had died after a fall in England). The Ten amateurs who followed Hawke out to India in the steamer *Bengal* were:

G.F. Vernon, J.G. Walker, H. Philipson, T.K. Tapling, G.H. Goldney, A.E. Leatham, E.M. Lawson-Smith, E.R. de Little, F.L. Shand, J.H.J. Hornsby.

The Honourable A.M. Curzon filled the gap left by the untimely death of H.E. Rhodes and A.E. Gibson, who had recently emigrated to India, was asked to make up the numbers when the news of Hawke's indisposition came through. It was a useful side, a mix of regular county performers, Oxbridge men and first-rate club cricketers. There was plenty of batting as well as bowlers of most types, indeed it was a side that would have held its own against an English minor county. Against the opposition it was likely to meet in India, Vernon's Team was a very handy combination. Moreover, it was a team full of characters; in addition to the double international, Vernon, there was J.G. Walker, the Middlesex batsman who had represented Scotland on the Rugby field, H. Philipson the captain of Oxford University, and T.K. Tapling, the sitting Member of Parliament for the Harborough division of Leicestershire.

By the time Hawke joined the side at Lucknow early in February 1890 the tourists had completed nine fixtures, winning seven and losing only one, against a surprisingly capable Parsee XI in Bombay. The tour had progressed from Colombo in Ceylon to Calcutta in the east, on to Bankipore in Behar Province, onward up to the North-West Frontier at Allahabad, thence to Bombay and now Lucknow, a town still redolent with echoes of the mutiny.

The team that represented Lucknow and district comprised eleven expatriates – civil servants and soldiers in the main. To the surprise of the tourists the only reverse that Vernon's men had suffered had been at the hands of the one ethnic Indian side it had encountered to date, the Parsees. For the main, cricket on the subcontinent in the 1880s remained an essentially British pursuit. Indian cricket played by native Indians was to prosper alongside the rise of Indian influence first in local government and then in national politics under the the the Raj. In Bombay the Parsees formed a distinct, relatively wealthy community that supported British rule. The Parsees were the trail-blazers' of native Indian cricket.

Few of the expatriate XIs had seriously tested Vernon's Team but Lucknow outplayed the tourists on the first day. Assuming the captaincy, Hawke had opened the batting, was bowled for a duck and saw his side dismissed for 79. The local XI replied with an innings of 125, an advantage of 46 runs. No sooner had Hawke gone out to bat on the second morning than he put up a catch to third man, which to his relief was promptly spilled. Taking courage from his escape he began to hit out, at one point carting three successive deliveries to long-leg for boundaries until at 45 he played around a straight ball and was bowled. The openers had put on 85 and the subsequent batsmen quickly took the total to 229. On a wearing wicket a target of 184 was never within the capabilities of Lucknow, whose fitful resistance came to an end 123 runs short of victory late that afternoon.

Vernon's Team then took the train to Agra. Illness and injury had taken its toll among the English amateurs; Goldney, Hornsby and Vernon were all unavailable and their places against Agra were filled by guest players. The tourists were much too strong for the local side – despite the dogged batting of W. Troup, the Gloucestershire batsman, who carried his bat through Agra's first knock – winning by an innings and 66 runs. Hawke's contribution to the victory was modest, a free-hitting 34 on the first morning that confirmed his return to fitness, if not his capacity to compile a high score.

A week later at Meerut, the redoubtable Troup was once more defying the tourists, on this occasion batting for Northern India in a drawn contest. Vernon's Team had forced the follow-on but the heat, the clock and the tenacity of their hosts' batting had always threatened to deny them. Before the team moved on from Meerut E.R. de Little's tour ended prematurely when he broke a collar-bone in a riding accident.

The final match of the tour was against the Punjab at Lahore at the end of February. The tourists won by an innings, Hawke contributing a handsomely struck 65 to his side's total of 325. Although illness had kept him out of the first nine matches, Hawke had the satisfaction of heading the tourist's batting averages, albeit by a mere fraction.

It had been a somewhat mixed few months for the seventh Baron Hawke. He had fallen under India's spell, experienced the pleasures and the vicissitudes that the subcontinent offered – and in the process had been changed for ever. Whilst he had been away from England events in Yorkshire had taken a new twist, a twist which was to lead him to question seriously his own involvement with the county club.

7

The Winds of Change
(1890–1893)

The annual general meeting of the Yorkshire County Cricket Club held at the Bramall Lane ground in Sheffield on Tuesday 7 January 1890 was an unhappy affair. The county's dismal showing in the Championship and the subsequent sacking of Grimshaw, Lee, Preston and Wade lent the occasion an air of crisis. Moreover, the Committee had to report that having commenced the year with a balance in hand of £139 16s. 9d., the club's funds had been reduced to a mere £7 9s. 10d.; Yorkshire cricket had made a loss for the first time in its history. It was a dark day in the shire of the broad acres. Had the Committee known that until a few days earlier Hawke had been desperately ill in Gwalior, it would have seemed a black day indeed.

Yet when the Yorkshire President, M.J. Ellison, got to his feet to move the adoption of the Committee's annual report and accounts, he had no comfort for the reformers. The Sheffield monopoly remained intact, Ellison spoke for Sheffield and so far as he was concerned Sheffield remained the heart and soul of Yorkshire cricket. If Yorkshire cricket was in the doldrums, it was because Yorkshire had failed Sheffield. In Hawke's absence the exasperated dissenters seethed as Ellison absolved himself and his Committee from blame. The Sheffield monopoly had lost touch with the mood of Yorkshire cricket, revolution was at hand in the Ridings whilst Ellison and his cohorts congratulated each other within the walls of their castle. Conservatism was king, Ellison spoke with the voice of the past and had he only opened his eyes he would have seen that the days of Sheffield dominance of Yorkshire cricket were numbered. *Cricket* faithfully reported Ellison's speech:

The Chairman remarked that he wished to say something with regard to the position which Yorkshire occupied last season in the world of cricket. They embarked upon the season of 1889 with the full expectation that they would be at the top of the tree. They all knew the lamentable failure they met with. For this result a large number of people who called themselves supporters of cricket were responsible. The great difficulty with which they had to contend arose from what he might call 'demon drink'. They had had to put out of the team one upon whom they had relied as a tower of strength for a great many years, and at a critical time they had to suspend another. In a great measure these occurrences were caused by those who called themselves supporters of cricket, who came to the ground, and who could not see a professional cricketer without wanting to give him a glass of drink. They never thought that if they gave him a glass a thousand others would want to do the same. If the grateful professional accepted the offer of one man and refused that of another he made himself enemies. People who have done this have been remonstrated with. This was one of the greatest difficulties with which they had to contend, and he wished its serious nature would be borne home to every one who frequented the ground. The most serious thing they could do to a professional cricketer was to offer him drink. It not only imperilled his immediate advantage in destroying his chance of being a member of the county team, but it endangered his future interests when he came to apply for a benefit. He hoped this would be brought home to the mind of every person who frequented the Bramall Lane ground. If it were, he was of the opinion that it would not be long before Yorkshire attained a high position among the counties.

The problems of Yorkshire cricket would, it seemed, disappear if the Sheffield public desisted in buying ale for professional cricketers . . . Only Sheffield folk were apparently true supporters of cricket. The problem was the 'frequenters' of Bramall Lane. It was, of course, arrant nonsense.

The Sheffield monopoly had complacently presided over Yorkshire cricket in decline, more concerned to preserve its own vested interest than to promote success on the field. It was Hawke who had taken up the cudgels against the 'demon drink', not Ellison, nor his Committee. The Sheffield monopoly had ignored, then tolerated drunkenness and individualism at the expense of the team for years and even now its conversion was half-hearted. Sheffield blamed the paying public, the professionals, 'demon drink' and the weather; only Sheffield was blameless. The Sheffield monopoly had backed itself in a corner from which there was no escape. It could no longer put forward a coherent case for its own continuation; instead it looked for scapegoats. It had no answers, all it could do was issue exhortations, pretend it was in control, hope and pray that nobody noticed the emperor was unclothed.

It was a self-defeating strategy that was to deliver Yorkshire cricket into Hawke's hands before the end of the decade. However, in the spring of 1890 Sheffield clung to its authority, as afraid of losing its supremacy as it was uncertain as to whom it might eventually be surrendered.

On his return to England Hawke put himself forward for military duties with the 5th West Yorkshire Militia, into which he had been commissioned in his Cambridge days and in which he now held the rank of captain. Because of this commitment he would be lost to cricket for between five and six weeks in the middle of the season. In 1890 cricket was to be his recreation while he contemplated hunting tiger in India and laying the groundwork for future overseas tours. Before his departure the previous autumn he had stirred up a veritable hornet's nest but, in the intervening months the flame of his reforming zeal had been largely extinguished. Once again events had revealed to him a life beyond cricket, reminded him that cricket was not the be-all-and-end-all. He had discovered the fascinating and dangerous thrill of hunting big game, suffered an illness that had almost killed him and travelled widely across India. There was no reason to believe that Yorkshire would be any more capable of challenging for Championship honours in 1890 than they had been in 1889; cricket would not have first call on him that year.

Nevertheless, under Hawke's purposeful leadership in May and June Yorkshire's record in first-class cricket confounded the critics. Victories were achieved against Gloucestershire at Bristol, Liverpool and district at Aigburgh, Sussex at Bradford, Kent at York, Middlesex at Lord's and the Australians at both Bramall Lane and Bradford. Set against defeats by Nottinghamshire at Sheffield and at Fenners to a powerful Cambridge University side, it was a brilliant opening to the new campaign.

Bobby Peel's bowling and George Ulyett's batting were the roots of the all-round team efforts that bore such promising fruit in the first two months of the season. In mid-June Yorkshire headed the Championship despite losing to Nottinghamshire by the apparently huge margin of 198 runs. The Trent Bridge men had enjoyed the best of the conditions, and the paucity of the Yorkshire batting had been cruelly exposed. Only against the light blues at Cambridge had the Yorkshiremen been truly outfought and outplayed. Ironically, in this match a 19-year-old freshman, the Yorkshire born and bred F.S. Jackson, burst upon the big stage of English cricket. In what was only his fourth first-class match, the Old Harrovian wrought havoc in both Yorkshire innings, registering figures of 5 for 61 and 7 for 53. Jackson was destined to become Yorkshire's most remarkable amateur and eventually succeed Hawke in the office of President of the county. It was not the last time Jackson's bowling would decimate his native county's batting.

Hawke had had his eye on Jackson for a couple of years; in the Eton and Harrow meeting at Lord's in 1888 Jackson's batting and bowling had overwhelmed Hawke's old school so comprehensively that it had earned him a degree of national celebrity. In the summer of 1890 Hawke extended an invitation to Jackson to join the county team when he came down from Cambridge later in the season.

Yorkshire's form fell away after Hawke went off to his Militia in July. George Ulyett had been named as deputy captain that year, more out of regard for the ageing but ever-geneal, near-legendary batsman than any failing on Louis Hall's part. When Ulyett was called away by England Hall stood in. Victory in the Championship proved equally elusive for both captains, with defeats at the hands of Lancashire and Gloucestershire and draws with Surrey and Lancashire. In other fixtures Yorkshire beat MCC at Lord's but suffered unnerving defeats to minor counties in second-class matches, losing to Warwickshire and to Derbyshire at home and away, respectively.

The Committee advanced the theory that the professionals were being asked to play too much cricket, but the congestion of the fixture list was the Committee's response to the previous year's financial losses. Hawke's return saw a recovery: mighty Surrey were beaten in a desperately close match at the Oval; Sussex were swept aside by an innings at Brighton; honourable draws resulted from contests against Nottinghamshire, Kent and Middlesex. At Lord's Hawke hit 74, including two sixes and four fours, on a treacherous rain-ruined wicket as every other batsman struggled.

At the end of the 1890 season, a season not without its controversies Yorkshire finished joint third with Kent in the Championship.

When it was discovered that Middlesex had refused to release A.E. Stoddart for the Oval Test, the Yorkshire Committee – at Hawke's prompting – swiftly retaliated by denying England the services of Ulyett and Peel. Since the two counties were scheduled to meet during the Test match northern feelings ran high at what was perceived as southern perfidy. Hawke made no apology for putting Yorkshire before England.

Yorkshire relied too heavily on Peel and Ulyett that year. The latter was no longer the fearless, happy-go-lucky hitter of former years, an element of sobriety had crept into his batting after a protracted lean period and had rejuvenated his career when it looked as if he must surely be nearing retirement. Peel took wickets all season long but often ploughed a lonely furrow. Only Wainwright provided regular support, claiming 37 Championship wickets to the master's 91.

If the revival of Yorkshire's fortunes in 1890 granted the Sheffield monopoly a year's grace, the disappointments of 1891 were to cause Ellison and his men to retreat further. In the Championship Yorkshire lost twice as many matches as they won, finishing eighth of the nine competing counties. Holmes wrote in *The History of Yorkshire County Cricket: 1833–1903*, 'loud and long were the jeremiads uttered by the press and the man in the ring'. Yorkshire cricket was the butt of too many jokes and questions were asked in the Press, such as, 'are batting, fielding, if not bowling, becoming a lost art among Yorkshiremen?' The 'frequenters' of Yorkshire cricket whom Ellison had so haughtily sought to blame for failings that were, root and branch, of his own making, turned their wrath on the Committee. The tenor of the debate can be gauged by Holmes' account of the demands of the reformers: 'Get rid of the present County Committee; smash up the Sheffield monopoly ... The present Committee is effete; it has lost touch with Yorkshire local cricket, if, indeed, it ever possessed it,' and 'What is wanted is a Committee, selected on a broad basis, in which not one town nor one district shall have a preponderance of voting power.'

English cricket watched uneasily as Yorkshire drifted towards undeclared civil war. Few men chose to voice publicly their support for either of the rival factions. Eventually, in its 1892 edition, *Wisden* pronounced:

The record for 1891 obtained by the Yorkshire eleven naturally created great dissatisfaction all over the county. The reason for poor result is, we think, amply accounted for in the moderate quality of the new blood that has been infused into the Yorkshire team of recent years. Great players, one after another, have dropped out of the team, and the men who have taken their places have proved inadequate substitutes . . . Possibly there are men in the county of first-class ability, but if so they are immensely difficult to discover, or else the County Committee is formed of a singularly incapable set of men. The present constitution of the Yorkshire Committee may be most undesirable, and the regrettable condition of Yorkshire cricket may be due to the lack of adequate representation for districts other than Sheffield. We hold no brief for the Yorkshire Committee, but we cannot forget how much Yorkshire cricket has owed in the past to Sheffield, and though the time may have come for the pre- ponderance of power being held by that town, the change should be striven for in a sportsmanlike manner, and not in a way such as last summer aroused all over England pity . . . for the Yorkshire County Committee and the Yorkshire County Eleven. The people of Yorkshire probably never showed to less advantage than in the attitude they displayed to their representative cricketers last summer. Of course it is very annoying in a county of such extent as Yorkshire, in which club cricket reaches so high a standard of excellence, to have to admit that the team, picked presumably from the best players the districts can produce, is inferior to that of a young aspirant to Championship honours like Somerset, or compares unfavourably with Sussex. The way, however, to remedy such a state of things is not by abuse of authorities and of players such as disgraced Yorkshire last summer, but rather by encouraging both to further effort. At any rate, we trust that any future attempt to reconstitute the Yorkshire Committee may be conducted with better taste and judgement than characterised the agitation of last season.

The oracle had spoken. Enough was enough; Yorkshire cricket was making an ass of itself and the time had come to call a halt.

Hawke had a torrid time with the bat in 1891. Up until the last week of July his highest score was 37. His seventeen innings had produced an average only slightly in excess of seven runs, and had included eight ducks. Before the match with Somerset at Taunton a friend, H.V.L. Stanton ('Wanderer' of the *Sportsman*), commented upon his poor run, spurring Hawke to open the batting in an attempt to find his touch. When he arrived at the wicket Lionel Palairet turned to S.M.J. 'Sammy' Woods, who was then perhaps the most lethal fast bowler in the land, and remarked: 'Here's a rabbit beginning his innings.'

Sammy Woods was a much wiser man than legend would have one believe. He hedged his bets: 'Don't lay too much on that, old son.'

Hawke went after the bowling from the start. He batted for just three hours, hitting 126 out of 233 scored while he was at the wicket, in an innings which included a six and nineteen fours. In the second innings he scored another 42 and Yorkshire proceeded to an easy victory. However, his luck soon deserted him. In the next match against Gloucestershire at Sheffield he took a painful blow on the hand. The injury was initially examined and diagnosed as bruising by none other than Dr W.G. Grace. Not wishing to flout the 'old man's' opinion Hawke batted on until he had scored 36, when his distress became so acute that he could hardly hold his bat and he threw away his wicket. He had in fact sustained a broken finger which kept him out of the game until Scarborough week.

While controversy rumbled around the county Hawke somehow managed to distance himself from the unseemly goings on. On the face of it he was scrupulously loyal to Ellison, if only by default, since to all intents and purposes he remained aloof throughout. In private the Sheffield camp were left in no doubt that any move they made to broaden the consensus within Yorkshire cricket would have Hawke's whole-hearted support.

In any case Hawke had other preoccupations: he was protective of the younger men who were coming into the Yorkshire side; he defended his colts against all criticism; then there was the tour he was busily trying to organise for the coming winter. At first he hoped to take a party of English amateurs back to India, but when that fell through he turned his sights west to the New World, from where an invitation from the Germantown Club of Philadelphia was soon secured.

Hawke was a rare man in Yorkshire; a man not totally obsessed with the internecine strife that was blighting the county's cricket. He had no taste for infighting and found the feuding and intrigue deeply offensive. At this stage of his life he would quite happily have become a country squire, an occasional city man, played his cricket for the Yorkshire Gentlemen and forsaken the English first-class game with few regrets.

The Winds of Change (1890–1893)

When, on Wednesday 16 September, he boarded the Inman Line steamer *City of New York* at Liverpool, he left the woes of Yorkshire cricket in his wake. The Germantown club had taken upon itself the considerable burden of the detailed organisation of the forthcoming tour, leaving him free to concentrate on his cricket and to enjoy the society that awaited the tourists on the other side of the Atlantic. American cricket, at least in Philadelphia if not generally, was played to a very high standard. During this period the Philadelphians were – as they proved on several visits to England – redoubtable opponents. Consequently, English cricketers held their American cousins in high regard.

The gentlemen cricketers who embarked with Hawke on his first odyssey to the Americas were:

H.T. Hewett, C.W. Wright, G.W. Hillyard, K. McAlpine, J.H.J. Hornsby, K.J. Key, G.W. Ricketts, G.E.M. Throwley, S.M.J. Woods, C. Wreford-Brown, H.A. Milles.

Lionel Palairet had originally accepted Hawke's invitation to join the tour, but stepped down late in the day to be replaced by Woods, who was to be the star of the side. It was a fairly strong team, although without the addition of Sammy Woods the bowling would have been little more than ordinary on a good wicket. Hawke, Hewett, Woods, Wright and Key were performers capable of holding their own in any company, but the balance of the side was essentially formed by good school and club cricketers. It was a party full of all-round sportsmen, full of characters, a band of brothers among whom it would be almost impossible to spend a dull evening.

Few characters in cricket history can compare with Sammy Woods. He had already played for Australia and before the end of the decade he would have played for England. H.T. Hewett, Wood's county captain at Somerset was a quick-tempered, high-principled man renowned for his prodigious hitting. He was known as 'the Colonel' on account of his bearing and commanding presence and was Hawke's vice-captain. G.W. Hillyard was a noted lawn-tennis player who at the age of 44 represented Britain in the 1908 Olympics. No more than a stock bowler, he was a fine golfer and redoubtable opponent on the billiards table. K. McAlpine, formerly of Haileybury, had few pretensions to greatness at the wicket, but in 1922 he became President of Kent. Kingsmill Key, the Surrey batsman, had toured in America as long ago as 1886 with Saunders's team. A double blue at Oxford (cricket and Rugby), he went on to captain Surrey from 1894 to 1899. Throwley was the future Lord Throwley, second Earl Sondes, and H.A. Milles was his half-brother. They were Kentish men, both handy club cricketers. C. Wreford-Brown was a renowned footballer. He played centre-half for Oxford, the Old Carthusians, the Corinthians and England. Later he was Vice-President of the Football Association and, legend has it, the man who first coined the expression 'soccer'.

After a stormy crossing and a warm welcome in New York the tourists boarded the train for Philadelphia. Then, with a single net session under their belts the English amateurs took the field against the immaculately turned-out Gentlemen of Philadelphia. On winning the toss Hawke sent Wright and Hewett out to bat. The tourists batted until shortly before the close, the last man departing with 259 on the board. Against expectations run-getting had been rather hard work on a true, if slow, wicket. Hawke had entered the fray at the fall of the first wicket, been cheered all the way to the wicket, and rewarded the crowd with an attacking innings of 74 that included an expansive demonstration of his crashing off-drive.

When the Philadelphians batted, a well-made 69 by their captain and leading all-rounder, G.S. Patterson, enabled them to compile a total of 248 runs. The home side were helped by an out-of-sorts Sammy Woods, whose bowling lacked its customary and remorseless hostility. The English amateurs had reached 85 for 2 by stumps on the second day, some 96 runs ahead. However, in the morning the wicket began to take spin and the last eight wickets added only 86 runs. Set 183 to win on a turning wicket the Philadelphians, after relatively few alarms, coasted to a notable victory by the handsome margin of eight wickets. Once Charles Wright had put down a sharp chance offered by Patterson off Sammy Woods the die was cast.

Within days the tourists had their revenge. In a low-scoring return encounter the Philadelphians were overwhelmed almost single-handedly by Sammy Woods. Bowling fast and straight, he claimed 15 wickets for 86 runs in the match. As the contest had been concluded inside two days the English tourists readily agreed to commence an exhibition match, which began late on the afternoon of that same day and continued on the next. In the time available – just over a day – Hawke's men scored 331 runs in the only innings of the contest, Hawke with 76 and Key with 50 not out thrilling the crowd with their lofted hitting near the end.

Moving on to Livingstone, the tourists met XVI of New York in a drawn two-day fixture. Hawke was absent from the opening day's proceedings, kept indoors by a chill. Without him his men ran up a total of 383 in front of a crowd of some two thousand, Sammy Woods (92) and Hewett (113) mercilessly exposing the limitations of the local bowlers. Not content with flailing the bowling to every point of the compass, Sammy Woods claimed ten wickets in the New Yorkers' reply of 122 all out. The home side then batted out the match with a deal of comfort. From New York the team entrained for Baltimore. Nearly half the fifteen hundred spectators present at the start of the match at Mount Washington against XV of Baltimore were women indicating the social notoriety of the game at that time. Winning the toss, Hawke batted, his team accumulating a useful total of 305 before Woods was unleashed on the home side. Baltimore were rattled out for 70 as Sammy added another nine wickets to his tour collection. The match was won by an innings.

From Baltimore the tourists travelled to Boston, thence to Chicago and north into Canada to meet first Western and finally Eastern Ontario. The weather turned cold and cheerless, there was snow in the air at Chicago. Nevertheless, the Englishmen carried all before them. The Philadelphians had proved themselves the equals of their guests, but elsewhere the English amateurs found themselves faced with club cricketers whose guiding aspiration was not to be too badly outclassed by their visitors. Everywhere they went Hawke's men were warmly received, welcomed with flags and bunting, always perfect ambassadors for their sport and country; missionaries in the cause of international cricket. Sammy Woods was indisputably the star of the enterprise, bagging 76 wickets at a cost of just seven runs apiece and hitting 260 runs at an average of 23.63. Of the other batsmen, Wreford-Brown averaged 31.00, Hawke 29.70 and Hewett 29.09. It was a happy, successful tour.

In a period when Hawke was captain of what was, by any standards, a moderate county side blighted by off-the-field rivalries the success of the American tour was seen very much as a personal triumph. His reputation increasingly depended upon aspects of his life that were separate from the strife within Yorkshire. It is ironic that Hawke's record as captain of Yorkshire until 1892 was an unbroken sequence of failure, failure that was in many ways hastened and exacerbated by initiatives and actions that were singularly Hawke's own responsibility. His leadership at Yorkshire had produced many things, but success was not among them. Had it not been for his involvement in overseas tours and the immense public curiosity that they aroused, his position in the early 1890s in Yorkshire would have been parlous. However, the Baron was in fact a burgeoning national hero, perceived as a born leader of men.

On his return from the Americas Hawke travelled via India where he spent eleven weeks hunting and fishing at the foot of the Himalayas, thousands of miles away from the persistent travails of the county club. Yet change was afoot in Yorkshire that winter. Castigated by *Wisden* for its intransigence, the Sheffield monopoly was at last beginning to think the impossible; of the day when all Yorkshire would have a voice in the affairs of the county club. Ellison, at the head of the monopoly, felt himself under attack from every quarter; the Committee was harangued by the Yorkshire public, the reformers campaigned with ever greater vigour and less grace and now *Wisden,* the voice of the game, had spoken against Sheffield. The one chink of light in the deepening gloom over Sheffield was that at no stage had Hawke, the county captain, publicly taken sides. Ellison doubtless realised that The Reverend E.S. Carter and the Yorkshire Gentlemen probably still saw Hawke as their man, but he knew also that Hawke had been scrupulously loyal to the Committee and the officers of the club, Ellison and Wostinholm included, throughout the traumas of recent years. Ellison liked and trusted the dashing young nobleman who captained his Yorkshire side. He admired Hawke's innate decency, Hawke's morality, his distaste for intrigue and his penchant for straight-talking; Yorkshire cricket would be safe in his hands in years to come.

That winter (1891–2) the Sheffield faction finally came to terms with the inevitable; that the monopoly could not be sustained. It had begun to crumble in 1883 when the Committee was originally expanded and further erosion had continued in the intervening years. Barnsley had been admitted in 1888, Wakefield in 1890 and Scarborough the following year. Before the changes of 1883 only Sheffield had been represented, now, in 1892, Sheffield held just thirteen of the twenty-two votes in Committee, although all the officers of the club remained Sheffield men. It was the last year of the Sheffield monopoly.

It might also have been the year that saw the end of Hawke's captaincy of the Yorkshire side. He had grown heartily fed up with the feuding behind the scenes and was exasperated with the apparent inability of his professionals to adopt the attitudes that he believed were essential if Yorkshire cricket was to be restored to its former position among the counties. The joys of touring, not least the company of like-minded men, and the constant stimulus of new places and new acquaintances were in sharp contrast to the grind of county cricket when often he was the only amateur in the side, a lonely, isolated figure in the pavilion.

The season of 1892 began hopefully, but then fell about Hawke's ears. Surrey were worthy champions as they had been for the previous two years; Yorkshire finished sixth of the nine first-class counties. The team had shown a degree of consistency in the Championship, winning as many matches as they lost, but there was little about the Yorkshire performance to suggest that much more could reasonably be expected of the team in the coming years – other than the fact that in ten matches against second-class counties, Yorkshire had won eight and drawn two, displaying a sense of purpose and application that had too often been absent in earlier meetings with lesser teams.

Hawke's batting was still erratic. Kept out of the side on many occasions by niggling injuries, he passed fifty just once in first-class cricket. He missed the two most memorable matches of the season, the desperately close match at the new Headingley ground in which Surrey secured victory with three minutes to spare, and the Somerset game at Taunton in which H.T. Hewett (201) and Lionel Palairet (146) put on 346 for the first wicket and thus improved the twenty-three-year-old record of 283, previously held by W.G. Grace and R.B. Cooper. It is worth noting that the men who would later dramatically raise this same record were both present in the Yorkshire side that day. Neither John Tunnicliffe or J.T. Brown were then regarded as potential world-beaters by their county captain; indeed in this match Brown batted at number nine in the Yorkshire batting order which had Ernest Smith and F.S. Jackson ensconced at its head.

Hawke had hoped for great things from Jackson and Smith in the latter part of the season. Unfortunately, neither man had yet come to terms with county cricket, runs came infrequently from their bats and on good wickets both men had much to learn about how to bowl at a well-set batsman.

Significantly, it was the last season that George Hirst was unable to command a regular place in the Yorkshire team. Unknowingly, Yorkshire had discovered a crop of brilliant young cricketers who would soon carry all before them; no one, certainly not Hawke, foresaw what was to come. In cutting out the dead wood and axing disruptive elements Hawke had cleared the way for a wealth of young talent to come into the county side. The new players had struggled to keep their heads above water, but now they were ready to strike out towards the horizon. The season of 1892 was the darkness before the dawn of a golden age of Yorkshire cricket. Yet that autumn when Louis Hall, the most trusted and respected of Hawke's professionals, decided to retire, the darkness seemed uniformly gloomy and the prospect of a new dawn more remote than ever.

The departure of Louis Hall, with whom Hawke inevitably felt more at ease than the irrepressible Ulyett, saddened an already worried captain who was seriously considering whether he really wanted to retain the job. Hawke's inner debate had not reached a conclusion by the time he set off for India on his next tour. While he was there he planned to fit in some shooting. It would be a chance to relax, to think things through and contemplate his future. However, he intimated to friends that he did not plan to return home at the end of the tour and that it was possible he might miss part, if not all, of the English season of 1893. The news was like an arrow aimed at the heart of the Sheffield monopoly and in Hawke's absence abroad that winter, sudden changes were enacted in Yorkshire to dismantle forever the Sheffield monopoly. After the years of procrastination and rancour it seemed as if Yorkshire cricket was about to lose the one man around whom all the warring factions would willingly unite. Almost by default Hawke had become the figurehead of the county club; without him Sheffield and the other districts were afraid the divisions that had brought the county so low would simply flare up again, irrespective of the defeat of Sheffield. Hawke left Yorkshire cricket in ferment, probably never realising the commotion he had caused.

He had drawn together a strong, well-balanced party of amateurs for his Indian trip. Several members of the team had toured with Hawke at least once before. Hawke's side was:

G.F. Vernon, G.A. Foljambe, J.A. Gibbs, A.B.E. Gibson, C. Heseltine, A.J.L. Hill, J.H.J. Hornsby, F.S. Jackson, A.E. Leatham, M.F. MacLean, J.S. Robinson, C.W. Wright, H.F. Wright.

It was a combination that was the equal of any of the English second-class counties and no doubt would have given one or two of the less fashionable first-class counties a run for their money. It was anticipated – with the notable exception of the Parsees – that few sides in the subcontinent would seriously test the tourists. The main problems would be the heat, the food and, of course, disease; the white man's burdens.

The tour itinerary envisaged a leisurely progress from Colombo in Ceylon to India and through the provincial centres of the Raj: Madras; Bangalore; Poona; Bombay; Calcutta; Mozenfferpore; Allahabad; Lucknow; Agra; Umballa; Lahore; and Peshawar. In many of the cities the tourists would play on elegant park grounds that are now massive concrete stadiums, such as Chepauk in Madras and Eden Gardens in Calcutta.

Only eleven tourists embarked on the P & O steamer *Kaiser-I-Hind* at Tilbury in October 1892; Hawke, Vernon and Gibson followed two weeks later on the *Shannon*. A chill had forced Hawke to delay his departure and meant that he and his two companions missed the opening matches of the tour in Ceylon. It was an inauspicious start for what was to be a gruelling, but largely happy tour. Hawke's team lost just two of its twenty-three matches, winning fifteen, mostly by wide margins. Of the two defeats one was at the hands of the Parsees in Bombay and was avenged in a subsequent return match and the other was in a minor game to a side who borrowed Gibson from the tourists to make up the numbers. Playing for Behar Wanderers, Gibson performed like a man inspired, scoring 33 and 55 and taking 4 for 22 and 7 for 43 much to his fellow tourists' discomfort.

Everywhere the team was taken into the houses and the hearts of the expatriate community and treated regally. To European society in India the coming of the English amateurs was the highlight of the social year, matches were banner-waving, drum-beating affairs accompanied by military marches and parades. In Madras the Governor, Lord Wenlock, invited the tourists to stay at his country residence. In Bombay the tourists were entertained by another illustrious cricketing patriarch, Lord Harris, who was as surprised as Hawke at the showing of the Parsees. In Bombay the Viceroy, Lord Curzon, was called from his office when it seemed as if Hawke was heading for a century against the Bombay Presidency. Hawke was out immediately for 79.

During the three months of the tour Hawke's health remained sound. He suffered a couple of sprains, but otherwise the tropical malaises that afflicted most of his men at some stage seemed to pass him by. His good fortune was shortly to desert him.

8

The Shape of
Things to Come
(1893)

Before the tourists went their separate ways the party visited the Khyber Pass. For an Englishman the beauty and the grandeur of the mountains was nothing compared to the fact that he was standing at the northern frontier of the Raj, at what he considered the very edge of civilisation. The foot of the pass was bandit country and the party's escort of Bengal Lancers eyed the high ground with more than a little anxiety. Back in England there was speculation that Hawke would remain in the subcontinent for some time to come. *Cricket* reported that:

> Lord Hawke intends to prolong his tour in India to a much greater extent than was at first intended. Indeed, my informant goes so far as to say that he will in all probability not be here to take part in English cricket during next summer.

Indeed when the touring party dispersed in the first week of March, Hawke, Wright, Heseltine, Hill and Leatham remained behind. Christopher Heseltine became a lifelong friend and was later to be Hawke's best man, while Albert Leatham was a fellow Yorkshireman. In their company, Hawke set off for Nepal in search of tiger. Heseltine travelled the world with Hawke, hunting and playing cricket; he was a confident, gregarious man who bowled fast and shot true. Leatham was a quirky character, the cousin of G.A.B. Leatham of Yorkshire and the Yorkshire Gentlemen, perhaps the finest amateur wicket-keeper the county ever produced. Hawke and

Heseltine quickly found their companion was something of a liability; his preference for loading his own guns and repeatedly wounding animals that ought to have been downed by the first shot vexed them both. Quite apart from the unnecessary suffering this caused the quarry, Heseltine and Hawke not unnaturally took exception to being continually endangered by their friend's penny-pinching reluctance to employ a loader. Leatham finally hired a loader when Hawke, in exasperation, led him aside and delivered an angry dressing down.

Unfortunately, this did not appreciably improve Leatham's fieldcraft. Hawke and Heseltine still found themselves having to dispatch wounded animals and worse, during one tiger shoot Leatham took it upon himself to blaze away at a passing deer. Since it was the strict rule that on a tiger shoot only tigers were targets, his companions took a decidedly dim view of Leatham's behaviour. However, he was eventually forgiven, his waywardness excused as 'keeness' and strained friendships patched up. Leatham went on to hunt all over the world and his trophies came to clutter the walls of the pavilion at Lord's.

Hawke and Heseltine made the best of things, thirteen tigers going down to the guns of their party. In fact it was during this period that Hawke shot the most impressive of the six tigers whose skins he brought back to Wighill Hall. Heseltine and he were having such good sport that they saw no reason to return home. They set themselves up in a boat at Srinagar, the capital of Kashmir – an ideal base from which to mount hunting forays, just close enough to civilisation so as not to be completely out of touch with the Raj and the old country, but sufficiently distant to be able to pick and choose which, if any, communication from outside to acknowledge. Hawke contemplated never going back, wistfully longing for a life spent travelling and hunting, free of the cares and responsibilities of his other existence in England.

His idyllic stay at Srinagar was cut short, however, when he was suddenly struck down by fever and was compelled to return home. If a man survived the first ravages of tropical disease, he was a fool to remain much longer in the same climate to await its return. This was the turning point of his life, a fact Hawke readily admitted in his *Recollections and Reminiscences*:

I know now that had I missed that cricket season [1893], it is extremely probable that I should have given up county cricket.

I was quite ready to give it up, for it had not been all beer and skittles if the truth is known, but all the great days of Yorkshire cricket, which I did not foresee, were to come.

Hawke's return to England corresponded with the opening of a new page in the history of Yorkshire cricket. The Yorkshire Committee had ceased to be a Sheffield monopoly and for the first time two vice-presidents had been elected, one of whom was Hawke, voted in by the new committee *in absentia*. The membership – and consequently the voting rights – of the new Committee were:

Sheffield (7 votes), Leeds (3 votes), Bradford (3 votes), Huddersfield (1 vote), Dewsbury (1 vote), Hull (1 vote), Barnsley (1 vote), Halifax (1 vote), Wakefield (1 vote), and Craven (1 vote).

Sheffield had surrendered its monopoly and a new breath of hope was blowing away the cobwebs of the last decade; for the first time in years Yorkshire approached the season of 1893 with genuine optimism. Nevertheless, the unexpected renaissance of Yorkshire cricket that summer was greeted with as much incredulity in the shire of the broad acres as elsewhere.

In May the warning bells began to sound up and down the land as Yorkshire, under the infectiously cheerful leadership of George Ulyett, ran up a string of early victories. F.S. Jackson's Cambridge side – a remarkably strong University team – momentarily halted the Yorkshire charge at Fenner's after Ulyett's young Tykes had beaten MCC at Lord's and Gloucestershire at Gloucester. Thereafter, the Australians at Sheffield, Leicestershire at Leicester, Sussex at Headingly and Middlesex at Lord's were all swept aside in quick succession.

In the return match with the Australians at Bradford at the beginning of June George Giffen hit 171 as the tourists compiled a total of 470. In former times the brittleness of the Yorkshire batting might have undone the county, but now Ulyett's youngsters fought out a gritty draw as the wicket deteriorated.

Hawke appeared only once for Yorkshire in June, in a minor match against Essex at Leyton in the second week of the month in a contest won in two days by ten wickets. The experience convinced him that he was not yet equal to the rigours of county cricket and he dropped out of the side for another month. He sat back and watched Ulyett lead his boys to further triumphs. Surrey were dispatched at

Hawke as a young man.

Tom Emmett, captain of the old brigade.

'Happy Jack' – George Ulyett.

'The Batley Giant' - Louis Hall.

Edmund Peate,
Yorkshire's first great
slow left-arm bowler.

Bobby Peel, Peate's
successor and the
last survivor of the
old brigade.

Hawke, captain of Yorkshire (MCC).

The new sword, the Yorkshire XI of 1893.

The strongest side Hawke ever took abroad, his
South African team of 1895-6.

'Jacker' – Stanley Jackson, Yorkshire's most
remarkable amateur.

Ernest Smith; 'Nobody ever sent a ball faster to the ropes.'

Hawke at the wicket.

George Hirst, the greatest county cricketer of his day.

Wilfred Rhodes; 'It was not the wickets he took, but his beautifully easy action that at once impressed us all.'

Jack Brown, the first Yorkshireman to score a triple-century in first-class cricket.

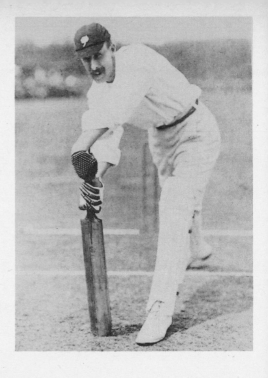

'Long John of Pudsey' –
John Tunnicliffe.

David Denton; 'If
Denton dropped a catch
the world wondered.'

Scofield Haigh; 'The stranger to despair, the enemy
of long-faced misanthropy.'

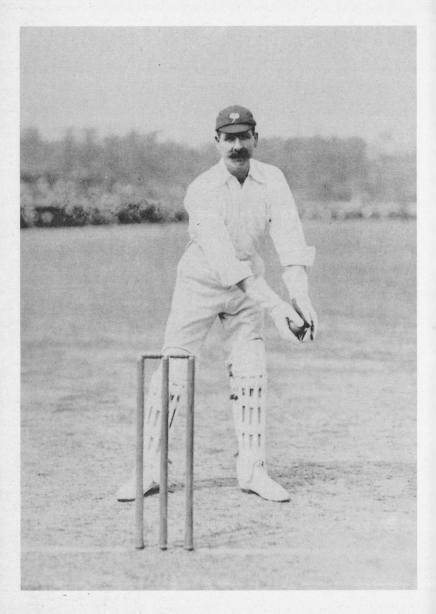

David Hunter, so perfect was his technique that his hands were as sound when he left the game as they were when he began his career.

Ted Wainwright, John Tunnicliffe's daunting partner in the slips.

Hawke in 1916.

Hawke in later life (MCC).

Sheffield, Somerset vanquished by an innings at Taunton before the bandwagon crashed into Lancashire at Leeds. Inspirational batsmanship from Archie MacLaren, mesmeric trickery from Johnny Briggs and blistering pace bowling from Arthur Mold overwhelmed Yorkshire in the Roses match. A week later Yorkshire faltered again against Warwickshire, who were then a second-class county. When Surrey inflicted a ten-wicket defeat on the Yorkshiremen at the Oval in the last week of June heads began to shake and Yorkshire's runaway stampede to the head of the Championship table seemed at last to have been checked. Hawke now took over the helm.

Ulyett had done a grand job, but Yorkshire's young lions had reached the point where inspiration was not, of itself, enough to sustain their form. At the Oval Yorkshire had fought tigerishly to the death but had been outplayed throughout. Hawke diagnosed a need for discipline and application and he recognised that 'Happy Jack' Ulyett was not perhaps the man to enforce it.

So it was that Hawke sent his men out to bat at Bradford against Nottinghamshire at the start of July. Yorkshire batted either side of a thunderstorm, suffered the worst of the conditions and were treated to a chanceless, five-hour innings of 150 by the Nottinghamshire batsman, William Gunn. In a match reduced to two days by the weather Yorkshire were left to bat out the draw which was duly achieved with a minimum of inconvenience. The rot had been stopped. Yorkshire cricket had discovered its inner steel.

In batting order (with the age of each man in parentheses) the side that Hawke led at Bradford was:

T.A. Wardell (31), A. Sellers (23), J. Tunnicliffe (26), M.B. Hawke (32), J.T. Brown (23), R. Peel (36), E. Wainwright (28), R. Moorhouse (26), G. Ulyett (41), G.H. Hirst (21), D. Hunter (33).

F.S. Jackson (22), the Cambridge captain, was engaged in the Varsity match at Lord's and Ernest Smith (23), a schoolmaster, was unavailable during term-time, but otherwise the XI was a representative Yorkshire side. The arrival of the two amateurs in the county side was eagerly anticipated.

Thomas Wardall had first played for the county in 1883 and his career was drawing to a close in 1893. He had never really established his place in the XI, despite heading the Yorkshire batting averages the previous season. A watchful, cautious batsman he was well-suited to the role of opener, the role that Louis Hall had made his own for a decade. Wardall's cricketing roots were firmly bedded in the Yorkshire of Tom Emmett and in the company of Hawke's young lions Wardall was the odd man out; he had little in common with the new generation, nor with the remnants of the old as represented by Yorkshire's senior professionals, Ulyett and Peel, both world-famous international cricketers. When in 1894 Stanley Jackson became available for his first full season it was Wardall's place in the Yorkshire side that he filled.

Arthur Sellers – the father of Brian Sellers who captained Yorkshire from 1933– 48 – scored two of the county's three Championship centuries in 1893; one was against Middlesex, the other was at Bramall Lane against Somerset on a wretched wicket. On that occasion he told David Hunter, as he went out to bat, 'I think I'll get a hundred.'

The wicket had begun to break up in the latter stages of the Somerset first innings and Hunter thought Sellers was joking, but he joined in the spirit of the thing. 'If you do I'll give you a canary.'

Every ball Sammy Woods bowled ripped up a piece of turf but Sellers got his hundred and, according to Yorkshire mythology, his canary, too. In the words of The Reverend R.L. Hodgson in *The Happy Cricketer* Sellers 'like a meteor flashed across the horizon of county cricket'. He was a batsman who knew his limitations and concentrated on making the best of his strengths. His business interests virtually ended his county career after 1894, although he made sporadic appearances in the first-class game until 1899 and was involved with the club for the rest of his life in various capacities, principally as a Committee member and as Chairman of the Selection Committee.

'Long John' Tunnicliffe was 25 years old when he first played for Yorkshire. Standing 6 feet 2 inches tall in his stocking feet and as thin as a rake, he began as an highly aggressive bat and a useful stock bowler. Later he would learn to curb his attacking instincts, becoming perhaps the finest opening batsmen never to play for England. In 1893 he was still intent on smashing the bowling out of the ground. This he did twice in one week, first at Bramall Lane and then at Bradford, matching feats previously only achieved by George Ulyett in his prime and prompting The Reverend R.S. Holmes to comment in *Cricket*: 'his shots may be few, but they are mighty'.

From the outset he was a brilliant slip fielder with an intuitive knowledge of where to stand on any kind of wicket. Like many men gifted with razor-sharp reflexes he was a deeply contemplative man. Like Louis Hall, he was a teetotaller and Methodist lay preacher, a man of intransigent views and unshakable beliefs. Almost inevitably, like Hall, he became Hawke's right-hand man among the professionals. In 1893 Tunnicliffe's batting rarely came off, yet it mattered not one jot to his captain. So far as Hawke was concerned 'Long John of Pudsey' was a peerless influence on his fellows and if he also scored a few runs that was bonus. Indeed, in the years ahead he became one half of the most famous opening partnership in the land.

His future opening partner, John Thomas Brown, was an entirely different character. Tunnicliffe was tall and thin; Brown was short and thickset. While Tunnicliffe was slow of humour, taciturn and deeply religious, Brown was impulsive, quick to anger and less of the team man. While Long John had to work for years on his batsmanship to arrive at a method that eventually produced thousands of invaluable runs, Jack Brown's batting suddenly clicked and the runs came in an irresistable tide without him ever really understanding how or why, for there was a touch of something infinitely precious, wholly intangible about John Thomas Brown that bordered upon genius.

1893 was the season when Jack Brown's batting clicked. When he was in the mood he was one of the most destructive batsmen of the era, impossible to contain. He was the master of the late cut and an instinctive, vicious hooker of short-pitched bowling. A tidy, neat, well-organised batsman, he played within himself until he was set, thereafter he tended to do what he wanted with the bowling, regardless of its direction, pace or spin. He went to Australia with Stoddart in 1894 and began to rewrite the record book; he carried on where he had left off in the Antipodes on his return to England.

Life and batsmanship were alike to Jack Brown: he never did anything by halves, his hundreds were more often than not big hundreds. Legend has it that Long John persuaded him to take the pledge, apparently convincing his partner that turning teetotal would help his batting. He was a hard man to know. H.D.G. Leveson-Gower said of Brown that he was 'a nice fellow when one gets to know him, but he always appeared to me to have a grouse against life'. Hawke always felt that Brown's success in Australia with Stoddart's team had 'turned his head'. At the end of the day nobody really cared whether or not Jack Brown had a chip on his shoulder, if he farmed the bowling he was readily forgiven. His moodiness was taken with a pinch of salt; the Yorkshire public worshipped Jack Brown.

Edward Wainwright had stepped into Billy Bates's shoes. He never aspired to equal Bates as a batsman – although he scored no less than nineteen first-class centuries in his career – but he was every inch as effective as a slow-medium off-spin bowler and, unlike Bates, he was a brilliant fielder in any position. A big, rugged man from Tinsley, he was a blunt, proud Yorkshireman with a talent for vivid invective and unashamed of it. On a wicket receptive to turn, he was a deadly foe and when the other batsmen were struggling Ted Wainwright could be relied upon to drop anchor and grind out an innings against the odds. Standing behind John Tunnicliffe's right shoulder at second slip he made a habit of clutching hold of improbable chances. He was chosen for England in 1893 but England never saw the best of him; as with George Hirst his best was saved for Yorkshire.

Robert Moorhouse was a wool spinner by trade and, every summer, a batsman who made up for his lack of technique by drawing upon an apparently bottomless well of courage. Yorkshire would send him out to stem the tide on a wet, kicking wicket when the fastest bowlers in England were flinging down their fiercest thunderbolts. His team-mates called him the 'man of Bruises'. His batting was built around a single precept: get into line first and play the ball second. Frequently the ball arrived long before his defensive bat. In reality, his method amounted to deliberately playing fast bowling with his body and he invariably took a fearful pounding. In an era when a batsman's only protective equipment was a pair of flimsy gloves and his pads (thigh-pads, boxes, arm-guards, chest-protectors and helmets are all modern innovations), it is almost impossible to imagine how any man in his right mind could combat the likes of Tom Richardson or Charles Kortright in such a fashion on the most benign, featherbed of a wicket; to attempt it on a weather-damaged surface smacks of a death-wish.

Bobby Moorhouse was a curious character, an unlikely man to find in Hawke's new guard. He was renowned for his lack of self-restraint, his short temper, his careless attitude to authority. His Yorkshire days were to end abruptly when he decided he could not be bothered to run to try and take a catch, which was altogether more than Hawke was prepared to tolerate.

Hawke regarded George Hirst as the 'greatest county cricketer of our time'. In 1892 Hirst had taken twenty-seven first-class wickets, the following year he took ninety-nine. Then there was his batting; it was in 1893 that Yorkshire became aware that their young left-arm fast bowler was a decidedly handy man to have batting down the order. After Hirst had played a short, brutal innings on a poor pitch against Gloucestershire at Huddersfield W.G. Grace was moved to comment: 'I'd no idea the beggar could bat, too.'

George Herbert Hirst had first turned out for Yorkshire as an 18 year old in 1889, but had had no real opportunity to establish himself in the side until the summer of 1892. In the opening match of the season of 1893, at Lord's against MCC he had taken 12 for 48. He never looked back. He bowled left-handed, batted right and was a superlative out-fielder, usually at mid-off. When he bowled he bounced to the wicket, his arm swung high and propelled the ball unerringly at the stumps. He was not an out-and-out speed merchant, he was more a subtle craftsman with innumerable variations up his sleeve; one ball would skid through, another rise that fraction higher than it had any right to rise, the next delivery might cut this way or than, might even be his sparingly deployed and heavily disguised slower ball. When he learned the knack of inducing swing he became the terror of the county circuit. Sammy Woods was once heard to protest that:

> I don't really see how one can be expected to play a ball which, when it leaves the bowler's arm appears to be coming straight but when it reaches the wicket it is like a very good throw coming in from cover point.

In 1893 George Hirst had yet to discover the secrets of swerve and his batting was promising rather than accomplished; he was a cricketing novice. By the time the season was finished he had established himself as one of the most feared bowlers in the land. Success left him untouched, nothing dented his innate good humour, his sense of fun was unquenchable. Yorkshire folk took him to their hearts and no man was a better ambassador for Yorkshire cricket. He was a man without side, the friendliest face in the county.

David Hunter was the same age as Hawke. He was a tall man for a wicket-keeper, standing a shade over 6 feet. He had come to first-class cricket relatively late in life, filling the place in the Yorkshire side vacated by the retirement of his elder brother, Joseph. Clog-dancer, huntsman, breeder of canaries (hence his gift to Arthur Sellers on scoring his century at Bramall Lane) weight-lifter and bell-ringer, he was the best stumper never to play for England, and probably the most capable batsman ever to bat at number eleven throughout a career of any length. Behind the stumps he was nimble and sure, the ball whispered into his gloves. So perfect was his technique that his hands were as sound when he left the game as they were at the start of his career. A compulsive talker he was an immense power for good in the Yorkshire dressing-room.

Hawke thought the world of David Hunter, together they grew into middle age fighting shoulder by shoulder in the cause of Yorkshire cricket, firm friends and allies. They shared in many last-wicket stands, their running perfectly atuned, calls superflous. David Hunter was the unsung hero of the first golden age of Yorkshire cricket.

As if the flowering of Hawke's carefully husbanded crop of young professionals did not promise a rich enough harvest, the Yorkshire captain also had up his sleeve two of the most remarkable amateur talents of the day in Ernest Smith and Stanley Jackson.

Ernest Smith was the older of the pair by a year and had come down from Oxford the previous season. A product of Clifton College he was a tearaway fast bowler and a dynamic batsman. He was not a wealthy man and his teaching severely restricted his career in the first-class game. Hawke was to heap extravagant praise on Ernest Smith's contribution to Yorkshire cricket:

Each August he came into the team, keen, fresh, vigorous, ready with his skill and his enthusiasm to hearten and prevent staleness. As a quick bowler he perhaps looked better than his figures showed him to be; in the field he was safe and quick; as a bat he was the unknown quantity. He might fail, and of course, did at times; but when he came off he made his runs fiercer and faster than anyone else on the side, and there was an audacity about the way he placed his scoring shots which completely perplexed the opposing bowlers.

'Nobody,' Hawke would declare, with pride and without fear of contradiction in the shire of the broad acres, 'nobody ever sent a ball faster to the ropes than Ernest Smith!'

In the very last major fixture of the 1893 season, captaining the North against the South at Hastings, Ernest Smith shared in a partnership with C.E. De Trafford of 254 runs in only 105 minutes. When he was out for 154 he had hit a six, a five and twenty-one fours in a shade over two hours. Lest it be thought it was an innings plundered from occasional bowlers, the roll call of bowlers tried against him that day reads like a *Who's Who* of English cricket; Tom

Richardson, William Lockwood and Walter Read of Surry, J.T. Hearne and A.E. Stoddart of Middlesex, J.J. Ferris the Australian, even W.G. Grace turned his arm over, his twenty-five deliveries punished to the tune of fifty runs. In *Great Bowlers and Fielders*, C.B. Fry was equally respectful of Ernest Smith's prowess with the ball:

> His bowling belongs to the class of pace of which consists in a strong, whizzing flight. The difference between this and ordinary so-called swift bowling can not be described in words; but there is a difference between bowling which is merely swift and bowling which is fast because the flight of the ball is strong.

Often his direction was awry and the bat prospered. Yet he was capable of bowling with a ferocity that ripped out the stumps of the most accomplished batsmen in the land. That was Ernest Smith, the essence of the man: all fire and thunder, the sort of cricketer who never took a backward step. If in total his achievements in the game were relatively modest, the way in which he played his cricket earns Ernest Smith a place among Cricket's immortals. Among Yorkshire amateurs he had only one equal, a man in whose long shadow he and a generation of English gentlemen cricketers lived and died: Francis Stanley Jackson.

Jackson was the second son of William Lawies Jackson, soon to be created the first Baron Allerton of Chapel Allerton. If there was ever such a thing as a born cricketer it was 'Jacker'. Sir Home Gordon, in his *Background of Cricket,* recollected:

> I saw him play his first match against Eton – as a fully-fledged cricketer: splendid bat, perfect field, excellent fastish bowler. All others I have heard or seen as cricketers developed, but 'Jacker' never did, simply because he never could – there was no scope. He passed from Harrow to Cambridge, thence to Yorkshire and so to England, merely adapting his own methods to the prevalent conditions but being distinctively the same player all through.

Excepting W.G. Grace, Jacker was the finest amateur cricketer of his or any other era. He was captain of Harrow School, Cambridge University and belatedly, England. In Yorkshire, however, it was his destiny to stand at Hawke's right hand, but no lieutenant in cricketing history has ever been held in greater awe than Stanley Jackson. When in 1905 Jackson scored his fifth century against Australia in Test matches in England he set a record that to this day still waits to be improved and has only once been equalled, by another highly individual Yorkshireman, Geoffrey Boycott. In the Gentlemen and Players match at Lord's in 1894 he hit the amateurs' top score and then bowled unchanged with Sammy Woods through both of the professionals' innings, recording figures of 12 for 77. From his bat, in 1905, came the first hundred scored in a Test match at Headingley. In 1902, playing for Yorkshire, his bowling – in partnership with George Hirst – routed the Australians for just 23 runs in eighty-four deliveries, snapping up the last four wickets in five eventful balls. During the Boer War Jackson was struck down by enteric fever and invalided home from the Transvaal. After a couple of gentle nets he turned out for the Gentlemen at Scarborough and plundered a brilliant century off the Players. When in 1905 he succeeded to the England captaincy he won the toss in all five matches against Joe Darling's Australians, won two and drew three of the five contests and topped both the batting and the bowling averages in the Tests. Then, at the end of the season, he took a hundred off the tourists at Scarborough and effectively bowed out of the first-class game at the age of thirty-four. Between 1893 and 1905 he had scored nearly as many runs in home Test matches as the next two most prolific English batsmen combined.

Of Jackson's batting C.B. Fry said; 'he had versatility and what, for want of a better name, we call genius'. Whether a wicket was plumb or false, wet or dry, Jacker watched the ball from hand to pitch and played it on its merits, invariably with the middle of his bat. He was renowned as one of the best players of fast bowling in England in an age when every county seemed to have at least one, and sometimes two, very quick fast bowlers. Upon the retirement of Shrewsbury, Jackson became the undisputed master of the art of batting on the rain-ruined wickets of the day.

He bowled off a shortish run with an easy, natural action that tended to hurry the ball on to the bat. Accuracy was his hallmark and he always pitched just short of a length in the area where the batsman was least certain of how to play the ball, on or just outside his off stump. His stock ball was his off-cutter; a wicked delivery that hit the seam and knifed back into the right-hander, scattering the stumps as the bewildered batsman floundered flat-footed. Like all the great bowlers of the period he was remorseless on a weather-damaged surface. Once the rain had fallen he would bowl a perfect line and length at his lively fast-medium pace and allow the vagaries of the wicket to do the rest. On a good wicket his faster ball was an unnerving weapon, he could bowl a cunningly disguised slower delivery, could sometimes conjure up swing, mix up his seamers with inordinate off-spin and slip in the occasional bouncer. Nobody in Christendom ever hit Jacker off his impeccable line; very few men even tried.

On the first day of his first Test match as England captain, at Trent Bridge, Australia had outfought and outplayed Jackson's men. Then, with the close approaching, he decided it was time he had a 'bit of a bowl'. In six deliveries he altered the whole course of the game, taking the wickets of Montague Noble and Clem Hill, who had been in full cry, and dismissing Joe Darling, his redoubtable opposite number, for a duck.

That was Jacker, an affable, intelligent man who combined the diverse roles of soldier, businessman, politician and gentleman cricketer with the grace and aplomb of one who was nothing if not to the manner born; he was the supreme all-rounder at both life and cricket. Gifted with the perfect temperament for the big occasion he was the ultimate man for a crisis, the man of the moment. When disaster threatened Yorkshire or England and Jackson emerged on to the scene a hush would descend. He was the man his captain would send out to hold the innings together on a mud-heap of a wicket, the man his captain would ask to bowl at two well-set, rampant batsman. Jacker was not like other men, for his reputation was built not upon classical batting on flat wickets, nor upon destructive bowling on rain-wrecked pitches; rather it was based upon his countless innings against the odds and his ability to break dangerous partnerships.

In Yorkshire cricket George Hirst, Jack Brown and men whose turn had not yet come, such as David Denton and Wilfred Rhodes, would loom as large if not larger than Stanley Jackson, but Jacker belonged to England and the Gentlemen as much as he did to the shire of the broad acres. There were times when his particular gifts needed a bigger stage than those offered anywhere on the county circuit, times when the challenges of Championship cricket left him cold. His record is littered with failures when Yorkshire had no need of his contribution, and, conversely, rife with matches that turned upon a battling, back-to-the-wall innings or an inexplicable spell of mean, destructive bowling seemingly produced out of nothing.

A.A. Thomson wistfully commented in *Cricket: The Great Captains* that 'Jackson, in personal character and in cricketing genius, was unique. There has been nobody like him since.' Jackson laid down his bat when he was at his peak. He left quietly, unannounced at the height of his powers, an English cricketing hero of a kind that Percy Chapman was to become many years later. He was too wise a man to contemplate ever rekindling the glories of 1905, his year of victories. As R.C. Robertson-Glasgow observed in *Rain Stopped Play;* 'Such a man was, rightly, not to be a re-tracer of his steps down the mountain side, a mere subject of kindlier memory.'

In later life Jackson entered Parliament, rising to be Financial Secretary to the War Office and, in the 1920s, becoming Chairman of the Unionist Party. In 1927 he was knighted and sent to India to replace Lord Lytton as Governor of Bengal. Robertson-Glasgow captured the spirit of the man and his age when he wrote; '. . . he is a chapter in history. For the true amateur has almost passed from cricket; and the proconsul will soon be a story.'

Jackson had taken wickets galore for Cambridge in the seasons of 1890, 1891 and 1892, but scored erratically. He had been widely regarded as a fine bowling prospect and a good-looking batsman who tended to flatter to deceive. In India with Hawke, Jackson had added durability and tenacity to his armoury and in 1893 he stepped serenely on to the big stage of English cricket, where he remained until he walked away from the first-class game a dozen years later. While Yorkshire's young professionals went about the business of winning the Championship that year, Stanley Jackson carried the flag of Yorkshire cricket into the Test match arena.

In 1892 Hawke's young lions had whimpered their last, in 1893 they learned to roar and English cricket trembled. The honour and the glory that had bled from Yorkshire cricket in the late 1880s and early 1890s now came flooding back. Nobody was more surprised than Hawke. He had given up hope, decided that hunting and touring foreign lands was his destiny and that the woes of Yorkshire cricket were not for him. Without warning, the seeds of revival – which in earlier years had seemingly been sown on barren ground – had burst through to the light in a spectacular blossoming. Hirst and Wainwright began to run through sides, the batsmen started to bat with an immense doggedness, but the biggest transformation was in the field. Their opponents were rocked back on their heels by the tigerishness of the Yorkshiremen in the field. Hawke's team fielded run down, like men possessed, every shot was run down, the throwing was ferocious. Impossible catches, no more than half-chances, barely chances at all to most players, disappeared into the hands of John Tunnicliffe and Ted Wainwright.

Like all great sides the Yorkshire XI of 1893 had been a long time in the making. Wainwright and Moorhouse had made their débuts as long ago as 1888, Hirst, Brown, Sellers and Smith in 1889, Jackson in 1890 and Tunnicliffe in 1891. Wainwright, Hunter, Jackson and Smith had been regarded as players certain to make their way in the county game from the outset, although the latter pair had done little in the Championship to confirm Hawke's high hopes for them prior to that season. Sellers had scored useful runs without ever threatening to dominate the best bowling. Moorhouse and Hirst had struggled to win a place in the side and, odd as it may seem now, neither Tunnicliffe nor Brown were considered more than journeymen in their younger days. After 1893 Hawke gladly recanted his view.

Hawke's own form was poor that year. He eased himself back into serious cricket playing in several matches for the MCC at Lord's, registering a best score of 59 against Oxford University. His illness had robbed him of his stamina and his basic fitness that season was never of a level to permit him to do justice to his abilities. Following the Nottinghamshire game Ulyett briefly stepped in to captain Yorkshire to a crushing victory over Somerset at Sheffield before Hawke returned for the rest of the season. The Australians beat the county comprehensively at Leeds, but Yorkshire obliterated the memory within a few days by trouncing Nottinghamshire at Trent Bridge by an innings. Gloucestershire at Huddersfield and Kent at Blackheath were roundly beaten at the end of the month.

Hawke had hoped to include F.S. Jackson in the Yorkshire side for these matches, but lost his services to England in the middle of the month. The Cambridge captain burst into international cricket with a dazzling 91 on his début, a feat he followed up with a century in his second Test a fortnight later.

Injury prevented Hawke from taking the field against Lancashire at Old Trafford, but the captaincy passed not to Ulyett, but to the senior amateur in the side, Ernest Smith. In a low-scoring game on a sodden Manchester wicket Yorkshire lost by five runs after being set 52 to win. The Yorkshire openers, Sellers and Jackson had collected 24 of the required runs when a disastrous misunderstanding meant that Jackson was run out. Some 22,554 people paid to enter the ground on the first day and another 9,599 the second.

Defeat in the Roses match was soon forgotten as under Hawke's captaincy Yorkshire won their last three Championship games, beating Middlesex at Bradford, Kent at Sheffield and finally Sussex at Brighton. F.S. Jackson had withdrawn from the third Test against the Australians to play for Yorkshire at Brighton, and fittingly was at the wicket when the winning run was hit. Yorkshire had won twelve of their sixteen Championship matches and taken the title by a considerable margin from their nearest rivals, Lancashire. Surrey and the southern counties had been eclipsed. Although Hawke had captained Yorkshire in only six Championship fixtures (winning five and drawing one), his leadership of a side that had faltered in mid-season was almost certainly the difference between winning and losing the Championship. His presence, his will, had picked up a tiring team and propelled it relentlessly forward to what, as the weeks went by, became a seemingly inevitable triumph. The glory was as much George Ulyett's as Hawke's, but for Ulyett it was by way of a swansong whereas for Hawke it was the key to the kingdom. At the end of the season Hawke had Yorkshire cricket in the palm of his hand, his to do with more or less as he pleased. The years of struggle were over; the glory years had begun.

9

The New Sword
(1894–1896)

Yorkshire came within an ace of retaining the County Championship in 1894. Needing to beat Somerset at Taunton in their last match to share the title with a rejuvenated Surrey, the northerners had dismissed their hosts for 99 when the rain put an end to the proceedings. Earlier in the season, at Huddersfield, Yorkshire had trounced the West Country side by an innings inside a day.

Yorkshire bore their misfortune stoically, as if the intervention of the elements was part of some fiendish southern conspiracy designed to deny the county its due. Yorkshire cricket had refound its sense of humour and although there was inevitable disappointment, nobody pretended it was the end of the world. Cricket in the shire of the broad acres had undergone a sea of change and optimism now ruled.

Hawke basked in the triumph of 1893, a happier, more relaxed captain than he had ever been before. In 1894 he found time to turn out for MCC in half a dozen first-class games and his appearances in county cricket were interspersed with weekends hunting or shooting. Although Hawke contrived to lead Yorkshire in twelve of their fifteen Championship matches, that year the county had no less than seven different captains in all their matches. When the season was over Hawke reflected that his young lions had done well, but they still had a great deal to learn. In a way the Championship of 1893 had been an accidental triumph, as much to do with the falling away of the leading counties as with the rise of Yorkshire cricket. The revival of Surrey in 1894 seemed to confirm his highly cautious view that the task of rebuilding the Yorkshire team was not yet completed.

At the end of 1893 Hawke, Ellison and Wostinholm had represented Yorkshire at the annual meeting of the county secretaries. Other than the arrangement of the fixture list for the next season, there were three matters on the agenda: the status of the first- and second-class counties; umpiring; and the question of whether to extend an invitation to the Philadelphians to come to England in 1894. The proposal that the Americans should tour England was not contentious and was supported by the meeting. The other matters – on which Yorkshire held decidedly strong opinions – did not lend themselves to a speedy conclusion.

Yorkshire believed that the existing County Championship based upon competition between the nine established first-class teams – Gloucestershire, Kent, Lancashire, Middlesex, Nottinghamshire, Somerset, Sussex, Surrey and Yorkshire – should be widened to include all those counties that had shown themselves capable of organising major matches and of performing to a sufficiently high standard. Broadly, this meant permitting Derbyshire, Essex, Leicestershire and Warwickshire to join the first-class club. No county had done more in recent years to encourage the minor counties than Yorkshire, as witnessed by the county's congested fixture lists. The expansion and development of the first-class game was seen as both a sporting and financial imperative by Ellison, and in Hawke he had a ready disciple.

Hawke himself became embroiled in controversial discussion when the subject turned to umpiring. The shortcomings of some of the umpires on the county circuit was a subject that had sent rumblings of discontent throughout the game. The Yorkshire captain pointedly told the gathering that the root of the problem was that the best men for the job were being discouraged, for a number of reasons, from becoming umpires. He suggested that match fees ought to be raised from £5 to £6, that many more men would come forward if they were allowed to stand in matches involving their own county and finally that there should be a list of approved umpires drawn up before each season. Nobody was left in any doubt that he spoke not just for Yorkshire, but also for the majority of the county captains.

The meeting ended inconclusively, reaching no decision on the vexed question of the reconstitution of the Championship and done nothing to allay disenchantment with the traditional system of appointing umpires. However, there was general agreement that these were pressing issues requiring action sooner rather than later. In the meantime the counties were asked to submit a list of umpires for the consideration of MCC, and the meeting committed itself to reviewing the status of the leading second-class counties when it next convened.

But in May 1894 the captains of the nine first-class counties took the law into their own hands. With W.G. Grace and Hawke in the vanguard they undertook to lay before the MCC at its annual meeting a resolution declaring:

> That the matches played by the following four counties: Derbyshire, Warwickshire, Essex, and Leicestershire against the nine counties at present styled first-class, and also against one another and against the MCC, should be regarded as first-class matches, and the records of the players engaged in these matches shall be included in the list of first-class averages.

The signatories were W.G. Grace (Gloucestershire), M.B. Hawke (Yorkshire), J. Shuter (Surrey), S.M.J. Woods (Somerset), J.A. Dixon (Nottinghamshire), F. Marchant (Kent), W.L. Murdoch (Sussex), A.J. Webbe (Middlesex), and A.N. Hornby (Lancashire). When MCC convened, the proposal – almost unopposed – became policy and the single most significant expansion of the English first-class game came into effect.

Hawke celebrated by raising his highest score to 157 when opening for A.J. Webbe's XI against his old university at Fenner's in mid-May. Cambridge were desperately short of bowling that summer but it was an innings that gave Hawke immense personal satisfaction. He gave a single chance when he was on 53 and was eventually out with the total on 294, his knock including four sixes and sixteen fours. In June, just before the Varsity match he plundered a hard-hit 64, playing for MCC, off the light blues, and then watched, horrified, as W.G. Grace set about the piecemeal destruction of the Cambridge bowling, scoring 196. Hawke was so infuriated by what he considered the great man's gratuitous run spree against the University, just before they faced Oxford, that he was moved to approach W.G. and inform him of the extent of his displeasure. W.G. was unrepentent. 'Testing the quality of the bowling,' he explained, 'good for young 'uns.'

Hawke was unimpressed. In the context of a match won by 374 runs he believed Grace's innings to be an indulgence, irrelevant to the final result.

Once again Hawke achieved little in county matches. In twenty innings he accumulated only 197 runs (one more than W.G. had scored in less than a day against Cambridge) at an average of 10.36. He went past fifty just once in the Championship when he hit 56 against Somerset at Huddersfield in July in a match that was over in a day. Earlier the same week the West Countrymen had lost in a day to Lancashire. At the St John's Ground they were bowled out for 74 and 94 and beaten by an innings and 5 runs. George Hirst (10 for 53), Ted Wainwright (8 for 85) and Stanley Jackson (2 for 7) took advantage of a damp wicket that was awkward but hardly spiteful, the rapid downfall of the Somerset batsmen owing as much to the exertions of the Yorkshire fielders as it did to the bowlers. *Wisden* reported:

> On nearly every occasion last season the Yorkshire eleven fielded in splendid fashion, but they surpassed themselves in this match, and it would probably be only the truth to say that rarely or never have so many fine catches been brought off in one afternoon. At any rate, it may be asserted with confidence that the work done in the field by the Yorkshire team during the second innings of Somerset has scarcely ever been beaten in a county match.

When Hawke spoke of the need to continue the process of rebuilding the Yorkshire team even after 1893, it was more than rhetoric. He saw it as being the county's one defence against a lapse into the bad old ways of the 1880s. He was proud of his Yorkshiremen and in many ways his young team's performance in 1894 had given him greater pleasure than the actual winning of the Championship in 1893: Yorkshire had consolidated their success and Hawke was at pains to ensure that everybody knew exactly how the county captain felt about his boys' deeds. The following extract is from a letter widely published in the Press at the end of the season:

> Yorkshiremen must be good sportsmen and bow to the element of bad luck that has attended them through the race for the premiership in 1894. Personally, I am quite satisfied with the work done by the team, and certainly I have never had the honour of captaining a better all-round eleven for Yorkshire.

The season of 1893 had been the closing chapter of the illustrious career of George Ulyett. His formidable powers had been in decline for several years, but his departure left a huge void in Yorkshire cricket. With Happy Jack gone Bobby Peel lost a friend and became senior professional, a role for which he was not ideally suited.

In all, Hawke tried twenty-four players in 1894, including seven amateurs. Among the new blood tried in county cricket that year was Frank Milligan the highly promising Cantab, Frank Mitchell, and a twenty-year-old batsman from Wakefield who would become a Yorkshire legend, David Denton. It has been said that Milligan was a cricketer in the nineteenth-century mould; all bustle and unthinking aggression. He bowled fast, batted with abandon and in the field was a bundle of reckless energy. His critics said he gave his wicket away too easily, that his bowling was too wild. Nevertheless, he was good enough to play with distinction for the Gentlemen against the Players. Though not perhaps a performer of the highest class, his whole-hearted cricket made him an instant favourite among the crowds. One of many cricketers to volunteer for duty in South Africa, he became a national hero when he was killed serving with the Rhodesian Frontier Forces at the relief of Mafeking.

Frank Mitchell made sporadic appearances for Yorkshire over several years. In 1894 he was a Cambridge freshman and by 1896 was captain of the University XI. He was not a stylish batsman, nor the most fleet-footed of men between the wickets or in the outfield, but he drove straight and to the off with disconcerting ferocity, defended stoutly, piled up the runs season after season. Like Frank Milligan he was also destined to play for England under Hawke. He, too, went off to fight the Boers, happily surviving unscathed. In fact he was so taken by South Africa that he emigrated to the Cape, returning to England as captain of the touring Springboks.

David Denton's style of batsmanship was not to everybody's taste, it seemed too flashy, too risky by half. Small-minded opponents called him 'lucky Denton'. One captain on the county circuit would wait until Denton was within earshot, look around his fielders and ask: 'Who's going to drop him first?'

If David Denton was a lucky batsman then it was because fortune favours the brave. He looked for runs from the moment he took guard, there were no dull moments when he was at the wicket. He was one of the last great self-taught batsman and in consequence his batting lacked the technical orthodoxy demanded by his critics. He suffered throughout his career by comparison with his Lancastrian contemporary, J.T. Tyldesley, who played the game as expansively as any amateur and in a fashion that was the envy of most; practically any batsman of any era would suffer by comparison with the Lancastrian wizard. When Shrewsbury retired Tyldesley and Denton were universally regarded as the finest professional batsmen in

England for the best part of a decade; Tyldesley was marginally the better player of slow bowling on a turning wicket, but as Plum Warner was to remark, Denton 'was the hardest hitter of his size and weight' he had ever seen. At one time only W.G. Grace had scored a thousand first-class runs in a season more often than *lucky* Denton. To this day only four men have scored more centuries for Yorkshire than David Denton's 61: Herbert Sutcliffe (112); Geoffrey Boycott (103); Sir Leonard Hutton (85); and Maurice Leyland (62).

Denton was picked for only four matches in 1894 and although his batting did not initially justify the reputation it had earned in league cricket in Wakefield, his fielding was a revelation. It is doubtful whether there had ever been as formidable a fielding side in the history of the game up to that time as Hawke's Yorkshire XI, yet even in such company David Denton was without equal in the deep.

'If Denton dropped a catch,' wrote A.W. Pullin, 'the world wondered.' It did not happen very often. Hawke could not recall him spilling a catch in the first dozen years he played for Yorkshire. Lightning fast over the ground, Denton was the master of the running catch taken at full-tilt, inches from the ground, and the prime exponent of how to pouch the steepling, swirling hit as he sprinted backwards.

On Saturday 8 September, scarcely a fortnight after Yorkshire's Championship aspirations had drowned in the rain at Taunton, Hawke assembled his second touring party to the Americas at Waterloo Station. Catching the 9.40 to Southampton, the English amateurs embarked that afternoon on the steamer *New York* for the Atlantic crossing. Hawke's companions in the venture were:

C.W. Wright, G.W. Hillyard, K. McAlpine, C.E. De Trafford, A.J.L. Hill, C.R. Bardswell, L.C.V. Bathurst, J.S. Robinson, R.S. Lucas, W.F. Whitwell, G.J. Mordaunt.

As with most amateur combinations the side's strength lay in its batting. The bowling looked distinctly fragile and liable to embarrassment on a good wicket, but the risk was minimal and in any event it was by the standards of the day, planned to be a short tour. In common with all Hawke's touring parties it was one that was bound to enjoy its own society.

Wright (Hawke's deputy), Hillyard, McAlpine, Hill and Robinson had toured with Hawke at least once before. De Trafford was the captain of Leicestershire, Bardswell and Bathurst were Oxford

blues, as was Mordaunt, who was also a noted long-jumper, Lucas
the Middlesex player, was an accomplished hockey player with
Teddington and Whitwell was an old friend of Hawke's and the
captain of Durham.

The *New York* made its fastest ever passage from Southampton to
the New World. The tour, which had been organised under the
auspices of the Merion and Germantown Clubs of Philadelphia,
began with a two-day match against New York on the ground of the
Staten Island club. There was such a growth of grass on the wicket
on the first day that Hawke insisted that the wicket should be cut
again before the match commenced. However, his fears about the
state of the pitch proved to be unfounded. After some early scares
the tourists hit a respectable score of 289, with A.J.L. Hill, who had
matched F.S. Jackson run for run and wicket for wicket in India
eighteen months before, leading the way with a chanceless innings
of 99. The rain washed out the second day of the game.

In Philadelphia a small crowd greeted the appearance of the teams
on the first day of the match against All Philadelphia on the ground
of the Merion club. However, interest picked up on the second and
third days, with some five thousand people watching the contest.
Any fears about the adequacy of the English attack were soon
dispelled; Whitwell, Bathurst, Hillyard and Hill were always in
control. Hawke was the pick of the batsmen; taking full advantage
of a let-off in the deep when he had scored 12, he went on to strike
up a cavalier 78 in the tourists' first innings of 187. He added another
39 hard-hit runs when the English amateurs batted a second time.
The visitors' eventual victory was by the comfortable margin of 131
runs.

A few days later at Mannheim, on the ground of the Germantown
club, Hawke's men defeated essentially the same Philadelphian side
– this time styled Gentlemen of Philadelphia – by an innings. On the
second day of the contest a crowd of over five thousand watched as
the home side was twice bowled out. Robbed by a finger injury of
the batting services of G.P. Patterson, their captain and best batsman,
the Philadelphians had no answer to Whitwell's fast-medium bowling.

Even in the 1890s a cricket tour of the United States was an
anachronistic endeavour. Apart from at a handful of beleaguered
clubs in the east, and north of the border in Canada, the cricketing
tradition had not taken hold in the New World. Here it was the
sport of the rich, a pastime that the fashionable middle classes
embraced without ever really taking it to their hearts. In England

and Australia cricket was as much the sport of the down-trodden masses as it was of the ruling classes, it was a social institution. In America it had never lost its exclusivity and as a result it was already, in the land of the free, beginning to atrophy. Philadelphia remains to this day the main bastion of cricket in the Americas. Whenever Hawke returned to North America after 1894 it was to hunt and not to play cricket. Headlines and comments such as those that had followed his earlier tour rankled.

Why do these big fine fellows want to waste their time playing that girl's game?

Cricket will never become a national game where baseball is understood, for one who knows baseball cricket must seem foolish.

From Philadelphia the tour progressed to Toronto where on a soggy wicket the Englishmen had much the better of the encounter with the Gentlemen of Canada. The match was drawn on the second day with the home side 33 runs ahead in their second innings with five wickets to fall, after following on 92 in arrears.

The last match of the tour was against XV of Massachusetts at the Oval at Lowell. Going out to bat after an overnight journey from Montreal the tourists hit 176 and had won by an innings within two days. Charles Wright who scored 3, hit just 25 runs on tour. On the trip back to England he was heard to remark that he had travelled eight thousand miles with an average of three runs per thousand miles. Cricket was indeed a funny game.

That winter Bobby Peel and Jack Brown went to Australia with A.E. Stoddart's side. Peel took twenty-seven wickets in the five Tests, Jack Brown won the fifth and deciding match of the series, hitting the then fastest century in international cricket. Set 297 to win at Melbourne England had tottered to 28 for 2 when Brown went to the wicket. He raised his fifty in twenty-eight minutes, and his hundred in just ninety-five. When he was finally out for 140 he had batted a shade over two hours. His partnership of 210 for the third wicket with Albert Ward had set a new record stand for any wicket in Tests.

Jack Brown had a season of mixed fortunes in England in 1895. He hit an unbeaten 168 against Sussex at Huddersfield and a string of fifties, but otherwise failed more often than not. Nevertheless,

John Tunnicliffe and he both hit over a thousand runs for the county that year. Yorkshire began the season badly, enjoyed a brilliant run in mid-season, only to fall away at the end to finish third in the reformed Championship behind an outstanding Surrey side and the old enemy, Lancashire. Moorhouse, Jackson, Denton and Hawke were consistently in the runs and Peel, Hirst and Wainwright plundered wickets wherever they bowled, aided and abetted to excellent effect by the ubiquitous Jackson.

As if Yorkshire did not already have bowling talents aplenty, a 24-year old right-arm medium-pace bowler from Berry Brow, Huddersfield, appeared on the scene that year. He had begun his career as a tearaway fast bowler before having a rethink and coming up with a method that was altogether more sustainable and effective. A.W. Pullin later said of him that he was '. . . the stranger to despair, the enemy of long-faced misanthropy . . . the sunshine of the Yorkshire eleven'. His name was Schofield Haigh.

Haigh's speciality was a brand of medium-pace off-spin that induced the ball to bite and kick back into the right-handed batsman off a good length. His yorker was all but unplayable, bowled two yards quicker than his normal delivery and devilishly accurate. He was to terrorise county batsmen for the best part of twenty years. On a wet wicket he was lethal. Always experimenting, always thinking, varying his flight, line and length, there were days when he mesmerised his quarry. Most bowlers have their stock delivery upon which all others are in some measure a variation, but not Haigh. He never gave the least indication what was coming next; a gentle off-spinner, fastish cutter, yorker, slower ball, bumper rearing at a batsman's throat – most things were possible when Schofield Haigh had a ball in his hands. It was not unknown for Haigh to force a batsman further and further back into his crease until eventually he trod on his wicket. He exasperated David Hunter, the wicket-keeper, with his unpredictability. Herbert Strudwick, the Surrey and England stumper, declared after keeping to Haigh for the first time: 'By gum, isn't Scof a funny bowler!'

Whimsical of face, a perennial smile in his eyes and gifted with a dry, imperturbable sense of fun, he was the joker in the Yorkshire pack. Modest to a fault, utterly unaffected by his or his team's success, his presence in the XI completed the first of Hawke's great teams.

In 1895 Hawke enjoyed his most prolific season with the bat, scoring 1,078 runs in first-class cricket including seven fifties. He played in all but one of Yorkshire's first-class matches that year, and top-scored in nine of the forty-seven innings in which he batted, vindicating the dictum that he restated in his *Recollections and Reminiscences*:

> It is the man who regularly gets thirties and forties who is of more use to his side than the one who makes two or three centuries and does nothing on a dozen occasions: that is the kind of fact which averages do not prove.

Confident in the state of Yorkshire cricket, Hawke wintered in South Africa. The side under his command was perhaps the strongest he had ever taken abroad, superior even to G.F. Vernon's Australian Team of 1887. Its members were:

Amateurs
H.T. Hewett, S.M.J. Woods (Somerset), H.R. Bromley-Davenport, T.C. O'Brien (Middlesex), C. Heseltine (Hampshire), C.B. Fry (Sussex), A.J.L. Hill, A.M. Miller (Wiltshire), C.W. Wright (Nottinghamshire).

Professionals
T. Hayward, G.A. Lohmann (Surrey), H.R. Butt (Sussex), EJ. Tyler (Somerset).

Hewett, Woods, O'Brien, Heseltine, Hill and Wright had accompanied Hawke on previous adventures, all were proven performers at the highest level. Bromley-Davenport had been a fixture in F.S. Jackson's remarkable Cambridge team of the early 1890s. A swift left-arm bowler and punishing batsman he was one of the few men of the period who played his cricket in spectacles.

1895 was the year Charles Burgess Fry came down from Oxford. R.C. Robertson-Glasgow described him as 'nearly the last of those turn-of-the century immortals, scholar-athlete, columnist, instructor of youth, ripostorial yet creative in wit and debate'. He was all that and more. Not yet the supreme batting technician, he was an ugly, flinging sort of fast bowler and a batsman of unusual promise. Hawke had invited him to tour on the strength of Ranjitsinhji's personal recommendation.

A triple blue at Oxford (cricket, football and athletics), Fry had held the world long jump record since 1893 with a leap that had moved the event into a new era, in the same way that Bob Beamon's phenomenal leap in the rarified Mexican atmosphere was to do in 1968. An intellectual, a man overflowing with ideas, sometimes garrulous, sometimes infuriating, never dull, he was a fascinating companion but one with whom Hawke could not relax. Like many of his contemporaries he found Fry a trifle overpowering. It is no coincidence that of all of Fry's England captains only one, F.S. Jackson, was to earn his enduring respect.

Jackson's winter in India three years before had been his finishing school; now Fry's time in South Africa was to add a new dimension to the Sussex amateur's game. Jackson had rocketed to the forefront of English cricket within months of his return; Fry's advance would be slower, but no less astounding. If his erratic bowling was destined to fall by the wayside, then his batting triumphs were to be legendary.

Audley Miller was the captain of Wiltshire, in terms of first-class cricket he was a bits-and-pieces player, a nagging medium-fast trundler and a useful lower-middle-order blocker or hitter, according to the needs of the moment. He belongs to that select club formed by men who have made their first-class débuts in a Test match, in his case, at Port Elizabeth in the first Test.

Of the professionals, George Lohmann – whose horribly deceptive medium-pace bowling was to torment and finally unnerve the Springbok batsmen – filled the dual role of tour manager and opening bowler; Tom Hayward had scored a thousand runs for the first time in 1895 and was obviously an outstanding prospect; Henry Butt was as sturdy and reliable a stumper as England had to offer; and Edwin Tyler's slow left-arm spin was expected to cause no end of havoc on the matting wickets of the Cape.

The tour had been sponsored by the financier, J.D. Logan, a pugnacious expatriate Scot who ran his business empire from his seat in the Karoo Riding near Matjesfontein. Logan had befriended George Lohmann when the Surrey professional was diagnosed as tuberculor, appointing him manager of one of his farms, hoping no doubt that the crystal-clear air of the Cape would work a cure. Through Lohmann's offices, Hawke had been approached and the tour mooted. However, what began as a purely cricketing enterprise soon fell victim to circumstance.

The main body of the party sailed from Southampton on the Union Line steamer *Guelph* on the last day of November; Hawke, Hewett and O'Brien following a week later on the *Moor*. Delayed by boiler trouble Hawke arrived too late to take part in the first match of the tour against Western Province, but just in time to be greeted by the repercussions of the Jameson Raid.

The Jameson Raid was a skirmish orchestrated by Cecil Rhodes. It was a deliberate provocation of the predominantly Boer population of the Transvaal. Under the extraordinarily inept leadership of Dr L. Starr Jameson, a close friend of Rhodes, a force of some five hundred adventurers and freebooters, mostly of British extraction, departed from Mafeking and rode on Johannesburg, hoping to spark an Uitlander uprising against Kruger. Jameson's raid came to an abrupt end in the the first week of 1896, Boer commandos out-riding and outfighting the invaders at Krugersdorp. The ease with which the Boers rounded up Jameson's men bred a contempt for the English and all things English, and with the grace of hindsight, Rhodes's folly must be seen as the first step along the road to a war which would cost tens of thousands of lives and turn the Transvaal into a wasteland.

Hawke's men found themselves treading warily through the fallout. The original itinerary was suspended as the team cooled its heels for ten days in Cape Town while wild rumours circulated and Rhodes worked to defuse the situation. The waiting came to an end when Hawke was approached with a view to the possibility of employing his side to distract minds from politics. As C.B. Fry noted, dryly, in his *Life Worth Living*:

> Presently it was deemed useful to send us to Johannesburg as an antidote to the inflamed melancholy of that distant city, then in the throes of not knowing what to do . . .

The team entrained for the thousand-mile journey into the Boer heartland at dusk and travelled north through the night. It was very much a journey into the unknown. At the frontier of the Transvaal Republic the train was greeted by a detachment of Boer commandos. The 'welcoming committee' was armed to the teeth and unwelcoming to a man. The English cricketers were ordered out of the train, their luggage inspected, duties levied on practically every item, including cricket bats. T.C. O'Brien's Irish temper flared early in the proceedings as he violently objected to the Boers rifling his baggage. Hawke intervened, soothing emotions, but then Hewett refused point blank to submit to being searched after one of the Boers suspected he was carrying a revolver. In fact it was Hewett's cylindrical toothbrush bottle rather than a gun. Nevertheless, Hewett had no intention of backing down. Armed Boers surrounded him and a heated exchange followed. Hewett was adamant and once again Hawke had to step into the circle, dispensing tact and diplomacy and radiating calm authority. Eventually, with handshakes and smiles all round Hewett was allowed to entrain unsearched; Hawke presented bats to customs officials, and goodwill prevailed.

The team arrived in Johannesburg a few hours after a train transporting dynamite had blown up the station. Hundreds were dead and injured, the Wanderers' ground had been turned into a hospital, Boer artillery was ranged on the city from the commanding heights of nearby hills, commandos patrolled the streets, When the team arrived at its hotel it found that Boer commandos had cut off the water supply. An impression of the atmosphere can be gauged from the fact that many of the city's leading citizens – exclusively British – had been summarily imprisoned and given the option of buying their freedom or rotting behind bars. Johannesburg was a city divided, a city under martial law, a city under the iron rule of Kruger.

Two matches had been arranged but the first of these was cancelled due to what *Cricket* quaintly termed 'the disturbed times'. In the midst of the chaos Hawke, O'Brien and Wright actually dined with several of the detained magnates in prison – and the tourists eventually took on a XV of Johannesburg. Crowds flocked to the match in their droves and £800 was taken at the gate over the two days. To the Boers the presence of the English cricketers must have seemed like a calculated insult. Hawke's men went about their business with the complacent assurance of the English abroad, they made a virtue of making the best of a bad deal, almost behaving as if there was no crisis. If the Boers had no time for them then that was their problem, the Boers were miserable beggars, anyway. However, Johannesburg was no place to play cricket and with a heartfelt sigh of relief the party travelled on to Pietermaritzburg where the tourists received a greeting of an entirely different kind to that which they had experienced in Johannesburg. Hawke was a guest at Government House, other members of the team were put up by the Hussars, the rest in the best hotels.

Two matches were played against a XV of Natal; the first was drawn, the second won by the home side. That the Natal side presented such formidable opposition was due in no small measure to the presence in the side of that redoubtable soldier-cricketer R.M. Poore, then a lieutenant. In the two games he recorded scores of 112, 0 and 107 not out. For Hawke's team Fry (153) and O'Brien (118) scored freely in the first encounter, but no man could match Poore in the return match.

If the Boer hinterland rumbled with discontent, elsewhere was calm. The tour settled down to a more normal tempo, one dictated by the speed of the train – or ox-cart – across the veld, or a steamer up the coast, rather than the political upheavals of the Transvaal. While most of the batsmen prospered on the matting wickets, Hawke floundered. The mat tended to be too slow for his forcing game, and took too much turn for his fallible defensive bat. He hated this type of wicket. He clattered up 59 in a game against odds at Craddock in early February, otherwise he struggled. By the end of the tour he had completely lost his touch.

At Pretoria members of the touring party were induced to visit Kruger and pay their compliments to the crusty old Boer. Early one morning the party trooped up to the President's villa in small groups to pay their respects. Kruger was singularly unimpressed by the gesture. He had no time for cricket nor the Englishmen who played it and he was not of a mind to conceal the fact. Hawke expressed his hope that the President would come and see the forthcoming match in his capital; Kruger grunted and uttered three words. The translator told Hawke that the President was very pleased to see Hawke and his team in Pretoria. C.B. Fry recollected later that Kruger had not looked pleased, and had actually said, 'No good here.'

Sammy Woods' first words to the President were: 'Well, Mr Kruger, we hope we find you well. We have come all this way to see you.' Kruger made no reply, contenting himself with giving the normally irrepressible Sammy the sort of look that told him in no uncertain terms that he had just made a terrible, irremediable blunder. Mightily glad to leave Kruger's villa in one piece Sammy complained to Fry that the 'old blighter was not very hearty'.

At Port Elizabeth Hawke's team met a South African XI. In the first of three games that were subsequently recognised as full Test matches, Hawke led his side to a crushing victory by a margin of 288 runs. The Springboks never found an answer to Lohmann who took 15 for 45 in the match. In the South African's second innings Lohmann took 8 wickets for just 7 runs as the home side were bowled out for 30 in 94 balls. The Surrey professional ended the match with a hat-trick.

Hawke had made a duck in the England first innings, and a handy 30 in the second. In the two subsequent representative matches at

Johannesburg and Cape Town he added scores of 4 and 12 not out. Fortunately, his batting was superfluous as the English bowlers, led by the impossible Lohmann, swept aside the Springbok batsmen with an ease that was at times a little embarrassing. The limitations of Hawke's batsmanship had been cruelly exposed on the mat, but the quality of his leadership throughout had been exemplary. Despite everything the tour had been a cricketing triumph.

10

Stormy Waters
(1896–1897)

Yorkshire took the Championship of 1896 in emphatic fashion. Sixteen of their twenty-six matches were won and only three lost. Lancashire, Middlesex and Surrey were left to compete for the minor placings long before the season was over.

Strangely, the northerners owed their success that year more to their prodigious batting than their bowling, which was often, according to *Lillywhite's Cricketers' Annual*, 'not so deadly'. Five men – Jack Brown (1,556), John Tunnicliffe (1,223), Bobby Peel (1,135), Stanley Jackson (1,030) and George Hirst (1,018) – scored over a thousand runs in the Championship that year and David Denton (852), Ted Wainwright (817), Robert Moorhouse (675) and Hawke (577) each scored at least one century during the campaign. Yorkshire's scoring was without precedent. In an age when a score in excess of 300 was considered to be a match-winning total in almost every circumstance, Yorkshire went past 400 on eight occasions in the Championship of 1896.

At Edgbaston in May Hawke's men struck up a total of 887 against Warwickshire that remains to this day both the highest and longest innings (650 minutes) ever played in the County Championship. During the course of the innings four Yorkshiremen – Jackson (117), Wainwright (126), Peel (210 not out) and Hawke (166) – scored centuries, the first time four men had achieved such a feat in a first-class innings. The stand of 292 for the eighth wicket between Peel and Hawke has never been bettered in England. At the time Yorkshire's 887 was the highest score ever recorded in first-class cricket.

Hawke's 166 was the highest score of his first-class career. It comprised 21 fours, 7 threes, 13 twos and 35 singles, most of the boundaries were driven straight or to the off and he gave no chance until he had reached 151. He had arrived at the wicket with the scoreboard showing the visitors at 448 for 7 shortly before the close of the first day's play. Not out on 3 overnight, the next morning he and Peel set about the systematic destruction of the Warwickshire attack. Hawke recollected that by the time he was out, bowled by the persistent Pallett, the fielding side had been 'played to a frazzle'. The depth of Yorkshire's batting may be appreciated by a glance at the Yorkshire scorecard at Edgbaston, which shows that upon Hawke's dismissal at 740 for 8, George Hirst emerged from the pavilion at number ten in the order to continue the mayhem.

A fortnight after the massacre of the Warwickshire attack Yorkshire scored 543 against Sussex at Bradford with Wainwright (145) and Peel (111) sharing in a fifth wicket stand of 198 after Denton had gone without troubling the scorers and the innings had faltered at 179 for 4. In the absence of Jackson, who was away nursing cracked ribs after an early encounter with the touring Australians, Tunnicliffe (87) – who had missed out at Birmingham – was like a rock at the head of the order. Down the list Hirst (90) again brutally plundered tired bowling.

In the following match against Middlesex at Lord's Jack Brown hit 203 in the first innings and 81 not out in the second as he and Tunnicliffe shared in opening partnerships of 139 and 147 to carry Yorkshire to victory by a margin of ten wickets.

Yorkshire's batsmen had occasional setbacks – the rain was always the joker in the pack – and wickets were not invariably prepared to encourage stroke-play. At Sheffield the pace of Ernest Jones put Hawke's young lions in their place; the Australians bowled them out for 118 and 136 and won by an innings. Later in the week, however, Yorkshire took 459 runs off Kent, with Hawke (110 not out) and David Hunter (41) sharing in a punishing last-wicket partnership of 118.

In mid-June at Grace Road it was Leicestershire's turn to suffer. Jack Brown (131) and John Tunnicliffe (79) began the torture with a stand of 139, Stanley Jackson (77) was next on stage, followed by David Denton (73). When Moorhouse succumbed for a modest 19, half the side was out for 371 and the weary Leicestershire bowlers briefly entertained visions of salvaging a little pride from the ruins. But then George Hirst, promoted in Hawke's absence to seventh in the list, crashed 107 in two hours as Yorkshire hurried to a final total of 660. For the first time every member of the Yorkshire side had reached double figures. Shell-shocked, the home side reeled to an inevitable innings defeat.

The next week in a minor match against Durham at Barnsley, a depleted Yorkshire XI without many of its regulars, crushed the visitors, thanks to Schofield Haigh's bowling. Haigh returned match figures of 14 for 50 and was immediately drafted into the county side: in what remained of the season he was by far the best of the Yorkshire bowlers, taking seventy-one Championship wickets at fifteen a piece.

If scoring runs was not a problem that afflicted Yorkshire in 1896, bowling sides out was. Two men, William Storer of Derbyshire and Ranjitsinhji of Sussex, each scored two centuries in a match against Yorkshire that year. Ranji, amazingly, did so on a single day, a feat that no man has ever managed to emulate.

Perhaps it was because the county had surged to the Championship on a tide of runs rather than on the success of their bowlers that the triumph seemed to fire the imagination of Yorkshire folk. It was as if Hawke's men had now shown everybody that they could not only bowl and field better than the rest, but also bat better, too. The last vestiges of self-doubt disappeared.

Hawke's personal reputation was now at its height and in Yorkshire the Baron could do no wrong. He was rightly seen as the man who had transformed Yorkshire cricket from the shambles of the late eighties to the triumphs of mid-nineties; now he acted to consolidate and build upon the success of Yorkshire cricket.

Hawke approached the county Committee with the proposal that his professionals should be remunerated during the off-season. As The Reverend R.S. Holmes records in his *History of Yorkshire County Cricket: 1833–1903* the Committee hurriedly acquiesced.

The Committee decided to give winter pay to the professionals in the team at the rate of £2 per week from 7th September 1896, to the opening of the cricket season in 1897, at the same time giving half that amount to their old scorer, H. Turner. This winter subsidy was paid to the professionals on 'the express condition they do not engage with any club or league during the summer'. It was subsequently resolved that the period for such pay extend from September to May the first following, and that 'one half of such pay be retained by the County Committee, and four per cent interest per annum be added thereto'. The accumulated sum will be paid over when a player retires from active county cricket, or a portion or the whole of it at any time 'if in their opinion it appears desirable to do so'.

Many years before, Hawke had done away with the old talent money regime under which bonuses were only paid for a fifty, a hundred or for five wickets in an innings. He had replaced it with his 'mark system'. Under the new regime marks, each worth five shillings, were awarded for good performances. In other words, a score of twenty or thirty on an awkward pitch or in a tight situation might now earn talent money, as might the capture of a valuable wicket, the taking of a sharp catch or a day's good work in the outfield. Hawke's marks were flexible, adapted to circumstance and, by their nature, issued much more liberally than the talents of earlier times. After every season Hawke would gather his professionals together at his country seat and ceremonially present each man with the bounty his accumulated marks had earned.

The introduction of the mark system had been one part of his campaign to instil discipline and inculcate a sense of personal pride and responsibility in the ranks of his professionals. Hawke's apparently ruthless treatment of disruptive elements and those who could not, or would not, curb their drinking had tended to distract attention from the quiet revolution he had worked in Yorkshire. All through the long years when Sheffield had fulminated against the rebels in the Ridings Hawke had gradually learned the art of captaincy and won the trust and respect of his professionals. By 1896 they regarded Hawke not just as their captain, but as their mentor and protector. With the coming of winter pay, Hawke had squared the circle; rewarding his professionals for their cricket and their personal loyalty to him, whilst binding them even more closely to his will.

Winter pay was seen very much as Hawke's own initiative. Other counties paid individual professionals retainers in the off-season, some made *ad hoc* payments to players in cases of hardship; institutionalised winter pay as a right was virtually unheard of, beyond both the slender resources and the wit of the majority of counties.

Hawke portrayed himself as merely his professionals' agent in carrying winter pay through the Yorkshire Committee, spoke as if it was simply a case of bringing the county into line with the rest of the game. In reality, Yorkshire cricket, in terms of its approach on the

field and its administration off the field, was streets ahead of the
pack. His modesty endeared him to his professionals and soothed
the doubts of the faint-hearted in Yorkshire who had lacked the
courage to challenge Hawke in Committee. However, interviewed
by W.A. Bettesworth, Hawke told the cricketing world – in so
many words – that he believed it was a county's duty to look after its
professionals, and that was that. This was the heir apparent to
Yorkshire cricket speaking for the future of the county club. W.A.
Bettesworth faithfully reproduced Hawke's declaration of intent in
his 'Chats on the Cricket Field' column in *Cricket* at the end of
December 1896:

> I have been chaffed about getting my players two pounds a
> week, but I found that in the very great majority of counties
> men are either being paid during the winter or weekly all the
> year round, and as my players expressed a wish to be also paid,
> I readily brought the proposal before the committee. I feel the
> captain is the proper person to represent the players. They
> know that we have a very substantial balance – if we had been
> in low water they would have waited until we were in a better
> position; and while they feel they are well paid during the
> summer, they do not like to be left unprovided for in the
> winter. One has to consider that men while playing cricket
> have very little opportunity for saving; you expect them to
> work hard for you all the summer and then cast them off to get
> whatever work they can. It has often been said to me that men
> are all the better for working during the winter, but apart from
> the fact that they cannot always get work, I don't believe in
> men going into hot mills for the winter. You cannot expect in
> common fairness a man to be the absolute gentleman he is in
> the summer, and then to like being turned loose for the rest of
> the season . . . Nowadays County cricket is really hard work,
> and a very great deal is expected of those who play it.

Hawke also used the opportunity to deal with the mooted revival of
the Cricket Council. Yorkshire felt that such a revival would
inevitably lead to alliances and feuding between the counties and,
mindful that Lord Harris was back in the country, Hawke commented
that:

> MCC are perfectly capable of deciding any questions with

regard to the counties. They have been somewhat diffident for many years, but they are beginning to see that cricketers look to them to go into matters of importance, and they are ready to do so.

Content with his year's work Hawke turned his thoughts to his next overseas adventure, his forthcoming tour of the West Indies. He had been invited to take a team to the Caribbean as long ago as the winter of 1894–95. On that occasion he had been unable to accept the invitation and R.S. Lucas had stepped in as a replacement. However, there was a problem. As he prepared to depart for the Caribbean, another rival tour was being planned. Haunted by the spectre of his first venture abroad, the doomed double tour of the Antipodes that had ended in financial disaster, and for him in personal grief, Hawke was not unnaturally livid to find himself in a similar position ten years later. Whilst in 1886 the primary obstacle to common sense had been the obstinacy of Melbourne and Sydney, in 1896 the authorities in the Caribbean would have been amenable to practically any solution that ensured that only one team toured the West Indies that winter. There was great embarrassment in the Caribbean when it was realised that separate invitations had been sent to both Hawke and Arthur Priestley (later Sir Arthur Priestley, Member of Parliament for Grantham from 1900 to 1918, who had toured the West Indies with Lucas in 1894–5) to bring out teams. Unfortunately, by the time Hawke, Priestley and their respective hosts in the faraway Caribbean realised what had happened, the two principals had already promised men places in their sides.

Hawke had developed his own very particular method of assembling a touring party. First he would sound out the availability of likely candidates. Next he circulated the list of names among his chosen band of brothers and asked – with a wholly unapologetic bluntness – whether anybody had any observations they wished to make before the party was finalised. A single dissenting voice was usually sufficient to bar a man, regardless of his cricketing pedigree. The process was time-consuming, unwieldy and deeply unsatisfactory to the man who later found himself left at home. To Hawke it was more important that a man was a good tourist than a good cricketer and he unashamedly placed comradeship and sportsmanship above all else. The result was that Hawke's tours were invariably happy.

To cut a long story short, when, in the autumn of 1896, Hawke and Priestley corresponded about the possibility of amalgamating the two sides, two men whom Priestley had included in his team proved unacceptable to all the members of Hawke's party and Hawke flatly refused to have them in his side. Matters came to a head after a highly publicised exchange of letters in the Press. Hawke peremptorily summoned Priestley to a meeting, no doubt hoping to clear the air. Priestley was in no mood to compromise and deeply resented Hawke's cavalier behaviour. The two men argued and parted with daggers drawn; an impasse had been reached.

Sir Home Gordon, a long-standing mutual friend of the two protagonists, wrote of the affair in his *Background of Cricket*:

> Arthur Priestley, known as 'the politician', was forced by family influence to represent Grantham in the House of Commons, which he hated. He was an impregnably slow batsman who once came into the limelight by taking a cricket team . . . to the West Indies at the same time as Martin Hawke led another. The latter was very intolerant at the idea of a rival tour, so sent for Priestley and bade him abandon the idea, adding that in compensation he would give him a place in his own side. The politician hotly refused, and they parted on pretty hostile terms. Only once on tour did the two sides run across each other and then they fraternized, but the respective captains held angrily aloof from each other. A couple of years later I reconciled them, but though they shook hands there was never more than the barest acquaintanceship subsequently in spite of both being intimate friends of Ranjitsinhji.

According to Home Gordon, Priestley was a man who 'held emphatic views on most subjects except politics, and was remarkably voluble on them'. He was a prickly character, easily angered. Like Hawke he was a confirmed bachelor whose life was ruled by family tradition and like Hawke he was a man accustomed to getting his own way in most things.

Two teams toured the West Indies that winter and undeniably the fault was largely Hawke's. He was the senior man. Had he dealt with Priestley in a less high-handed fashion, treated him more as a friend and ally in the cause of spreading the cricketing gospel than as an upstart interloper, reason might have prevailed. Had Hawke stepped down from his pedestal and enlisted Priestley's support rather than his antagonism, cricket would have applauded him; instead, the débâcle marked a watershed in Hawke's career.

Since Yorkshire's triumph in 1893 Hawke's reputation had soared. It had seemed that the Baron could do no wrong. His treatment of Priestley heralded the end of the honeymoon and when, within a year, the sacking of Bobby Peel rocked English cricket, the bubble burst with a vengeance.

That winter Hawke led the weaker of the two touring sides. Those who accompanied him to the Caribbean were:

H.R. Bromley-Davenport, C. Heseltine, P.F. Warner, H.D.G. Leveson-Gower, G.R. Bardswell, R. Berens, J.M. Dawson, A.E. Leatham, W.H. Wakefield, A.D. Whatman, R.D. Wickham.

Priestley's side included Sammy Woods and A.E. Stoddart, performers seemingly of an entirely different calibre to the men in Hawke's army. Nevertheless, men like Bromley-Davenport, Heseltine and Bardswell had had their day on the big stage of English cricket, even if five members of the party – Berens, Wakefield (Oxford Authentics), Dawson, Wickham (Yorkshire Gentlemen) and Whatman (Eton Ramblers) – were club cricketers who would never aspire to play first-class cricket in England. Of the other tourists, Leatham had been Hawke's and Heseltine's companion in India with bat, ball and gun; Leveson-Gower, formerly of Winchester College and Oxford University, was a Surrey batsman of considerable promise and also an accomplished leg-spinner in club cricket; and Warner, too, was a batsman who was threatening to make his way in the first-class arena. Leveson-Gower and Warner were both later to join that most exclusive of all cricketing clubs; of cricketing knights.

H.D.G. Leveson-Gower, known as 'Shrimp' on account of his diminutive stature, had made his name as captain of the Winchester XI that had beaten Eton on their home ground for the first time in ten years in 1892. He was a competent batsman who was to serve Surrey for many years, but his great contribution to his county, MCC and England was as an administrator. A lifelong friend and confidant of Hawke, Leveson-Gower was for fifty years a leading figure behind the Scarborough Festival.

Pelham Francis 'Plum' Warner – batsman, Ashes-winning captain, selector, administrator, journalist, chronicler and broadcaster – was 23 when he boarded the Southampton train at Waterloo on 13 January 1897 and set off on his first cricket tour. His father was for many years the Attorney General of Trinidad and Warner had been born in Port of Spain, the youngest of eighteen children. He had left Trinidad at the age of 13 and now, ten years later, via Rugby, Oriel College, Oxford and the Bar of the Inner Temple he was returning to be the star of the tour. His batting illuminated the XI's passage through the Caribbean, but, just as significant, so did his writing. Warner's batting was the product of application and of years of dogged perseverence; his literary light was uncovered by chance.

Just before the S S *Don* sailed for the Caribbean H.V.L. Stanton of The *Sportsman* asked Hawke if it would be possible for somebody to send home accounts of the matches. Whether by accident or design Hawke turned to Warner. 'Plummy, you're the last from school,' he said, mindful of Warner's recent call to the Bar, 'why shouldn't you do it?'

It was a fateful suggestion. Warner was not perhaps the great author that Cardus was, but his gentle anecdotal, profoundly optimistic writing chronicled the deeds of generations of English cricketers in a way that was quite unique. The pages of his books speak for the romanticism and the magic of the game. A.A. Thomson said of Warner in his *Cricket: The Great Captains:*

> There have been greater performers but no one has in his person more truly symbolised cricket; its pageantry, its dignity and decency, its sense of 'civilization under the sun' than that very perfect gentle knight . . .

Warner and Hawke became firm friends in the Caribbean. When Hawke's appetite for leading cricket tours waned Warner picked up the torch, the perfect heir, the ideal ambassador. Hawke later ensured that Warner was appointed captain of the first team sent to the Antipodes by MCC in the winter of 1903–4. But in 1897 Warner was no more than a promising University batsman, technically sound, otherwise unremarkable.

On the first day of the opening match of the tour against the Queen's Park club at St Clair, Trinidad, Warner hit 119 including fifteen fours as Hawke's team raced to 428 all out. Warner's was the first century recorded in an important match in Trinidad. Intriguingly, the home side was captained by his elder brother, Aucher.

In the West Indies cricket had already lost much of its exclusivity. Whereas in India cricket was mainly the preserve of the expatriate community, or in America a pursuit of the wealthy, in the Caribbean gentlemen expatriates, civil servants, officers and businessmen played shoulder to shoulder with amateurs and professionals drawn from the local population. The most obvious manifestation of this mixing of the classes and races in West Indian cricket was that both Hawke's and Priestley's sides found themselves facing a battery of black professional fast bowlers. Even at this early stage in the development of West Indian cricket, many of the best batsmen and practically all the best bowlers, were Afro-Caribbeans. At the end of the tour Hawke was so impressed by the quality of the Caribbean game that he campaigned to bring a West Indian side to England.

Hawke's team had a taste of what West Indian cricket had to offer in the second fixture of the tour, at Port of Spain against Trinidad. Warner again shone, scoring 74 in the tourists' first innings, but otherwise the pace of Cumberbatch and Woods swept away the English batting. In the second innings Hawke's team were put out for just 59. There were murmurings about the standard of the wicket and suggestions were made to the effect that on a good wicket Cumberbatch and Woods would have presented few problems, but within a few days Trinidad had comprehensively defeated the tourists a second time on the same ground. Again, the fearsome Cumberbatch and Woods wreaked havoc amongst the battered and bewildered English batsmen.

By the end of the second week of February the tourists were glad to escape to Grenada. The St George's Club were easily conquered. Hawke's lobs claiming 4 for 34 on a relaxed second day. Grenada put up little resistance, beaten by an innings in the following days. On St Vincent Warner scored 156 to overwhelm the local side. Severer tests awaited in Barbados where a hard-fought draw and a narrow victory resulted from two tight games against the island's team. Warner's purple patch continued, his 113 not out being the difference between victory and defeat in the second match. He registered another century, 110 in the second innings against Antigua at St John's, then hit 81 against St Kitts at Basseterre in matches won by huge margins.

Up until the eleventh match of the tour, at St Lucia, Hawke had batted very moderately. In Trinidad he had been as hapless as the rest against the fast bowlers; in other matches he had clattered a few boundaries and holed out with monotonous regularity. Against St Lucia Hawke smashed 108 runs in quick time. He was brought down to earth in Georgetown, however, ten days later, suffering the indignity of being run out without troubling the scorers in the victory over British Guiana. In the return match at the beginning of

April he managed 26 in his only innings to finish with a respectable tour average of 22.37.

Warner's form had been of a different order. He had scored four centuries and accumulated 984 runs at an average of 51.78. He had scored more runs than the next two most prolific batsmen combined. By comparison, the leading light of Priestley's team, A.E. Stoddart, had scored 1,079 runs at an average of 53.95. Such things were expected of the magnificent Stoddart; Warner, on the other hand, had been almost unknown before the tour.

While Hawke was in the West Indies the controversy over the rival tours had continued unabated. In the spring of 1897 Hawke was widely seen as the villain of the piece. The events of the coming English season were to do little to redress the damage. Yorkshire slumped to fourth in the Championship behind Lancashire, Surrey and unfashionable Essex. Once again, the batsmen dominated, six of them scoring over a thousand runs in the competition: Jack Brown (1,431), Ted Wainwright (1,372), David Denton (1,328), George Hirst (1,212), Stanley Jackson (1,089) and John Tunnicliffe (1,077). Against Sussex at Sheffield in the second week of July Brown (311) and Tunnicliffe (147) had put on 378 for the first wicket in 270 minutes, improving by 32 the record of Palairet and Hewett against Yorkshire five years before. To Jack Brown went the honour of being the first Yorkshireman to hit a triple-century in first-class cricket. In all he batted for 375 minutes and hit forty-eight fours. Surrey's Bobby Abel and William Brockwell bettered the record by a single run in August, but Yorkshire's 681 for 5 (declared) remained by far the best score of the year. The problem, as before, was the bowling. Although five men claimed at least fifty wickets no man sustained his best form throughout the season. For Lancashire Johnny Briggs took 140 wickets and W.R. Cuttell 102, and for Surrey the indefatigable Tom Richardson took 238. Yorkshire's top wicket-taker was George Hirst with 84.

Hawke was plagued by lumbago during the first half of the season and the captaincy passed into the eminently capable hands of F.S. Jackson. Hawke returned to preside over the surrender of the title. His own form with the bat was a model of respectability, his 436 Championship runs were struck at an average of 31.14. Nevertheless, the Championship slipped inexorably from Hawke's grasp.

This was also the year that Bobby Peel was sacked. Inevitably, it was said that Peel's departure lost Yorkshire the Championship but an examination of the evidence quickly dispels this myth. When Hawke led Peel off the field and out of Yorkshire cricket two matches remained of the county's Championship programme, one of which was won and the other drawn; had both been won, Yorkshire would not have taken the Championship. Much more damaging to the county's cause had been Peel's absence through injury and then illness in July and August, denying the Tykes his services in nine of the ten matches before his suspension on the first day of the penultimate Championship fixture, against Derbyshire at Bradford.

Yorkshire had won nine of their first fourteen Championship matches and been well placed to retain the title by mid-July, but in Peel's absence – which coincided with a spell of dry weather – the Yorkshire attack struggled to bowl sides out. Untimely injuries to other key players, Hawke included, robbed the side of balance and continuity over the final twelve matches, four of which were lost, and with them Yorkshire's grip on the Championship. After losing to Essex at Huddersfield by a single run, the rot had set in against Gloucestershire at Harrogate at the end of July when Gilbert Jessop had thrashed 101 off the Yorkshire bowlers in forty minutes.

Hawke was undoubtedly shaken by the vehemence of the outcry over Peel's sacking. It was as if he had not realised that Bobby Peel was a living legend in the shire of the broad acres, a working-class hero whose deeds had long since become an integral part of the mythology of Yorkshire cricket.

In later years Hawke was to refer to his dismissal of Peel as 'the most decisive action of my whole career'. He was still defending himself in the 1920s, claiming in his *Recollections and Reminiscences* that 'it had to be done for the sake of discipline and the good of cricket'. However, when he declared that 'nothing ever gave me so much pain,' the sceptics were unconvinced, no doubt remembering Edmund Peate. The fact of the matter was that as a disciplinary exercise the departure of Bobby Peel was an object lesson *par excellence*; no one, not even Bobby Peel, was indispensable. In fact, it was the Yorkshire Committee that suspended Peel on the first day of the Derbyshire match at Bradford, the Yorkshire Committee that decided in committee to discharge Yorkshire's senior professional, a decision whole-heartedly and publicly endorsed by M.J. Ellison who remained the titular figurehead of Yorkshire cricket. However, everybody knew that all Yorkshire now bowed before the will of the county captain, that when Hawke spoke all Yorkshire instantly obeyed any request. This was too much for Hawke's critics. It seemed as if, to paraphrase Voltaire, Hawke had sacked one professional to encourage the others. The Sheffield grinders had a field day.

In reality, of course, Bobby Peel was the architect of his own downfall. It was hardly unknown for Bobby to arrive at a ground drunk. He was the last survivor of Hawke's old brigade, less respectful of the county's noble captain than his younger fellows, wiser in many things than the rising stars of the new guard, sometimes a shade jaundiced at the zeal of Hawke's young lions. He had become an outsider, a legend growing old in a time of change. However, his powers were undimmed and whatever his faults he had been a great servant of the county for many years; he deserved better. Hawke ought to have found a way of saving Bobby Peel from himself. As it was, the Bradford incident followed close on the heels of Peel's self-induced 'indisposition' on the last day of the previous match against Middlesex. Once Peel had publicly disgraced himself at Bradford Hawke felt he had no choice in the matter and Peel had to go. Bobby had paid lip-service to the new order, but never taken it onboard. In August 1897 his folly caught up with him.

Wounded by personal criticism and suddenly aware that the affair threatened to reawaken the internal rivalries that had lain dormant in Yorkshire since 1893, Hawke went to the Committee with a proposal that promised both to improve the financial security of his professionals, and to tie them even closer to the county. He proposed that a bonus fund be set up by which:

> Each professional cricketer, who shall take part in a fixed number of matches arranged by the County Committee shall, in addition to such payments, talent monies and benefits as have hitherto been the custom, be credited with a bonus of £2 for each County match in which he has played since May 1st 1897.

In times of need a player could apply to the Committee to draw a certain amount, otherwise the bonus would be paid as a lump sum when a player retired from first-class cricket. Yorkshire cricketers would never again be left to fend entirely for themselves in their declining years. However, there was a caveat:

> Dissatisfaction with the conduct of a player or with his reasons for leaving their service might forfeit any accumulation to the credit of the player.

11

Imperial Cricket
(1898–1899)

The Peel affair left Hawke bloodied but unbowed. He emerged in 1898 determined to assert Yorkshire's rights and to put the discord of the previous year behind him. English cricket was looking forward to the next visit of the Australians one year hence, in 1899, and the time was right for full-scale reform of the chaotic *ad hoc* arrangements which had until then governed the administration and conduct of major tours.

At Bedale in the first week of May, just before Yorkshire's trial match against the local XVIII, Hawke fired the opening broadsides in the campaign for change. The occasion was a gathering to welcome George Hirst and Ted Wainwright back from Stoddart's tour to Australia, but within the county it was widely known that Hawke planned to use the forum to set out Yorkshire's stall. Hawke's dislike for public speaking lent itself to brevity and a directness that went down well in the Ridings. First there were the pleasantries; nobody was left in any doubt about how delighted his Lordship was to have Hirst and Wainwright safely back in the fold. Next, he told his audience how much he admired Australian cricket. This was safe ground, but a moment later he threw caution to the winds. Cricket, carried a full report of his speech.

> In my opinion . . . the Committee of the Marylebone Club should select the team for each Test Match, and also choose the grounds on which they should be played. Lord's must, of course, have one match, but the Oval and Manchester should not be allowed to take the other two Test games. In Yorkshire we have a ground second to none – two or three grounds, in

fact, capable of accommodating 30,000 persons – and it is only fair that Yorkshire should have a share of the Test Matches.

As if calling for the end of the Lord's/Oval/Old Trafford monopoly of Test matches (and of course Test receipts) was not enough, Hawke asked for an end to the undignified debate over the appearance money paid to professionals chosen to play for England. At the Oval in 1896 five players had threatened to strike over what they considered to be a derisory match fee; two men had actually refused to play, including Surrey's George Lohmann. Payment, Hawke declared:

> '. . should be absolutely in the hands of the MCC. I am one of those who think the players should be paid liberally. Ten pounds, with five pounds for travelling expenses, has been suggested, but I think twenty pounds should be allowed and have done with it.'

Then he struck at the heart of the English game's most treasured vested interest. Commenting on the view that only fifteen per cent of the takings should be held by the ground staging a Test match, Hawke remarked the he felt twenty per cent was a better figure. He believed that, in future, 'the balance should be divided among the clubs who had representatives in the English team'. At the time it was a startling idea. Hawke being Hawke, proceeded to hammer home the point:

> For years the gate-money has gone to the clubs on whose grounds the matches are played, and we in Yorkshire have allowed our players to take part in the games year after year, and have never had a Test played in the county. If the matches in future were arranged on the principles I suggested, I am sure they would give satisfaction to the cricket world in general, and there would be an end of cavilling.

In the unlikely event of Yorkshire's proposals going unheeded, Hawke, moderating his tone as befitted a loyal committee member of MCC, was moved to issue a veiled threat to the other counties:

> If a change is not made Yorkshire will take a strong stand, and will not allow their players to take part in a Test Match unless it is

arranged by MCC, to whom we owe allegiance as the head of cricket.

Hawke finished with the comment, 'As the other counties are being asked for their opinions on these matters, it is as well that those of Yorkshire should be known.'

It deserves to be noted that when Hawke spoke for Yorkshire at Bedale it was without the formal sanction of his county Committee, although this was freely, if belatedly, forthcoming at the end of May. Yet if Hawke was the self-appointed leader of the crusade to bring Test matches and tours under MCC control, he was hardly isolated in his views. He had powerful friends and allies, among them Lord Harris and many of his fellow county captains.

In mid-July the first-class counties met at Lord's and a majority voted in favour of Hawke's proposal that MCC should 'appoint a Board to govern future Test matches between England and Australia at home'. Moreover, when it was suggested that 'such a Board be comprised of the President of MCC, five of its club Committee, and one representative from six of the first-class counties selected by the MCC with 'the President of MCC always to have the casting vote,' this, too, was carried. *Cricket* observed that 'The resolution gives the MCC a majority, so that the counties will, in future, practically have no control over the matches.' The counties had effectively surrendered their old ways. Hawke had made the initial breach, Lord Harris now stepped into it. In October that year Harris, encouraged by Hawke, induced the counties to formalise the arrangements that would govern the Australians' forthcoming tour in 1899.

Any residual resistance in the counties evaporated when Harris proposed that for home Test matches:

MCC should not stand on their strict rights, and should accept a position of equality with the counties on the money question . . . After payment of half the gross gate money to the Australians, the net gate money should be divided equally among the first-class counties and MCC.

Agreeing that the ground or county staging a match should retain twenty per cent of the gate receipts, Harris carried the day. Later it was decided that five three-day Test matches would be played against the Australians, with Trent Bridge and Headingley being added to the traditional Test match venues of Lord's, the Oval and Old Trafford. The England team would be selected by MCC, probably by a delegated selection committee. Professionals would henceforth receive a match fee of £20.

The year of 1898 was Hawke's year. Yorkshire romped to the Championship and were never at any stage seriously threatened. Hawke missed only one county match, when he was attending the funeral of M.J. Ellison, the Yorkshire President, who died on 12 July. Ellison was buried in the churchyard of St Bede's at Masborough four days later (the day on which Yorkshire suffered their first defeat of the season, at the hands of Kent at Maidstone). The Duke of Norfolk and the Earl of Effingham were among the mourners, few of Sheffield's notables were absent.

Ellison's death sent a wave of uncertainty through the county. The *Daily Telegraph* fuelled old fears when it suggested that the death of the Yorkshire President might 'have an unfortunate effect'. It went on to comment that the danger lay 'in local rivalries' and asserted that:

There is a strong wish in some directions to shift the head-quarters of the county club from Sheffield to Leeds, but whether desirable or not, such a change could not be brought about without a great deal of friction and heartburning. The Sheffield people in the middle of the sixties made the County Club, and it is not in the least degree likely that they will, without a struggle, forfeit the position they have held for so long. It is to be hoped that, with Yorkshire doing such great things on the field, dissension will be avoided, but a very prominent member of the eleven confessed the other day that he felt a little uneasy as to the immediate future.

Hawke stepped into Ellison's shoes and 'local rivalries' withered on the vine. Yorkshire closed ranks behind him. The question of removing the club's offices to Headingley was temporarily set aside. On the field the team marched on.

Ironically, Hawke had not entertained the highest hopes for the season of 1898. Bobby Peel's absence from an attack that had struggled to bowl sides out in 1897 boded ill for the coming campaign. Both Hirst and Wainwright returned from Australia tired and jaded and neither had set the world ablaze with either their batting or their bowling that winter. With Peel gone and Hirst and

Wainwright clearly out of sorts, Hawke's hopes for 1898 had been modified accordingly. As it turned out events were to mock his early pessimism.

If Yorkshire's batting was predictably formidable, their bowling was a revelation. It hardly seemed to matter that Hirst and Wainwright, previously rocks upon which the attack had been built, were mere bit players, for three other Yorkshiremen claimed over a hundred first-class wickets that season: Stanley Jackson; Schofield Haigh; and a 20-year-old newcomer who as a boy had played in the same Kirkheaton XI as George Hirst. His name was Wilfred Rhodes.

The legendary deeds of Edmund Peate and Bobby Peel had spawned a host of would-be immitators in the shire of the broad acres. When Peel went there was a whole host of pretenders awaiting the call to arms, but only two were offered a trial, Rhodes and Albert Cordingley. Cordingley hailed from Eccleshill, Bradford, and was by some years the older of the pair when he and Rhodes appeared in opposition at Bedale at the beginning of May 1898. Rhodes was selected for the Yorkshire XI, Cordingley for the Bedale and District XVIII. This in itself was significant, for it gave Cordingley the opportunity to impress against Yorkshire's daunting batting line-up, whereas Rhodes had little chance to shine brightly against the local batsmen. Rhodes returned match figures of 6 for 37, Cordingley 5 for 75. Cordingley's victims included David Denton and Jack Brown; there were no such immortals in Rhodes' tally. Round one had gone to Cordingley. Three days later Rhodes and Cordingley were again under the microscope, this time on the same side, bowling for Yorkshire's Colts against Nottinghamshire's at Trent Bridge. Rain washed out the second day's play, but on the first Rhodes excelled, taking four wickets to Cordingley's one.

Undecided as to which man should fill the vacant slow left-armer's place in the Yorkshire side, Hawke included both men in the party that embarked on the Tykes' southern tour at the outset of the new season. Yorkshire were due to commence their first-class programme against MCC at Lord's at the end of the second week of May, and it was in the Nursery ground nets on the first morning of the match that Hawke turned to Stanley Jackson and asked him to test out Cordingley and Rhodes before the team was finalised. Hawke favoured Cordingley, feeling that Rhodes needed more experience and that Cordingley would probably be steadier under fire than the younger man. No doubt he hoped Jackson would confirm his judgement. In what must have been a nerve-wracking duel Cordingley and Rhodes wheeled away at Jackson. After W.G. Grace, and perhaps Archie MacLaren or A.E. Stoddart, there was no more daunting batsman in England than Jacker. Rhodes withstood the pressure better than Cordingley and much to Hawke's chagrin, won Jackson's vote.

Hawke and Jackson retired out of earshot. Hawke argued for Cordingley; Jackson for Rhodes; but Jackson would not yield. The discussion grew heated. Although Hawke endorsed Cordingley on the basis of what he had seen of him in match conditions Jackson was adamant; Rhodes was the best bowler and ought to play. Rhodes played.

It is often assumed that Hawke and Jackson were, if not from the start then certainly throughout their latter playing days, the closest of friends. This is not, in the strictest sense, accurate. They were from the outset the keenest of comrades in the cause of Yorkshire cricket, but friendship came much later and the road to it was strewn with pitfalls. Jackson admired Hawke and supported him loyally and without exception. Yet they were distanced from one another for between them stood the question of the Yorkshire captaincy. In the spring of 1898 Jackson's business and political interests were already encroaching upon his cricket and with his path to the Yorkshire captaincy and thus that of England too – apparently barred by Hawke's presence. Indeed his commitment to county cricket was always liable to decline with the passing years. For Hawke Yorkshire cricket was his life; for Jackson it was never more than his sport. Jackson was too gifted, too self-assured, too much Hawke's equal for him to ever be Hawke's confidant whilst they were fellows in the Yorkshire XI. Yorkshire cricket was only just big enough to accommodate them both. Inevitably, there were occasions when Hawke felt somewhat threatened by the presence of the illustrious Jacker.

Yorkshire defeated MCC under the captaincy of W.G. Grace by 99 runs, with Jackson (6 for 45) and Rhodes (4 for 24) bowling out the Premier Club for 69 in the last innings of the match. Hawke comments in his *Recollections and Reminiscences:*

> It was not the wickets he took, but his beautifully easy action that at once impressed us all. Both W.G. Grace and W.L. Murdoch were opposing, and both great judges told me how highly they thought of him. Not since A.G. Steel, twenty years before, had a bowler come out so perfectly master of his art.

Wilfred Rhodes had come to stay. No Yorkshire XI would be complete without him for three decades. Yet he had almost been lost to the county. With Bobby Peel in harness he had taken up the post of professional with Galashiels and had applied for a trial with Warwickshire who, for reasons best known to themselves, had rejected him!

He was an intense young man and, like Bobby Peel before him, a relentless plotter of a batsman's downfall, a remorseless opponent. A man of few words and fewer vices, he was a cricketer shrewd beyond his years. C.B. Fry summed up the young Rhodes for the *Strand Magazine*:

Hostile meaning behind a boyish face – ruddy and frank; a few quick steps and lovely swing of the left arm and the ball is doing odd things at the other end; it is pitched where you do not like it, you have played forward when you do not want to; the ball has whipped away from you so quickly; it has come straight when you expected break; there is discomfort.

From Lord's the Tykes travelled west to Bath where Somerset were their next victims. On a bowler's wicket Yorkshire were at one stage reduced to 42 for 6 on the first day, before Hawke (50) and Haigh (39 not out) put on 73 for the ninth wicket. When Somerset batted *Cricket* recorded that Rhodes 'was much too difficult for the Somerset men,' who were bowled out for 104. Set 234 for victory the home side – which included the Palairets and Sammy Woods – was bustled out for just 35 runs. According to *Cricket*, Rhodes 'was again irresistable'. Wilfred Rhodes had taken 13 for 48 in the match.

1898 was a relatively wet season, and many of Rhodes's early triumphs were on weather-damaged wickets. Unfairly, this earned him the reputation of being a wet-wicket bowler for he took wickets on every kind of pitch, his command of line and length progessively undermining, imprisioning and eventually demoralising batsmen. Few sides had an answer to the combination of Rhodes's classical slow left-arm spin, Haigh's idiosyncratic medium-pace off-breaks and Jackson's swift and deadly accurate seamers.

It was a season packed full of incident. The batsmen had every right to despair as time and again they went out to risk life and limb on rain-ruined wickets. David Denton's form deserted him so badly that, but for Wainwright's absence through illness, he might have been dropped in August, although Tunnicliffe (1,538), Brown (1,389) and Jackson (1,326) each scored over a thousand runs in the Championship. In a remarkable six-week period in June and July Jackson hit no less than five Championship hundreds. Hawke himself enjoyed his most successful county season with the bat, notching up two centuries (107 not out against Kent at Sheffield in June and 134 against Warwickshire at Edgbaston in August) and accumulating 797 runs at an average of over thirty. At the end of the season J.N. Pentelow was moved to remark in *Cricket* that Hawke:

> . . . like good wine, seems to improve with age. He was, doubtless, nearly as good a batsman about a dozen years ago in [1886–7] as he is know; but there have been seasons since when he has been very much below his level of the last year or two. One of his great characteristics is that he is 'good at need'.

Hirst and Wainwright, rather the worse for their winter in Australia, struggled for much of the season, with one notable exception. In the wet against Surrey at Bradford, Hirst battered a brilliant unbeaten 130 between the showers and Wainwright snapped up eight wickets (5 for 43 in the first innings and 3 for 10 in the second) and with Rhodes (7 for 24) was instrumental in bowling out the visitors for a mere 37 on the last day, sending Surrey crashing to an ignominious innings defeat. This season also saw Hawke and David Hunter put on 148 for the tenth Yorkshire wicket against Kent at Sheffield, a new record. However, it was a record that was soon put into the shade by the deeds of Jack Brown and John Tunnicliffe.

Yorkshire came to Chesterfield to play Derbyshire in the third week of August with the Championship in their pocket. The home county had nominated the match as Walter Sugg's Benefit. Hawke won the toss and elected to bat. Curiously, F.S. Jackson, who had been short of runs after his mid-season glut, had opted to bat down the order and Hawke, mindful of David Denton's patchy form, had decided to bat at number three in the list.

It was not, of course, uncommon for Brown and Tunnicliffe to keep the next batsman waiting – only the year before they had put on 378 for the first wicket against Sussex – so Hawke was not unduly disconcerted to watch his openers quietly take the measure of the home bowlers for the first hour. After a couple of hours he was less sanguine, after three he was exasperated. Brown and Tunnicliffe batted on and on. Indeed Hawke was to recall, somewhat ruefully: 'I actually kept my pads on from noon until tea-time, and then gave it up as a bad job.'

At the close of play on the first day the Yorkshire total stood at 503 for no wicket, with Jack Brown on 270 and Long John on 214. The latter's innings was all the more remarkable given the circumstances leading up to it. Hawke was proud to recount the tale of how Tunniclfffe, 'having been directed to a dirty inn, sat up all night sleepless rather than run the risk of a damp bed,' and how 'subsequently he could get no breakfast before catching the early train to Chesterfield,' and, not unnaturally, 'did not fancy a substantial meal just before going in,' and thus commenced hostilities on an empty stomach. It got worse, because during 'the luncheon interval the arrangements were so chaotic' that the batsmen 'could only get a small sandwich'. It was not until Evershed, the harrassed Derbyshire captain, made the suggestion that the slaughter might be halted to allow a tea interval, that 'a drop of moisture' finally passed Tunnicliffe's lips.

On the second morning of the match Brown and Tunnicliffe added a further 51 runs before the latter departed for 243, caught slogging the occasional leg-breaks of William Storer, normally Derbyshire's stumper. Jack Brown had by then reached 292 and the stand had realised 554 runs. Thereafter Jack Brown raised his 300 and promptly knocked down his wicket and the remaining batsmen slogged merrily to destruction to allow the bowlers to get on with their business. Yorkshire, who were all out for 662 by one o'clock, eventually won by an innings and 387 runs with time to spare on the third day.

The record was the icing on Yorkshire's cake. At their best Hawke's men were invincible, a wonderful amalgam of relentless efficiency and headstrong genius. When they were struggling – a rare state of affairs – the Tykes summoned up every ounce of native grit; when they were on top – most of the time – they ran riot with an abandon that tended utterly to demoralise the vanquished.

To Hawke went the laurels of victory. If he was no longer the popular cricketing hero of earlier years, the events of 1898 seemed to him to be the final vindication of everything he had worked for in Yorkshire. Success was sweet indeed and when The Reverend Egerton Leigh, vicar of Kirkstall, penned a poem whose form aped that of Newbolt's *Admiral's All*, Hawke treasured it:

In eighteen hundred and ninety-eight,
When Hawke came swooping from the west,
All Yorkshire determined, victorious of late,
From Lancashire the Championship to wrest,
The grounds were all o'ercrowded, the people all here,
At last has come the day to Yorkshiremen so dear;
For bragging time was over and fighting time was near,
When Hawke came swooping from the west.

'Tis just past noon when our battles first begin,
When Hawke came swooping from the west;
He faced the best of bowling, determining to win,
With certainty of victory in his breast,
For our fielding was the smartest in the world.
Haigh and Stanley Jackson, Rhodes and Wainwright hurled
The four champion English bowlers, how they twisted, how
    they curled,
When Hawke came swooping from the west.

The enemy dropped catches here and there,
When Hawke came swooping from the west;
Some were beaten by our innings and to spare,
Defeat by many wickets took the rest;
The balls that should have routed us were smacked and smashed
    for four,
The men who should have mastered us will master us no more,
For Yorkshire was Yorkshire and a mighty brood she bore,
When Hawke came swooping from the west.

There was no time for Hawke to rest on his laurels. On the first
Saturday of December he embarked for the Cape on what was his
last major overseas tour as captain. The tour was mounted at
relatively short notice. Originally, he had hoped to take a team back to
the West Indies, but the depressed economy of the Caribbean and the
devastation wrought by a hurricane foiled him. He had invited his
hunting soulmate Heseltine, and the two footballer-cricketers E.H.
Bray and C.J. Burnup, to join his tour. However, Heseltine declined
due to ill-health and the latter pair had prior commitments, compelling
him to look to the ranks of the Yorkshire Gentlemen for suitable
replacements. Inevitably, his second South African team was not
perhaps, the equal of his first. Nevertheless, it was formidable enough:

Amateurs
Lord Hawke, F. Mitchell, C.E.M. Wilson, F.W. Milligan
(Yorkshire), H.R. Bromley-Davenport, P.F. Warner
(Middlesex), A.G. Archer (Free Foresters).

Professionals
W.R. Cuttell, J.T. Tyldesley (Lancashire), S. Haigh (Yorkshire),
A.E. Trott (Middlesex), J.H. Board (Gloucestershire).

Only two of the tourists, Warner and Bromley-Davenport, had
been abroad with Hawke before. Of the others, Frank Milligan and
Schofield Haigh were Yorkshire favourites. Frank Mitchell had
captained Cambridge and thus been lost to the Tyke cause in recent
times. C.E.M. Wilson was another Yorkshireman, an accomplished
all-rounder who had hit 115 for the light blues in that year's Varsity
match. A.G. 'Gunner' Archer, a close personal friend of Hawke,
was an enthusiastic weekend stumper, but had failed to make the XI
at Haileybury. Like Audley Miller on Hawke's previous tour to
South Africa, he was to be called upon to make his first-class début
in a Test match. J.H. Board had kept wicket for Stoddart's side in
Australia, going abroad most winters, coaching when he was unable
to secure a playing berth. W.R. Cuttell had achieved the double in
the last English season for Lancashire. Sheffield-born, he had pur-
veyed his hustling leg-breaks in two second-class matches for
Yorkshire as long ago as 1890 and somehow slipped through the net.
If Cuttell was among the leading professional all-rounders of the
day, the foremost was probably A.E. Trott, then at the height of his
powers.

Albert Trott was an Australian, the younger brother of G.H.S.
Trott, the captain of the 1896 Australians. He had played for his
native land in the winter of 1894–5 against Stoddart's team, but been
left out of the side that came to England in 1896. Disappointed, he
had paid his own passage and applied for a position on the Lord's
ground staff, intent on showing the selectors the error of their ways.
A tall, brooding man who batted with a barely controlled, savage
violence that could subdue any attack, Trott's forte was actually a
form of lethal medium-fast bowling. He hit the seam hard, came on
to the bat quicker than he had any right to and every now and then
induced the ball to knife back into the right-handed batsman with
devastating results. This last delivery was a wicked weapon, unleashed
out of the blue, sometimes skidding, sometimes rearing high, virtually

unplayable. It was said that even 'the smoke from Albert Trott's cigarette broke in from the leg'. Hawke thought Trott the best professional all-rounder in the world at the time, although he saw the flaws in the man behind the formidable cricketer: 'Trott was rather like Tom Emmett, full of drollery and too apt to take his batting lightly, . . . one of those who through too short a life could not resist temptation.'

Posterity remembers Trott as a sad, lonely man who took his own life in July 1914. In 1898 he was a man with an immense chip on his shoulder and, briefly, it drove him to deeds few men have ever matched. Something of his sheer animal strength can be gauged from the fact that no other man has ever struck a six *over* the pavilion at Lord's.

The last member of the party was John Thomas Tyldesley. He had come into the Lancashire side at about the same time David Denton had emerged in Yorkshire, scored 152 in his second county match against Warwickshire at Edgbaston and never looked back. His was a very special talent. In the years ahead nobody begrudged Johnny Tyldesley his rightful place in an England batting order packed with crack amateurs.

Springbok cricket had changed in the three years Hawke had been away, moving forward in leaps and bounds. Unfortunately, whilst it had advanced on the field, off the field it was blighted with provincial rivalries. South African cricket was dominated by the alien influence of imported English professionals; for example, in Cape Town alone, Jack Brown, Frank Gutteridge of Nottinghamshire, George Lohmann, formerly of Surrey and England, Fred Tate of Sussex and Sydney Barnes, nominally of Warwickshire, were in the employ of local clubs. It was a dominance that spread jealousy and resentment throughout Springbok cricket. Hawke stepped off the boat at Cape Town straight into the cross-fire.

During Hawke's earlier visit to South Africa cricket had been played against a backdrop of turmoil. Then he had been the perfect cricketing ambassador; diplomat, sportsman and man of affairs, the man who had led his men into the lions' den and played the game under the muzzles of Kruger's cannon at Johannesburg in the aftermath of the Jameson Raid. Since those days antagonism between the British and the Boer communities had become deeply, bitterly entrenched. Around the Cape, in Natal and north in Rhodesia the imperial writ held sway; in the Transvaal and the Orange Free State, Paul Kruger spoke for the Boers. Kruger still hoped for peaceful coexistence within the Empire, independence without blood-letting. While South Africa drifted towards civil war Hawke stumbled on to the scene. He came with the best of intentions, convinced of the healing powers of his beloved cricket; he was to leave chastened, his faith sorely tested.

'There was a good deal of unpleasantness in connection with the tour,' he was to recall. It began even as the Union steamer *Scot* berthed in the shadow of Table Mountain. Hawke was immediately aware of the rumours circulating in the Cape about the status of his amateurs. Affronted, he made a statement that 'All the amateurs simply had their hotel and travelling free and paid for their own drinks and washing.' Hawke's amateurs were *not* paid men. It was a matter of honour; accusations of shamateurism were stiffly refuted: 'otherwise there would have been the impression that we were a commercial movement, a thing against which I have invariably set my face in all my tours, and which I have never allowed'.

The second match of the tour, against a Western province XI, including Jack Brown, Gutteridge, Tate and Barnes, was scrapped when the Western Province Union could not agree terms with the English professionals. It was whispered that Hawke had been instrumental in hardening the professionals' demands, a notion strengthened when it became known that Hawke had previously made representations to the authorities to the effect that his 'object was to develop and meet South African cricketers, not to encounter some we met year by year on our own grounds'. It was his view that 'when English teams go overseas, other Englishmen should not be pitted against them, for it nullifies the sporting interest'.

At the wicket the Englishmen – mightily assisted by that honourary Englishman, Albert Trott – were too strong for the Springboks in both the Test matches. In the provincial and country games, invariably against odds, Hawke's team terrorised the opposition. When the Transvaal dared to put an XI into the field at Johannesburg, the tourists won by an innings and 201 runs with Mitchell (162), Tyldesley (112) and Trott (101 not out) plundering centuries before Hawke declared at 539 for the loss of only six wickets. Elsewhere Trott and Haigh, abetted by the excellent Cuttell and the frenetic Milligan were irresistible.

The two Tests were played at the Old Wanderers' ground, Johannesburg, in February, and at Newlands, Cape Town, at the beginning of April. Of these, the first was an enthralling affair decided by the slim margin of 32 runs. J.H. Sinclair, the Springboks' premier all-rounder hit his nation's first half-century in international cricket as the home side bettered England's first inning's total by over a hundred runs. It was Plum Warner who saved the day. Playing in his first Test he carried his bat for 132 priceless runs in an English second innings total of 237. It was Warner's finest hour: W.G. Grace and Ranjitsinhji had both scored hundreds for England on their débuts, but no Englishman has equalled Warner's feat of carrying his bat through a completed Test innings in his first match for his country. Trott, Haigh and Cuttell did the rest, cutting down the Springboks for just 99 in the last innings of the match. When the two sides met again at Newlands, some six weeks later, England won by 210 runs after Sinclair (106) had again carried South Africa to a useful first innings lead of 85 runs. This time it was the turn of Johnny Tyldesley to parade his genius on the big stage. His 112 was the foundation upon which England built a match-winning score of 330. Set 246 for victory, Haigh (6 for 11) and Trott (4 for 19) scythed down the Springbok batting with a mere 114 deliveries for 35 runs.

Distracted by off the field 'unpleasantness', and never able to come to terms with batting on matting wickets, Hawke had another wretched tour with the bat. In the Test matches he recorded scores of 0, 5, 1 and 3. At Newlands he placed himself at the foot of the England batting order. Batting on the mat was quite unlike batting on a normal wicket. The mat was slower and took more turn than grass wickets. By custom the mat was secured at the commencement of an innings and allowed to loosen off as an innings progressed. The later batsmen often found themselves batting on a loose distorted carpet. Hawke made no excuses; he had no answer to the bowlers on the mat. He was a fast-wicket batsman and no amount of bloody-minded application could transform him into the master of the mat. Warner, Mitchell, and Tyldesley revelled on the mat, but they were batsman of another class. Once again, the mat had defeated Hawke's bat, and politics had mocked his good intentions.

On 3 May 1899, shortly after his return from the Cape, Hawke was formally elected President of the Yorkshire County Cricket Club, a position he was to hold for the rest of his life. He was thirty-eight years old.

12

Years of Triumph
(1899–1901)

Hawke's presidency of the county club began with a gesture that was wholly characteristic of the man and his methods. He immediately proposed that the disbursements made to the grounds which staged Yorkshire matches should be harmonised, suggesting that in future not less than twenty per cent of the gross takings at the gate should be paid to the host club. It was a shrewd step, removing painlessly a thorn that might otherwise have poisoned the fragile unity of Yorkshire cricket.

At the same time as Hawke was elevated to the Yorkshire Presidency he stood down – by rotation – from the Committee of MCC. F.S. Jackson was nominated as one of the seven candidates for the four vacant seats that spring and was duly elected in his captain's stead. Thus Yorkshire retained a voice in the Long Room at Lord's and Yorkshire had first call on its President; to an observer it would have seemed like an eminently satisfactory situation.

However, things are rarely everything that they seem to be; life would be somewhat tedious if they were. What was not generally appreciated at the time was that Stanley Jackson was neither Hawke's, nor Yorkshire's man; he was his own man. It was not a state of affairs that rested easily with Hawke, nor can it be discounted as a contributory factor in the first of many controversies that were to dog Hawke's participation in the selection of the England team.

In 1899 MCC took on board the responsibility of selecting the England XI for home Test matches against the touring Australians. The men MCC delegated to undertake this onerous task were: W.G. Grace, the England captain; Hawke; and H.W. Bainbridge, the captain of Warwickshire. The triumvirate was given the authority to co-opt two leading amateurs to assist in the deliberations and so F.S. Jackson and C.B. Fry were duly co-opted. A.C. MacLaren, after W.G. and Jackson the most senior of England's amateurs, had not appeared in first-class cricket prior to the Tests and was therefore not invited to join the Selection Committee.

Almost immediately, the Committee was presented with a crisis. An immensely powerful England batting side – Johnny Tyldesley could get in no higher than number seven – was rocked back on its heels by the terrifying pace of Ernest Jones in the first Test at Nottingham. Fry had fought his way to fifty in England's first innings, Ranji had saved the day in the second with a brilliant unbeaten 93, but nobody else had come to terms with Jones. Hawke had queried the inclusion of both men and, to his chagrin, had found himself in a minority of one as W.G.'s wishes inevitably prevailed. The unity of the Committee was brittle from the outset, and was soon to be tested, almost to destruction.

When the Committee convened at the Sports Club to discuss the team for the Lord's Test, W.G. Grace announced that he had decided to resign the captaincy. Hawke and Bainbridge tried to talk him round, but to no avail. W.G. felt he had to go, and that was that. At Trent Bridge he had been jeered for his stiffness in the field. *Anno Domini* would not be denied. He had not achieved all that he had simply to be remembered as a sad relic of former glories, an old man long past his prime humbled by younger generations who once hung on his name in awe. In a desperate attempt to persuade W.G. to reconsider Hawke and Bainbridge put it to him that he should continue so long as his batting warranted his place in the team. If he stood down it should only be if there was a better man to replace him. W.G. agreed to rethink his position if this was the unanimous opinion of the full Committee. The three men awaited Fry's arrival.

As the Sussex amateur belatedly made his entrance W.G. looked at him and, without preamble, asked:

'Do you think MacLaren should play at Lords?'

The old man had neatly outwitted his fellows. It went without saying that if the brilliant, irrascible MacLaren was available then he should be picked and that Fry would instantly concur. W.G. took Fry's agreement as final.

'That settles it,' W.G. said, confirming his intention to stand down. Thereafter, the Committee's deliberations on the XI for Lord's were, to say the least, conducted in a strained atmosphere. The fifth member of the Selection Committee, F.S. Jackson, was absent. Since the Nottingham match he had had ample time to acquaint Hawke with his views on the composition of the XI for Lord's, hardly suspecting that the occasion would signify the end of an era. The first England XI of the post-Grace age showed five changes from the Nottingham match; as if such wholesale surgery was not enough, the committee compounded its folly by appointing Archibald Campbell MacLaren as captain. In so doing the Committee passed over the senior amateur in the England side, Stanley Jackson.

Many years later Fry was to write in his *Life Worth Living*:

> It was quite forgotten that by order of seniority and on the score of at least equal merit, F.S. Jackson ought to have had the reversion of the captaincy.

If the others had forgotten, Hawke should have reminded them. Hawke's silence at the moment of decision is perhaps best described as inexplicable. It was an act that smacked of betrayal, a thing that was utterly alien to his otherwise innate sense of personal honour. Whatever his motives, it was an act he was to live to regret, bitterly.

Needless to say, England lost the Lord's Test and the Ashes. A lesser man than Stanley Jackson would have despaired, refused to play on, taken his grievance to the nation. Jackson's friends reported his anger, while he kept his feelings very much to himself. His relations with MacLaren were nothing if not friendly and his straight bat served his country truly: at Lord's he cracked 73 as Jones smashed through the rest of the order; later in the summer he scored a classic century at the Oval.

The Australians, under the pugnacious leadership of Joe Darling, sailed home with the Ashes. In England Stanley Jackson looked anew at his association with Yorkshire and inevitably concluded that the time had come to get on with the rest of his life. In future he would save his energies for the big occasions: Test matches; Gentlemen versus Players meetings; Championship contests against the strongest counties – Lancashire, Surrey, Middlesex and Nottinghamshire; play just enough cricket to keep trim and retain his rightful place in the England side. 1899 was Stanley Jackson's last full season for Yorkshire. It was the measure of the man that despite the decision to appoint MacLaren over his head (and a string of minor, but persistent injuries) he turned out in all five Test matches and in as many as sixteen of Yorkshire's Championship fixtures, finishing tenth in the national batting lists.

It was no fault of Stanley Jackson's that in the Championship stakes the Tykes stumbled at the penultimate fence. In his *History of Yorkshire Cricket: 1833–1903* The Reverend R.S. Holmes was to write of that year's campaign that it 'was a season of disasters, J.T. Brown being kept out of the August matches, whilst F.S. Jackson bowled but little owing to a damaged shoulder'. It was rather overstating the true extent of the county's woes. Granted that Jackson's bowling was below par, that Brown was afflicted by the first stages of a terminal illness which would tragically put him in his grave within five years and that both Rhodes and Hirst were called away to play for England, Yorkshire's honourable third place in the Championship behind a remarkable Surrey side, and a respectable Middlesex one, hardly constitutes 'a season of disasters'. In fact Yorkshire were unlucky not to win the Championship for until the last week of the county programme the title race was wide open, there for the taking by Surrey, Middlesex or Yorkshire. Had the county won their last two matches they would have been champions; history records that they were beaten fair and square in one and were held to a draw in the other.

It was another batsman's season. Mitchell (1,502), Hirst (1,454), Denton (1,409), Wainwright (1,324), Jackson (1,149) and Tunnicliffe (1,135) all made over a thousand runs in the Championship. Wilfred Rhodes again led the attack, taking 129 wickets in county matches, but unlike the previous year, he was often unsupported. Haigh managed to take only 68 wickets, Wainwright – his bowling powers now in decline – managed a haul of 54 and had it not been for the emergence of a tearaway fast bowler from Darfield, John Thomas Brown (the namesake of his illustrious team-mate), Yorkshire might have struggled in the field that year.

'Darfield' Brown, or J.T. Brown (jun.), to avoid confusion with the elder J.T. Brown, who hailed from Driffield, was the fastest Yorkshire bowler of the era. This was his most spectacular season; afterwards his pace was eroded and eventually destroyed by injury. He had turned out for the county in 1897, without making his mark. In the opening Championship match of 1899 against Worcestershire at Worcester he burst upon first-class cricket like a thunderbolt, shattering the home team with a forty-five ball spell of 6 for 19 when it seemed Yorkshire were drifting to an inevitable defeat. Holmes records that during a match later on that same season against Gloucestershire 'a ball from young Brown sent the bail a distance of 48 yards'.

In May the younger Brown was as powerless as any of his seniors to halt the carnage as Gilbert Jessop thrashed an unbeaten 171 in just 105 minutes, in the county's game against Cambridge at Fenner's. Jessop's runs came out of 206 scored while he was at the wicket and his innings included twenty-seven fours. Usually, it was Yorkshire's batsmen who handed out the punishment. When the Tykes batted against the light blues Jack Brown (168) and Stanley Jackson (133) undid the harm Jessop's innings had wrought and sent the students crashing to defeat. Later in the season George Hirst scored centuries in three successive innings and in July and August David Denton hit double or treble figures on nineteen consecutive occasions. Against Surrey at the Oval in August Ted Wainwright (228) and Hirst (186) put on 340 for the fifth wicket and helped to carry Yorkshire to 704 all out against Surrey, who replied with 551 for 7, Tom Hayward (273) and Bobby Abel (193) saving the home side with a fourth-wicket stand of 448.

Hawke gave a good account of himself with the bat, averaging 25.63 and contributing several invaluable knocks when his side was *in extremis*. He scored 127 against Hampshire at Southampton, putting on 225 with Wainwright (91) in 145 minutes, after the first five wickets had fallen for a meagre 83 runs. As he himself said: 'having been useful when things are parlous forms a pleasant memory'. His later days were to be littered with useful innings played when things were indeed parlous. He rarely exerted himself whole-heartedly unless the situation was dire.

He made another big score in the match which ultimately decided the Championship. Yorkshire came to Tonbridge to meet Kent in the second half of August knowing that nothing short of victory was good enough: the Tykes lost by eight wickets. Kent took a lead of 205 runs on first innings and Yorkshire were soon in trouble when they batted again. At stumps on the second day Yorkshire stood at 208 for 7, three runs ahead with Hawke and Wainwright at the wicket. Hawke was unwell, as he recounted in his *Recollections and Reminiscences*.

I do not mind confessing that I did not want to go in on the second afternoon, because I felt I had a fever coming on. However, I was not out. The father of Manley Kemp asked Frank Mitchell, Ernest Smith and myself to dinner. I was obviously out of sorts, and Miss Kemp pressed me to have a bottle of champagne all to myself. Out of decency I left the last glass.

In the morning Wainwright went to his century and Hawke battled to 81 before Alec Hearne bowled him out. Kemp suggested that if he had finished the bottle he, too, might have made a century. However, Hawke was distinctly unamused as the Kent batsmen knocked off the runs and prised the Championship from his grasp.

That winter the Boers finally rose against the British in South Africa. In Britain events in the faraway Transvaal were greeted with a mixture of horror and shocked indignation. The fact that the Boers had been driven to rebellion by years of criminally inept diplomacy and that had they not rebelled their heartland would probably have been invaded anyway, was conveniently forgotten in the headlong rush to war. Scores of cricketers ran to the colours, among them three of Hawke's men; Stanley Jackson, Frank Mitchell and Frank Milligan. Before the season of 1900 began Milligan was dead, mortally wounded serving with Plumer's column in the battle to relieve Mafeking, Jackson was struck down by enteric fever and invalided home from the Cape and Mitchell alone survived untouched.

Without Jackson, Milligan and Mitchell Hawke was gloomy about Yorkshire's prospects for the first season of the new century. Before battle was joined he was often overly pessimistic, a hangover from earlier struggles, earlier humiliations. It was almost as if he was unwilling to believe in what he had created in Yorkshire. What he had created was a magnificent all-round county side whose strength in depth was without equal in England. Yorkshire had won the Championship three times in the previous seven years, had been in the running for honours in each season since 1893 and with a little luck might have lifted the title in two or three of the four seasons in which they had been denied. The first great Yorkshire side – Hawke's side – was now approaching its peak. Even without men of the calibre of Jackson and Mitchell the Yorkshire juggernaut was now virtually unstoppable.

The Tykes went through the county programme of 1900 unbeaten. Twenty-eight Championship matches produced sixteen wins and a dozen draws. Lancashire clung on tenaciously until the end of July, but afterwards Yorkshire proceeded serenely to the title. Some idea of the dominance of Yorkshire can be deduced from the names of *Wisden*'s five cricketers of the year: Schofield Haigh, George Hirst, John Tunnicliffe, Tom Taylor and an interloper from Worcestershire, R.E. Foster. Hirst (1,573), Tunnicliffe (1,428) and Denton (1,111) topped a thousand runs in county cricket, while

Taylor, the Cambridge wicket-keeper, contributed 740 runs at an average of a just under fifty to head the Yorkshire lists. The true match-winners, however, were Rhodes (206) and Haigh (145) who took 351 Championship wickets between them. The next most successful bowler was George Hirst, with a haul of 49 wickets.

Holmes was moved to remark, somewhat unkindly, that while Hirst was 'greater than ever with the bat,' he was a 'complete failure with the ball'. Schofield Haigh was a more than adequate substitute. George Hirst was now a formidable batsman. Hawke said of his batting that year; 'He hit like a kicking horse, always getting off the mark brimful of confidence, and some of the punishment he meted out was of the severest type.' Once again, the real star of the Yorkshire XI was Wilfred Rhodes. In all first-class cricket that year he took an amazing 261 wickets. Already the brilliance of Rhodes was taken for granted in Yorkshire; he was the youngest man in the side yet he was the rock upon which Tyke invincibly was now founded. *Wisden* decided: 'The best proof of the strength of York-shire's bowling in 1900 may perhaps be found in the fact that in twenty-eight county matches the team only had two scores of over three hundred hit against them.'

Great bowlers, be they lightning quick or masters of flight and spin, tend to hunt in pairs. It seemed that if George Hirst's bowling arm failed him, Schofield Haigh stepped in to partner Rhodes as he did in 1900. Of the three, Haigh was often cast in the role of unsung hero. He hung on George Hirst's every word, but his amiability never broke down Wilfred Rhodes's austerity. Of the three, Haigh was the least confident, the least self-possessed. Hawke said of him that he was 'one of the best-tempered, happy souls I ever came across,' but sometimes he grew 'a little down in his luck and needed bucking up'.

Hawke knew his men. Hirst and Rhodes could be left to go about their business uninterrupted but Haigh was different; there were chinks in his armour. He disliked bowling with the new ball, and was inclined to underuse his wicked yorker when the batsmen were on top. Hawke would choose his moment: 'Now, Schofie, time for a yorker!'

A few minutes later another well-set batsman was tucking his bat under his arm and trudging back to the pavilion, the latest victim of Haigh's fast, dipping yorker.

Of the immortal threesome, Haigh was perhaps the ultimate exponent of the wet wicket. When he thought the conditions were in his favour he would go out and minutely inspect the wicket; his team-mates could tell immediately what the day held in store by his expression when he came back to the dressing-room. If Scofie's face was wreathed in smiles it signified that mayhem would surely follow.

Only one man really disturbed the Tykes' equanimity in 1901. Inevitably, that man was Gilbert Laird Jessop. In the last week of July at Bradford, Jessop's sustained hitting carried Gloucestershire to the very brink of an unlikely victory, Yorkshire eventually emerging victorious by the margin of forty runs. After the home side had hit over four hundred in their first innings, Jessop had smashed 104 in seventy minutes. Gloucestershire, 140 in arrears on first innings, then contrived to bowl out the northerners for 187. Hopes of denting Yorkshire's unbeaten run were low when Jessop came to the wicket on the last day with five wickets down, just fifty on the board and Rhodes and Haigh in total command. There was no such thing as a lost cause while Gilbert Jessop was at the crease. In the next ninety-five minutes he carted Rhodes and Haigh where he pleased. He was particularly severe on Rhodes, despatching him for six sixes. When finally he holed out to John Tunnicliffe in the deep, Jessop had made 139. It was a match of remarkable deeds. George Hirst had hit 111 in a hundred minutes in the Yorkshire first innings, and 92 in rapid time in the second and Rhodes, despite Jessop's hitting, still claimed 14 for 192 from the 225 balls he bowled. In the return match at Cheltenham three weeks later Yorkshire won by an innings, with Hawke hitting his season's best score of 79 going in first, Hirst cracking another hundred and Rhodes twice removing the dreaded Jessop before he had reached double figures.

The cooling of relations between Hawke and Stanley Jackson, who had been the vice-captain since 1894, had concentrated Hawke's mind on the matter of who should succeed him in the captaincy. Jackson's departure for foreign parts had lent an urgency to the question. Hawke had become rather stiff in the field. He suffered from recurrent lumbago and his general health – following bouts of fever overseas – was far from robust. W.G. Grace's decision to resign the England captaincy the previous year had left its mark; Hawke had no intention of clinging to the Yorkshire captaincy just for the sake of it. The problem was that there was no obvious candidate to replace him. After Hawke, Ernest Smith was the most senior of Yorkshire's amateurs, but he was unavailable for much of the season. Another contender, Frank Mitchell, was off in South Africa with Jackson fighting the Boers. At first glance the ring seemed empty. His hopes passed down to the next generation.

Thomas Lancelot Taylor had first appeared for the county the previous summer. He came to Yorkshire via Uppingham and Cambridge, an accomplished wicket-keeper and gifted batsman. Some observers thought Taylor a better stumper than David Hunter and many sides would have discarded the professional in favour of the amateur. Hawke would have none of it; Hunter was the Yorkshire keeper and so Tom Taylor came into the XI as a specialist batsman – and his batting was undoubtedly good enough to justify his inclusion. Joining the side after the Varsity match in July, he was Yorkshire's most consistent batsman in the latter half of the season. Hawke later said of Taylor; 'I always meant him to be my successor as captain.' It was not to be, although when Jackson returned to assume the vice-captaincy, Hawke still clung to his hopes for Taylor.

Stanley Jackson had returned to England in time to score a famous century for the Gentlemen against the Players at Scarborough at the end of the season, but duty had called him back to the Cape before the start of the 1901 season. However, Yorkshire's other soldier, Frank Mitchell, laid down his gun and shouldered his bat for the new campaign.

Four Yorkshiremen topped a thousand runs in the Championship in 1901, Mitchell (1,674) leading the way with seven centuries, followed by Jack Brown (1,263), Hirst (1,174) and Tunnicliffe (1,075). Six other batsmen managed aggregates of over five hundred. As always, the Yorkshire bowlers had plenty of runs to bowl at and with Rhodes taking 196 wickets in county matches, Hirst 135, Haigh 49 and J.T. Brown (jun.) 43, few sides withstood them for long. Again Rhodes was the pivot upon which the attack turned. The Reverend R.S. Holmes recalled: 'it was Hirst, not Haigh, who helped Rhodes, Haigh's knee giving him a lot of bother. Rarely, if ever, has a bowler been able to make the ball swerve in the air as Hirst did in match after match.'

In June Yorkshire trapped Nottinghamshire on a wet wicket at Trent Bridge and bowled them out for just 13 runs. The bowling figures of the executioners were:

	Overs	Mdns	Runs	Wkts
G. Hirst	1	0	1	0
W. Rhodes	7.5	4	4	6
S. Haigh	7	2	8	4

In the Nottinghamshire second innings Hirst made up for missing out in the first by taking 6 for 26. *Cricket* noted that 'rain never by any chance comes at an unfortunate time for Yorkshire,' and 'after the rain the wicket was in a hopeless state'. Before the rain the northerners had hit a total of 204 on a wicket on which batting was never straightforward. The fates were against the Trent Bridge men from the outset, for they had lost the services of their master batsman, Shrewsbury, with a split hand on the first day. Even though Hawke generously allowed the Nottinghamshire twelfth man to replace Shrewsbury and play a full part in the contest, the absence of the man acknowledged as the finest wet-wicket batsman in the world had much to do with the ease of the Tykes' eventual victory.

However, Yorkshire did not have it all their own way that year. At Bradford when Surrey were the visitors Hawke and Haigh stone-walled for over an hour to stave off defeat at the death. In Jack Brown's benefit match at Leeds when Lancashire were the visitors, the Red Rose county had much the better of things, with Archie MacLaren scoring a century.

It was in mid-July at Leeds that Somerset actually inflicted defeat upon their hosts. The men from the West Country had given Yorkshire a fright earlier in the season; at Headingly they achieved what they had earlier threatened. The match had begun as most Yorkshire matches began, with the Tykes firmly in control, Rhodes running through the Somerset batting and dismissing the visitors for a miserly 87. Yorkshire had batted without a great deal of conviction, but late interventions from Hirst (61), Haigh (96) and Rhodes (44) carried their total to 325 at stumps on the first day. When the Somerset openers – L.C.H. Palairet and L.C. Braund – went out to bat the next morning 238 runs in arrears, it seemed the match would be over by tea-time, and a very early tea at that. However, cricket being cricket, things worked out rather differently. Hawke recollected:

> We all knew Braund was out, caught at slip by the fairest of catches before the hundred went up. Mycroft could not see, and Walter Wright gave it against us. After that I never seemed to get my boys going again. Unfortunately, the wicket began to crumble badly at the end of the second day, and when Sammy Woods, having only two or three wickets to fall, put on the heavy roller next morning to make it worse, I remember telling him that I really thought he was a better sportsman, for he well

knew that we never had 'an earthly' to get the runs . . . only John Tunnicliffe rose superior to the conditions, and it was absolutely the only occasion during all my captaincy when I could not make my side buck up.

At the end of the second day Somerset had scored 549 for 5 and were 311 runs to the good. Palairet had scored 173 in 220 minutes, Braund 107 in 140 minutes and F.A. Phillips had chipped in with 122 in 170 minutes. Palairet and Braund had put on 222 for the first wicket and the later batsmen had cashed in. Sammy Woods (66) and V.T. Hill (54) had completed the piecemeal demolition of the Yorkshire attack. *Cricket* reported: 'for once the Yorkshire bowlers were treated as if they belonged to some small suburban club'. Wilfred Rhodes restored an element of sanity to the proceedings on the third morning, picking up the last five wickets at a personal cost of 37 runs. Somerset were all out for 630.

On a wearing wicket Yorkshire were bustled out for 113 and beaten by 279 runs. If the Tykes needed to be reminded to keep their feet on the ground, it had been a timely object-lesson. In a year in which Yorkshire won no less than ten of their Championship matches by an innings, only one other county managed to put Hawke's nose out of joint.

At Brighton near the end of the season Sussex batted for most of the first two days, C.B. Fry (209); and E.H. Killick (200) putting on 349 in 310 minutes at the heart of the southern county's 560 for 5 declared in 192 overs. After the northerners had been bowled out for 92, Hawke instructed his batsmen to stonewall until the close. The result was that Jack Brown and John Tunnicliffe successfully batted out eighty-two overs, scoring just 107 runs, infuriating the opposition and the crowd and raising the odd eyebrow amongst the gentlemen of the Press. Hawke said the match was 'one of the most rotten' he had ever played in.

Yorkshire's dominance had reached such proportions that the majority of the other counties either played for a draw from the first ball or, worse still, simply went through the motions in the belief that not even a draw was a realistic possibility. Hawke was too ready to condemn opposing captains for their temerity, too willing to castigate others for making the best of their relatively slender resources, too self-righteous by far about how *he* thought cricket ought to be played. Hawke's Yorkshire XI was an outrageously gifted combination whose supremacy was based upon tenacity at the wicket and ruthless efficiency in the field; just as nowadays few teams have the least idea of how to combat the West Indians, so in 1901 few had any idea how to cope with the Yorkshiremen. Like the modern West Indians, Hawke's team had an answer to every strategem. If the batting failed then Rhodes, Haigh and Hirst turned the screw tighter still; if, unaccountably, the attack let the opposition off the hook, inevitably, one or two of the batsmen would make a long score. It was one thing for Hawke to expect his men to adopt a positive approach; another altogether for him to expect his opponents to follow suit unerringly. There were one or two counties in England capable of matching Yorkshire ball for ball, or stroke for stroke, but not one that could hope to compete in every aspect of the game. Yorkshire could afford to play to their strengths for they had – in county cricket, at least – few weaknesses; the rest were not so fortunate.

When Hawke condemned Sussex's tactics in the Brighton match he was criticising the opposing captian, Ranjitsinhji, for doing no more than making the most of his own side's strengths. Not surprisingly, and with every justification, Ranji was deeply offended. Nobody would dispute that in the best of all worlds cricket should always be played purposefully and that both sides should always strive for a positive outcome. In practice, of course, the theory rarely applies. Two teams are seldom evenly matched and the real fascination of cricket is to watch as the opposing XIs attempt to take control by playing to their own particular strengths. Hawke's arrogant expectation that every team should play the game the way his magnificent Tykes played it was wholly unrealistic, for in the main it implied that opposing captains had a duty to bow to his will from the outset. Ranji was no keener than the majority of his fellows to serve up his men as cannon-fodder to the Yorkshire attack. Sussex were a strong batting side, and by batting on and on into the second day of the Brighton match, Ranji was doing everything in his power to make that batting strength count. The fact that Yorkshire were bowled out for under a hundred, rather suggests that it was Ranji, and not the Baron, who demonstrated a superior understanding of the tactical niceties.

Hawke was his own worst enemy. He was intimately involved with MCC's inept, somewhat lack-lustre, and eventually abortive, attempt to raise a team to send to Australia that winter. For years he had been advocating that the premier club alone should select and sponsor overseas tours by England teams. However, when the invitation from the Australian authorities arrived at Lord's for MCC to send out a side in the winter of 1901–2, Hawke's efforts to collect a truly representative side failed dismally. For a variety of reasons, Stanley Jackson, C.B. Fry, Ranjitsinhji and Archie MacLaren were unavailable, as were a number of the other leading amateurs, and MCC decided to abandon the idea of dispatching a side to the Antipodes. Hawke had anticipated leading the party, combining the roles of manager and captain for perhaps one last time. The tour might have laid to rest the ghost of his first, unhappy visit to Australia. When the enterprise was thwarted he was bitterly disappointed; later, when the Melbourne Club asked MacLaren to bring over a side in place of the doomed MCC venture and the Lancashire captain accepted, Hawke was enraged.

MacLaren was not a wealthy man and six months away from England might have bankrupted him. His initial unavailability owed much to the fact that had he gone with an MCC team under Hawke, he would have received his expenses and little else. Hawke's intransigence in these matters was renowned; beyond the costs of travel, board and miscellaneous petty costs, no amateur in Hawke's side could expect to receive any remuneration or consideration. Hawke was a rich man, he could afford his amateur scruples; MacLaren could not. In any event, MacLaren was the current captain of England and had no wish to play, let alone tour, under Hawke's leadership. The abandonment of the MCC tour changed everything. Hawke seemed to understand little of this:

> On my advice, my County Committee decided that neither Hirst nor Rhodes should go to Australia with a team under private enterprise. I then said that if a side went officially under the auspices of MCC, which I persistently urged, it would be a very different matter.

MacLaren soon discovered that the Surrey professionals Bobby Abel, William Lockwood and Tom Richardson were similarly 'unavailable'. Hackles were raised when Hawke goaded MacLaren and his backers, commenting that he did not see 'why our players should go merely to put money in the pockets of the Melbourne Club'. MacLaren retaliated, observing at length in *Cricket*, that England would do well to learn from the Australians in the matter of the selection of the national side: namely, the opinions of practising cricketers ought to take precedence over those of mere spectators.

The battle lines were drawn and neither man would countenance compromise. Within a year their feud would have blighted successive quests to regain the Ashes.

Hawke was standing up for what he thought was right. The problem was that in this, as in many other cases, there was no right solution. Without the presence of Ellison in the background or Stanley Jackson beside him in the field, Hawke's public persona grew steadily less temperate. His autocratic manners cast him in the role of bully, people remembered his treatment of Peel and Peate and slowly but surely Hawke's reputation began to tarnish. He was a victim of his own success. The very attributes that had enabled him to shape the destiny of Yorkshire cricket now proved his undoing.

The same man who had unfairly accused Sammy Woods of unsportsmanlike behaviour at Leeds in July then ensured that William Lockwood's benefit match was replayed in September after the original fixture in July had been washed out. That was Hawke: quick to anger, arrogant, self-righteous, yet always capable of an act of crushing generosity. Hawke was a well-meaning ogre. Sometimes he was less lovable than others, but at heart, he was never less than well-intentioned. He was a much misunderstood man wrongly assumed to be wholly in command of his own destiny.

In 1901 the world acknowledged that the phenomenon it knew as Wilfred Rhodes had come to stay. The *Sheffield Daily Telegraph* wrote of him:

> Season after season one wonders whether we have come to the end of his improvement; it is difficult to say even now that such is the case. One can only wonder what measure of success would be his if he had a wet season to bowl through, such as once came to Emmett and Peate. It is sufficient to point to Rhodes' position, clear at the top of the averages, as justification for the remark that he still has no peer in the country as a bowler.

Yorkshire's cricketing season ended with a personal triumph for Wilfred Rhodes, who scored his maiden first-class century (105, batting ninth in the list) against MCC at Scarborough in the last week of August, and a collective drubbing at the hands of a formidable Rest of England XI at Lord's a fortnight later. In this latter encounter Gilbert Jessop thrashed 233 in 150 minutes and C.B Fry, Yorkshire's chief tormentor at a game in Brighton the previous month, hit 105, his sixth – and record-breaking – hundred in successive innings.

Hawke did not set much store by the results of 'friendly' matches. Contests such as these were social events, trial games and little more. His players were not unaware of his Lordship's views on these non-county fixtures, and though they gave of their best, the razor-sharp cutting edge of Yorkshire cricket was more commonly applied to the Championship than to festival matches. At Lord's Jessop had been dropped twice! Ted Wainwright had spilled a sharp chance when the batsman had made 81 and John Tunnicliffe had dropped a straightforward catch off Rhodes shortly afterwards, when Jessop had advanced to 155. Hawke did not begrudge Jessop his glory, Jessop played the game with a violence and a passion that was thoroughly commendable. Over the years he became quite used to suffering his annual 'dose of Jessop'.

13

Indian Summer
(1902–1905)

In April 1902 Hawke was at Crystal Palace to watch Sheffield United draw with Southampton in the FA Cup Final. The Bramall Lane club had been part and parcel of the Sheffield fiefdom he had inherited from Ellison. Sheffield clung to the vestiges of its former influence; Wostinholm, the secretary of the county cricket club, remained the secretary of Sheffield United, unmoved from his Bramall Lane chambers. As long as he carried on, Hawke was unwilling to move the county club's headquarters from the city. Wostinholm was an old man and Hawke patiently awaited his retirement.

Yorkshire were without Frank Mitchell and Ted Wainwright in 1902, the former having returned to South Africa, the latter having come to the end of his distinguished career. In their absence Hawke was able to call again on the services of Stanley Jackson, although inevitably, he was selected for all five tests against the Australians. Likewise, Rhodes, Hirst and Taylor were, at various times, called to the colours and periodically lost to the Yorkshire cause. Hawke himself missed a number of matches around the time of the coronation – electing to turn out for MCC whilst he was in London – and was then side-lined with a damaged thumb in August. Nevertheless, Yorkshire's strength in depth insured that they were never seriously threatened in the Championship. Curiously, their solitary defeat was once more at the hands of lowly, unfashionable Somerset, this time at Sheffield.

These were glory days, indeed. In Yorkshire, Hawke's men were cheered on to victory after victory, fêted and mobbed as they calmly went about their business. With the exception of George Hirst no man's appearance on the field provoked a greater roar from the massed ranks of the Yorkshire faithful than Hawke.

In a bowler's year only three batsmen topped a thousand runs in the Championship, Taylor (1,276), Tunnicliffe (1,079) and Hirst (1,025), but Yorkshire batted solidly all down the list, five other men registering at least five hundred runs in county cricket; Denton (934), the stylish left-hander, Washington (908), Jack Brown (868), Haigh (573) and Jackson (544 in his sporadic county outings). The bowling was in the hands of three men, Rhodes (140), Haigh (123) and Hirst (53), abetted occasionally by Jackson (36). Jackson's county form was patchy, mediocrity interspersed with brilliance. Typically, Jackson gave of his best only when England and Yorkshire had need of it. In the Roses match at Sheffield in May Jackson emerged with bowling figures of 3 for 5 and 5 for 8; in June he and George Hirst bowled Yorkshire to victory by dismissing the Australians for 23 in just 84 balls.

Jackson's contributions were the gloss on Yorkshire's season. At a dinner given in honour of the whole Yorkshire team by the London Yorkshire Association at the Holborn Restaurant on Saturday 23 August (the day John Tunnicliffe held his five hundredth catch) Hawke said of his men:

'The team does not care for records; they play for the game's sake, and as an eleven, not as individuals. I could have done nothing without the loyal support of the players . . . It has been said that English cricket is on the decline. I have played for twenty-one years in the Yorkshire XI, and I do not believe it for a moment.'

Many years later Hawke was to recant his former intolerance of the attitudes of opposing captains and reflect in his *Recollections and Reminiscences* upon the effect Yorkshire's dominance had had upon the rest of the county game: 'I do not think our prolonged triumph was really good for cricket. There was too little of a struggle against us, too broadcast a feeling that other sides were outmatched when they came into the field to play our eleven.'

Such considerations were far from his mind in 1902, however. Yorkshire's unprecedented success contrasted cruelly with Hawke's unhappy career as Chairman of Selectors. MacLaren's weak England side had, not surprisingly, failed to regain the Ashes. Nevertheless, MacLaren was again appointed to captain England that summer.

The XI chosen for the first Test at Birmingham was probably the strongest batting side ever to represent England. As the season progressed and Joe Darling's Australians gradually asserted their overall superiority, relations between MacLaren and Hawke worsened, the selectors tinkered with the batting and, disastrously, with the attack. Bowlers came and went apparently without rhyme or reason. The Reverend R.S. Holmes was one of many who questioned the machinations of the Selection Committee: 'the non-inclusion of Haigh,' he declared, 'one of the three greatest bowlers in the world in 1902, was universally dubbed an irreparable mistake.' He concluded that 'someone had blundered in not picking a bowler who hit the stumps as often as Haigh did'. Hawke and MacLaren's differences reduced the Committee's deliberations over the team for the Manchester Test to a farce.

MacLaren wanted Haigh to be included – as a wet-wicket specialist – among the men from whom the XI would be chosen on the first morning of the fourth Test. Hawke would have none of it; Yorkshire already stood to lose Jackson, Hirst and Rhodes and he refused to countenance the thought of having Haigh kicking his heels as twelfth man at Manchester when he could be playing for the Yorkshire team. The fact that MacLaren's veiws were shared by several of his fellow selectors was totally disregarded by Hawke. Unable to include Haigh, the Committee therefore opted for Fred Tate of Sussex. Gilbert Jessop, the best England batsman at Sheffield, was dropped.

Archie MacLaren despaired: 'Look what they've given me!' he complained. 'Do you think we're playing the blind asylum?'

Against Hawke's expectations MacLaren actually included Tate in the XI. The man excluded, and thus left 'kicking his heels' when he could have been playing for his county, was George Hirst. In his eagerness to spite Hawke, MacLaren became the architect of his own downfall.

The match was a personal disaster for the England captain. On the first day Tate's bowling was carted all over the field; on the second day Tate spilled a vital catch; on the third day Tate was the last man out with victory agonisingly close. MacLaren and England drew consolation from an unlikely victory won against the odds from the bats of Gilbert Jessop and (to a lesser extent) Stanley Jackson – at the Oval in the fifth Test. If MacLaren had been foolish to try and play Hawke at his own game Hawke's foolishness was of another order. Hawke as Chairman of Selectors had taunted MacLaren with his

Yorkshire-first policy, high-handedly overruled all objections and put MacLaren in an impossible position.

It was an eventful season for Hawke. On the last day of June he had fulfilled one of his dearest ambitions. Opening the batting for MCC with W.G. Grace against Oxford University he had finally scored a hundred at Lord's. Moreover, in hitting his unbeaten 107 in 210 minutes he had carried his bat through a completed innings for the first time in his career. It was an effort that gave him even more satisfaction than his hard-hit 126 against Richardson and Lockwood at the Oval a month later, during the course of which he was missd three times in adding 165 with Haigh (62) for the eighth wicket, and damaged his thumb so badly he had to drop out of the next six Yorkshire matches.

That winter Hawke had hoped to lead a team to New Zealand. However, when his mother fell ill he turned over the captaincy to Plum Warner. He toyed with the idea of following on later, but shortly before he was due to see off the team from Liverpool he fell while riding with the York and Aincty Hounds and sustained a broken collar-bone.

However, Hawke was far from idle that winter. It was a time of change in Yorkshire, the end of one era and the dawn of another. J.B. Wostinholm, for nearly forty years the power behind the throne of Yorkshire cricket, resigned the secretaryship of the county club. Yorkshire were deluged with applications for the vacant post – which carried the then princely salary of £350 per annum – when it was advertised in December 1902. Eventually, a short list of three men remained, one of whom was E.H.D. Sewell, the Essex professional and assistant secretary who had played against Hawke in India in the early 1890s. Sewell tells of the final reckoning in his *Well Hit Sir!*:

One bleak morning at the Station Hotel, Sheffield, I was one of a trio, to which number the Committee had reduced the 140 odd applicants for the post. One of the others was that popular Sheffield journalist J.H. Stainton, but directly I saw the third, F.C. Toone, I knew my number was up anyway.

But I determined to die as game as possible, so when Lord Hawke, who did the questioning of the victims before surely the mightiest committee in the world (those who've seen only the League of Nations of UNO ought to have taken a dekko at the full Committee of the YCCC when the war drums are

throbbing!), put the vital questions; 'Do you go in for betting?'
I replied at once; 'Well, sir, I had a bet yesterday, that I
shouldn't get this job.'

Sewell was right; the job went to Fred Toone. Almost immediately,
the headquarters of the county club moved into new premises at
Park Square, Leeds. No sooner was the move completed than Toone
set about a complete modernisation of the club's administration. He
insisted – to the chagrin of local officials – that he should take
responsibility for the organisation of all the county's matches, that
he should oversee player's benefits and that the club's rules should
be extensively rewritten and revised. Even-tempered, tactful, immensely shrewd, Toone quickly became Hawke's closest lieutenant.
Writing in the 1920s, Hawke was to say 'Toone is Yorkshire cricket
to the backbone.' It was nothing but the truth. Just as Wostinholm
before him had been a power not just in Yorkshire but in England,
so too, was Toone. Fred Toone managed three England teams in
Australia after the Great War, and he sat in the Home Office
committee which considered crowd management in the wake of the
Wembley Stadium fiasco of 1923 which had turned the FA Cup Final
between Bolton Wanderers and West Ham United into a chaotic
lottery only given a semblance of organisation by a famous policeman
on a white horse. Yet Toone was much more the servant of his
membership than Wostinholm, much freer of partisanship and able
to devote all his efforts to the cause of Yorkshire cricket. In Toone's
time no Yorkshire member was permitted to retire without receiving
two, or sometimes three, personal letters from him. Benefits were
organised like military campaigns, every district had its own committee, no contribution was too small to collect. It fell to Fred
Toone to consolidate Hawke's work in Yorkshire.

Yorkshire began the season of 1903 with a trial match against an
XVIII of Northallerton and district. As a trial the contest was not a
great success, particularly for the county's batsmen. In the Yorkshire
innings of 313 all out, only two men progressed beyond double
figures, Stanley Jackson with 112 and George Hirst with 122.

During this match at Northallerton Hawke vented his exasperation
with the old guard within MCC who steadfastly blocked every
attempt of the reformers – among whom Hawke was the leading
light – to carry the game forward into the twentieth century. The
two burning issues of the day were the debate over the leg before
wicket law and the width of the stumps. In the previous twenty

years the bat had gradually gained an ascendency over the ball which Hawke believed would, if unchecked, ruin the game. Speaking on 7 May he announced that he was disappointed that the proposal to increase the width of the wicket had not received the requisite two-thirds majority at the recent meeting of MCC, and complained:

> It seems to me that cricket reform is at a standstill, and for this reason: many gentlemen of standing, of ripe experience in cricket, and of a certain age connected with the MCC, think they will teach the younger generation that the leg before wicket rule should be altered. Present-day cricketers fought against that proposal and it was defeated . . .

Yorkshire could only finish third in the Championship; an element of complacency had crept up upon them. Illness robbed them of Washington who had contributed useful runs the previous year and a freak injury ended Darfield Brown's career as a fast bowler. Stanley Jackson played infrequently and the calls of the business left Tom Taylor little time for cricket. Taylor had toured New Zealand with Warner amidst rumours that he planned to retire from first-class cricket in the near future. The editor of the *Yorkshire Post* had cabled him in Auckland: 'Reported here you retire from Yorkshire team. Cable yes or no.' Taylor had replied: 'Probably.'

In the event Taylor was abroad in 1903 and when Jackson did play he was strangely out of sorts. Luck was not on Yorkshire's side; batting frailties accounted for most of their reverses, while the weather denied them more than one victory. Nor was the Yorkshire cause aided by the fever that struck Hawke down in June when he was in the best of form. He played a string of invaluable, fighting innings – including 76 at Worcester against Worcestershire, 79 in the Roses match at Manchester and an unbeaten 61 at Bradford against Sussex – as Yorkshire made a disastrous start to their county programme, losing three of the first seven matches. The cruellest blow was the injury to J.T. Brown (jun.) – a dislocation of his right arm – after the Tykes had opened the campaign with handsome victories over Essex and Gloucestershire. It happened as Brown was bowling at Sammy Woods, who described the unhappy incident in his *My Reminiscences*:

> I took off my boot and tried to put it (the shoulder) in at once, but couldn't manage it, although I had someone to sit on his head and others to hold him down. He was very sweaty from

bowling, I couldn't get a firm grip of his arm, so he had to go to hospital and have it done. I am certain to this day that had he kept still it would have saved a lot of trouble.

Despite the fact that George Hirst performed the double in Championship matches, scoring 1,367 runs and taking 118 wickets, it was still not enough. By the time Yorkshire rediscovered their winning ways the title was lost, claimed by a fine Middlesex side.

Hawke wasted no time mourning the loss of the Championship. Instead, he concentrated on the positive aspects of the year. Foremost among these he counted the guarded *rapprochement* that had come about in his relations with Stanley Jackson. The process had begun the year before and was cemented that autumn when Hawke invited Jackson to captain the team MCC was sending to Australia that winter. In the event business and political commitments made it impossible for Jackson to tour and he was compelled to decline the invitation. Since Archie MacLaren's financial situation would not allow him to tour under the 'expenses only' regime that MCC were likely to enforce on the forthcoming tour the captaincy passed, by default, to Hawke's protégé, Plum Warner. It was a case of 'cometh the hour, cometh the man', for Warner duly recaptured the Ashes. Two years before Hawke's intransigence had denied MacLaren the services of Hirst and Rhodes. On Warner's tour the two Yorkshire-men made all the difference. At Sydney, Hirst's unbeaten 60 carried England to victory and at Melbourne Rhodes took 7 for 56 and 8 for 68, fifteen wickets in the match despite having no less than eight catches dropped off his bowling.

Many expected Yorkshire to reclaim the Championship in 1904, but although George Hirst (scoring 1,848 runs and taking 105 wickets), and Wilfred Rhodes (1,082 runs and 104 wickets) both achieved the double in county matches, it was not to be. Lancashire went through the season undefeated and the Tykes had to settle for second best as early as the first week of August. By then the Red Rose County had already won fifteen out of their nineteen fixtures.

That spring Stanley Jackson publicly demanded – politely, yet doggedly – that Yorkshire should have a county ground. He was worried about the development of young players, and commented that 'the present system seems hopelessly wrong'. His views were given a wide and sympathetic hearing in the pages of *Cricket*. 'Promising players,' he said, 'should be kept and watched and not sent out recklessly to a place where they lose any advantage they may have gained at the county practices, and where they scarcely ever bowl to a really good batsman, or get a chance of batting against a really good bowler.'

Jackson, a member of an old and powerful Leeds family, was unashamedly advocating that Headingley should be the county ground, but Hawke had not dismantled the Sheffield monopoly just to see power pass into the hands of Leeds. It was a political rather than a cricketing question. Hawke saw the sense in adopting Headingley as the home of Yorkshire cricket, yet knew the time was not yet right and chose to defer judgement confident in the knowledge that Stanley Jackson was a man who would go to almost any lengths not to split Yorkshire cricket over such an issue.

Yorkshire's season began with an experimental trial match against Nottinghamshire at Leeds in the first week of May (the contest has become known as the 'time limit' match). It was arranged to test one of Hawke's many theories about how best to improve county cricket as a spectacle. To this end the two counties agreed to play under a set of rules which stipulated, among other things, that each (of the four) innings was to be limited to four-and-a-half hours, boundaries were not to exceed sixty yards, and that the match would be won by the side scoring the most runs in the available time, regardless of the number of wickets that had fallen. In the event of rain the bowlers' and batsmens' footholds were to be covered, but play was to resume immediately the rain ceased unless the captains were in agreement that it was impossible to continue. As fate would have it none of the time constraints actually came into force and the match was played out to a normal pattern, to sighs of relief throughout the county game.

Afterwards, Hawke took the XI up to Northallerton for a three-day trial match against the local XVIII led by R.W. Frank, the captain of the Yorkshire second XI. Wilfred Rhodes took wickets with his first two deliveries and later claimed a hat-trick in taking 12 for 21 in the home side's first innings!

In April Warner, fresh from his Australian odyssey and obviously flushed with the heady wine of victory, had seen fit to make one or two vaguely disparaging remarks about the importance of county cricket as he looked forward in glowing terms to the forthcoming contest between his touring side and, he hoped, a full-strength Rest of England XI.

He had touched a raw nerve in Hawke. During luncheon on the opening day of the match at Northallerton, the Yorkshire captain got to his feet and set about putting his erstwhile protégé in his place. *Cricket* reported every word:

> 'I would wish to ask Mr. Warner one question, and to ask it publicly. How was it that the Middlesex county club thought it worth while to import Albert Trott if they did not think county cricket was of importance? It is all very well for Mr. Warner to say that Yorkshire ought to give up five or six players to play in a match between his team and the Rest of England, but that would mean that Yorkshire would have to go down to Worcester with an "A" team and perhaps lose the match, and the Championship might then go to Middlesex.'

That would never do.

1904 was the year in which Fred Toone's new broom stirred the dust of old rivalries, the year that brought Yorkshire down to earth with a bump. Sixteen of Yorkshire's twenty-seven Championship matches ended drawn, the twenty-eighth, against Kent at Harrogate having been abandoned on the second day after persons unknown had tampered with the pitch overnight. Two isolated defeats illustrated Yorkshire's dilemma; still almost unbeatable, they had lost the winning habit. The side suffered a body-blow when in mid-season it was revealed that Jack Brown had been forced to retire from the game due to ill-health. Dissent fed on disappointment and the Yorkshire faithful grew restive.

No man was in a better position to hold the line in Yorkshire than Hawke. He knew the rumblings in the dales were as much the result of Toone's administrative reforms as the county's erratic form on the field. Toone had his unequivocal support; short shrift was all he offered the detractors. Yorkshire's professionals and Yorkshire's balance sheet swiftly reaped the rewards of Fred Toone's labours. The protective umbrella of the county club extended over practically every aspect of the players' lives, from arranging the special railway coach that the Yorkshire XI used to travel to away matches to the masterminding of benefits; Toone had his finger in every pie. His management of Yorkshire's home matches – previously a task undertaken by local club committees whose primary preoccupation was the promotion of their own ground rather than to swell the coffers of the county club – was a triumph of sound business practice. He insisted that the privileges of the county's members should take precedence over those of local clubs, removing at a stroke the ludicrous situation that had seen Yorkshire members treated as second-class citizens on some grounds. Inevitably, many parochial feathers were ruffled, but the proof of the medicine was to be seen in the fact that the county's membership continued to increase.

George Hirst's benefit match would doubtless have been a hugely successful event without Toone; with him, it was turned into a bounty of a kind never before witnessed in English cricket. The Roses match at the beginning of August was set aside for Hirst's benefit and over the three days 78,792 paid to pass through the Headingley gates. When the final accounting was done the benefit showed a net profit of £3,703.

The highlight of Hawke's personal season was his battling, unbeaten innings of exactly 100 against Leicestershire at Bradford. Like so many of his best knocks it was struck up in good time (135 minutes) when his side was in need of runs. It was his thirteenth and last first-class century.

Yorkshire missed the presence of Jackson, Taylor and Mitchell in the middle order; Hawke missed their company. Often, the captain was the only amateur in the side, a lonely, isolated figure. On the field John Tunnicliffe and David Hunter had become Hawke's right-hand men, men with whom Hawke felt totally at ease. But without the society of fellow amateurs in the team cricket was less fun, almost a chore. Moreover, after 1902, there was really very little left for Hawke or Yorkshire to prove. The towering heights – such as they were – of English county cricket had been scaled and conquered in a manner that was nothing if not conclusive and not even Hawke really believed his now ageing team could reclimb the mountain. As strange as it may seem, Yorkshire lacked a sense of direction that year. While Toone's reforms would immeasurably strengthen the county club in years to come, in the short term the process of change was deeply unsettling to many people. Coming at a time when Yorkshire appeared to be entering a period of decline on the field, Hawke went on to the defensive. Nobody was allowed to say a word against his professionals, nor against Toone; he assiduously courted Stanley Jackson's support, railed against amateurs who wrote for newspapers, castigated boys for pestering cricketers for their autographs and stamped on any hint of dissent within the county.

That autumn Bradford cricket club broke ranks and publicly attacked Hawke over the curtailment of the rights of local members and the general financial arrangements which now governed the staging of county matches in Yorkshire. Hawke held back until the Annual General Meeting of the county club. These were sad days, for in the first week of November Jack Brown had died. He had suffered from rheumatism from his youth, been plagued by asthma and later heart disease. Hawke was convinced Brown's heavy smoking was a contributory factor. In the last half-dozen years of his life his health steadily deteriorated and in July 1904 he tendered his resignation to the Yorkshire Committee:

> It was with great regret that I had to write to Lord Hawke and let him know that the doctor had told me it would be impossible for me ever again to stand the strain of first-class cricket.
>
> I feel the severance very much, but we cannot stand against illness, and I shall have to make the best of it. I am glad to say that I am much better and can go about comfortably at present, and I feel sure that I shall be able to do some coaching next year, if I am lucky enough to find a place.

It was not to be. His death stunned Yorkshire. W.A. Bettesworth wrote of Jack Brown in *Cricket*:

> He never was satisfied with his performances. No matter how finely he played, or how great had been the difficulty of making runs, he shook his head and thought of what he might have done. And yet like many cricketers he had something of the Calvinist about him; he thought that on any particular day he was either predestined to make runs, or not to make them. Hence, perhaps, his indifference to circumstances. If the wicket was ever so bad, it might be that he was predestined to score well; therefore, why get excited or nervous?

When Hawke got to his feet at the Annual General Meeting he prefaced his remarks by commenting that Bradford's complaints came at an 'inopportune' time. This said, he launched into a withering dismissal of the club's case: 'The county matches played at Bradford this year,' he explained, 'had cost the county £188.' Furthermore, 'if the percentage paid to the Bradford Club, a percentage which was perfectly satisfactory to other clubs in the county, had been greater . . . the loss to the County Club would have been greater also'. Whilst he was prepared to concede that it had been 'said that the curtailing of the members' privileges had cost the Bradford Club two hundred half-guinea members,' he reminded Bradford, 'that so far from the County getting any of the Bradford membership, there had actually been a decrease' in the county's membership in the Bradford district.

Both the timing and the nature of Bradford's outburst incensed Hawke and he made no bones about it. He recalled angrily that 'in 1903 the Bradford Club received £900 from the County,' and concluded his remarks with the assertion that 'the attack upon the County comes with ill-grace from a Club for which Yorkshire has done so much in the past'.

Hawke approached the following season (1905) with as relaxed an attitude as he had approached any season. Leaving Stanley Jackson to fight Yorkshire's corner on the Board of Control for the matches between England and the Australians, Hawke set off for India to get in some big-game hunting. His plans were vague. Initially, it seemed unlikely that he would be back in Britain before mid-May at the earliest, despite his appointment as Chairman of the England Selection Committee. In the event he reached Plymouth on 3 May and was batting for Yorkshire – helping Rhodes (201) put on 151 for the eighth wicket in ninety minutes – in the opening match of the Championship at Taunton, the next day. By the standards of the age his fifty-two day absence from England (thirteen days out, twenty-five days on land, and fourteen days back), was a whirlwind trip.

While Hawke was away from Yorkshire Jackson had carried two significant resolutions through Committee. The first prohibited Yorkshire players from writing for newspapers. The second increased the proportion of the gate receipts retained by the clubs staging home county matches from twenty-five to thirty-five per cent. Hawke had no intention of sacrificing the unity of Yorkshire cricket for the want of sensible regulation and penny-pinching. Both proposals were welcomed throughout the shire of the broad acres.

No sooner had Hawke arrived at Taunton than he made an unprecedented announcement to the effect that:

So far as I am concerned Yorkshire cricket for the coming summer will be subservient to the claims and interests of England, and whether the Championship be won or lost will make no difference to us so long as the Test matches are won.

It came as no surprise when Stanley Jackson was named captain of

England for the forthcoming series. It was to be a famous year, Jackson's year. Under Jackson England won two tests and drew the other three, with the captain himself topping both the batting and the bowling averages. While Jacker hogged the headlines, Yorkshire, after a fitful start dominated and eventually won the Championship.

The Tykes had won eight and lost three of their first fourteen county matches; in the second half of the campaign they won ten and drew the remaining four fixtures. It was a superb all-round team effort. Denton (1,963), Hirst (1,713) and Rhodes (1,117) all topped a thousand runs in the Championship and five others scored at least five hundred runs. Rhodes was the first man to the double in 1905 and was Yorkshire's leading wicket-taker in county matches with 126. He was never without support, with Haigh (97 wickets), Hirst (88), as well as two unsung seamers, Hubert Myers (62) and William Ringrose (60), always pitching in with wickets.

George Hirst scored 341 at Leicester against Leicestershire, hitting 212 runs in boundaries and giving just one chance. Years later he would mock his own prowess by telling the story of how he thought he was out leg before wicket before he had scored. He was so convinced that he was plumb in front of the stumps that he had almost begun to walk before he realised that the umpire had turned down the appeal. At Sheffield it was Rhodes and Haigh who stole the limelight, bowling out Nottinghamshire for 39. At Harrogate the Tykes brushed aside Somerset and in the mêlée dismissed Sammy Woods for a pair for the first time in his career.

As the season drew to a close Yorkshire were cruising to the title, or so it seemed. At Leyton against lowly Essex the well-oiled Yorkshire machine faltered, and very nearly came off the rails. Without Jackson and the injured David Hunter Yorkshire struggled against Essex as the southerners piled up over five hundred runs and were themselves then bowled out for a mere 98. The main destroyer was J.W.H.T. Douglas, the future captain of England, with a remarkable eight-ball spell in which he took five wickets – all bowled – without conceding a run, including a hat trick. Following on 423 runs adrift Yorkshire began the third day at 15 for 1. Tunnicliffe (59) and Hirst (90) batted with immense patience and obduracy, the latter surviving nearly five hours at the wicket before, with an hour remaining and three wickets to fall, Hawke and Ernest Smith came together in the middle. Defeat might have handed the Championship to Lancashire. The two veterans blocked for an hour. Ernest Smith, among the most savage of firm-footed hitters, did not score a run. Together they saved the match and clung on to the Championship that three days earlier the Yorkshiremen had mistakenly taken for granted. Hawke was unbeaten on 9 when the draw was declared.

Jackson's leadership of the victorious England XI was the stuff of legends; Hawke's leadership of a rejuvenated Yorkshire team was in many ways no less extraordinary. Stanley Jackson virtually bowed out of the first-class game at the end of the season. He made no announcement, he simply bade his farewells to the big stage of English cricket and got on with the rest of his life. Speaking in Northallerton in October 1905, Jacker said of Hawke:

> 'Cricketers in Yorkshire are extremely fortunate to have a leader who set such a wonderful example as Lord Hawke. His Lordship is one of those captains who realise that there are lessons to be taught off the field as well as on. He inspires confidence in himself as a man as well as a cricketer, and it was to that circumstance that his success and influence for good were due.'

In the years ahead Hawke was to have no stauncher ally than Stanley Jackson.

14

Yorkshire First
(1906–1938)

The problem of the Yorkshire captaincy dogged Hawke's last years in the first-class game. After 1905 he was acutely aware that he was – at least in playing terms – something of a passenger. He hated it. He summed up his unenviable situation in his *Recollections and Reminiscences:*

> As it was, whilst seeking a successor I continued through several seasons, believing that I filled a gap for lack of a better, and not like an old actor who could not bear to quit the boards.

His critics accused Hawke of clinging on to the captaincy for the sake of it. He was doing nothing of the sort. Many said he ought to have handed over the captaincy long ago, and that this would have averted the troubles he now faced. It was nonsense. Had the captaincy passed to Stanley Jackson, Tom Taylor, Frank Mitchell or even Ernest Smith at any time during the previous five years, Yorkshire would have been in exactly the same position in 1906. Jackson had virtually retired, Mitchell had gone abroad, Smith was only available for a handful of matches each year and although Taylor came back into the Yorkshire side in 1906, business commitments would soon finish his playing career. Nevertheless, it cannot be said that Hawke was completely blameless in the matter. He certainly gave a great deal of thought to who should follow him in the captaincy, but he never really planned the succession. Some have claimed that Hawke was unlucky, the victim of circumstance. The facts do not support this view. He only ever really considered two men as long-term successors, Stanley Jackson and Tom Taylor. His differences with Jackson came to a head at the worst possible time and his hopes for Taylor were always too optimistic.

So Hawke soldiered on in 1906. In the event he missed thirteen of the twenty-eight county matches, side-lined from lumbago, committee work and the call of the hunt and the grouse shoot! Four other men captained the team at various stages of the season in his absence: Ernest Smith led the side on five occasions; Tom Taylor and John Tunnicliffe four times each; and Stanley Jackson emerged from retirement to grace Johnny Tyldesley's benefit match at Manchester. The season of 1906 saw George Hirst performing the unique feat of scoring 2,348 runs and taking 208 wickets in first-class cricket. It also saw Yorkshire lose the Championship by a single run, fate taking a hand in their penultimate county fixture at Bristol against Gloucestershire.

Gilbert Jessop, that perennial thorn in Yorkshire's side, bowled the ball that trapped the last Yorkshire batsman leg before wicket one run short of a tie, two adrift of victory. Either result would have given Yorkshire the Championship; instead, defeat gave Kent the title.

During the Yorkshire players' annual outing to Wighill, Hawke's eldest sister, intent on making polite conversation, turned to the tall young man next to her, and asked, 'Who was the wretched man who got out when only two runs were needed?'

The tall young man blushed. 'It was me, ma'am,' confessed William Ringrose.

The season also included a moment of farce. In the first week of July Yorkshire gave a début to a young professional, C.H. Parkin, against Gloucestershire at Leeds. Cecil Parkin was a flamboyant, gifted right-arm spinner who later played for Lancashire and England. Unfortunately, he was born in Eaglescliffe on the County Durham side of the Tees, some twenty yards over the Yorkshire border; Hawke knew this when Parkin was selected to play at Leeds. Summoning him into his presence on the morning of the match Hawke told him that:

'We are not particular about a few yards. You play today!'

It was Parkin's only match for Yorkshire. MCC telegraphed its formal objection to his qualification and Parkin disappeared into the leagues for eight years before recommencing his first-class career with Lancashire in 1914 at the age of twenty-eight.

The affair infuriated Hawke. Unjustly, the rumour spread that the Lincolnshire-born captain of Yorkshire had dismissed the young professional when he found out he was a Durham-born. Parkin himself attempted to set the record straight in the 1920s: 'I did not get into the Yorkshire team under false pretences. And it was not, as the story goes, Yorkshire that got me disqualified. The MCC did the disqualification.' Nobody listened, by then Hawke's reputation was set in stone. When A.W. Pullin discussed the matter in his *History of Yorkshire County Cricket, 1903–1923*, he perpetuated the notion that as soon as Yorkshire discovered that Parkin was not Yorkshire-born, he 'was forthwith dropped,' because 'the Yorkshire Committee and Lord Hawke did not require to be told their duty in the matter'.

In 1907 Yorkshire slipped from second to third place in the table. A.W. Pullin commented: 'Yorkshire were not a Championship side this year. The process of blending old and new had not yielded satisfactory results.' The weather disrupted the season and at one stage a whole month went by without a single Yorkshire match reaching a natural conclusion. Although, only two Yorkshiremen (Rhodes and Tunnicliffe) made centuries in the Championship, both Hirst and Tunnicliffe passed 20,000 runs in first-class cricket that season. When Hawke departed for Canada that winter on a hunting expedition he little suspected that his ageing, seemingly vulnerable 1907 side, would perform so valiantly the following summer.

The omens for 1908 were not propitious. At the end of the previous season John Tunnicliffe had retired to accept the post of cricket coach at Clifton College. Long John's departure was widely perceived as symptomatic of the break up of the great side of former years. Jackson, Taylor, Mitchell, Brown, Wainwright and now Tunnicliffe were gone and the others were no longer young men. The stalwarts of the side were Hunter (aged 48 at the start of the 1908 season), Hirst (36), Haigh (37), Denton (33) and Rhodes (30); the Tykes were badly in need of an infusion of new blood – and the hour brought forward two new heroes.

Both had struggled for some years to establish themselves in the Yorkshire XI, neither was in the first flush of youth and after 1908 both disappointed. Yet without their contributions that summer Yorkshire might not have won back the Championship. One was W.H. Wilkinson, a solid left-handed batsman, the other was a 28-year-old all-rounder who had first played for the county in 1903, J.T. Newstead. Newstead was the find of the season; in Championship matches alone he scored 733 runs and took 115 wickets.

A.W. Pullin later wrote of him: 'After the doubts concerning the county's cricket felt at the close of the 1907 season, the campaign of 1908 created as much surprise in Yorkshire as it did throughout the country.' Yorkshire celebrated the twenty-fifth anniversary of Hawke's captaincy by going unbeaten throughout the season.

Hawke's personal popularity in Yorkshire may be gauged by the success of two funds set up to mark his twenty-five years of captaincy. The county club raised over a thousand pounds and the *Yorkshire Evening Post's* 'Tyke Fund' another £824, mostly by public subscription. When in July the Earl of Wharncliffe presented Hawke with a clutch of mementoes and works of art to commemorate the event, he knew he was speaking for Yorkshire when he said:

> 'Lord Hawke had not adopted the methods of a martinet, but by firmness, by unvarying courtesy, by kindness, by a sincere love of the game, had brought Yorkshire cricket to the highest degree of efficiency, and had also earned the confidence and affection of the men.'

The Championship of 1908 set the seal on Hawke's captaincy in his last full season. He scored 50 not out against Gloucestershire at Sheffield in July, his final first-class half-century. Generally, however, he struggled with the bat and in the field he was stiff and slow. He would stand in the slips and chat through the day with David Hunter, two old warriors in the twilight of their careers. Hunter in fact, was a famous talker. Plum Warner would tell the tale of how once when he was batting against Wilfred Rhodes at Bradford, Hunter remarked, 'Ah, Mr Warner, you play Wilfred better than any of the others.'

A moment later Hunter paused and whipped off the bails. 'How's that?' he asked.

Then, as Warner – comprehensively stumped – put his bat under his arm, 'Good afternoon, Mr Warner, what a pity when you were playing Wilfred so well.'

Hawke and the faithful stumper had a perfect understanding. Hunter remembered that whenever they batted together '. . . we never used to have to call to each other when we set off, we saw where the ball was and if there was a run in it we ran and said nothing about it at all'. It was no coincidence that when David Hunter finally retired at the end of the 1909 season Hawke, too, bade his farewell to county cricket.

Illness and injury kept Hawke out of the Yorkshire XI for much of the following season (1909). He was Chairman of the England Select-ors again that year, but went off to Aix in mid-summer in search of a cure and was absent while his fellow selectors – Archie MacLaren, C.B. Fry and H.D.G. Leveson-Gower – perpetrated a series of blunders that doomed the English cause. Restored to a semblence of fitness Hawke returned in August to lead Yorkshire in seven Championship matches. Yorkshire's form was erratic and the title won so brilliantly a year earlier was meekly surrendered. Hawke captained Yorkshire in the Championship for the last time against Sussex at Brighton at the end of the month. An injured leg prevented him from batting and he played little part in the contest. Hawke had appeared in eight Championship matches in 1909, scoring 71 runs at an average of 8.87 Although he did not formally resign the captaincy for another year, his serious playing days were over.

The captaincy passed to E.J. Radcliffe. A good club player, Radcliffe's batting lacked the durability demanded by county cricket. Answerable to Hawke off the field and to the professionals on the field, the Yorkshire captaincy was a job a man took on at his peril. Radcliffe had led the Tykes through June and July 1909 and would continue in the post for the next two years. His captaincy marked a period of rebuilding which saw Yorkshire slump to eighth place in 1910 and seventh in 1911. He was not helped by Hawke's exhortation at the Yorkshire Annual General Meeting of 1909 to the effect that: 'I would sooner we had lost matches by sporting cricket than that they should be drawn by unattractive play.'

Unless a captain was willing and able to stand up to Hawke he was destined for the wilderness. Such was the fate of many of Radcliffe's successors. The captain of Yorkshire was often a very lonely man. The story is told of how one such passenger captain had to be 'rounded-up' by a kind-hearted professional who thought he ought to 'come in,' because 'Wilfred has declared'.

Hawke played in a handful of matches in 1910 and 1911, his last appearance in a first-class fixture in England being for Yorkshire against MCC at the Scarborough Festival. In his fifty-first year he acquitted himself honourably, scoring 20 – bowled out by the Leicestershire professional W.E. Astill – and 8 not out. Fittingly, for a man who had done so much to spread the gospel of cricket across the globe, his first-class career concluded overseas.

In February 1912 Hawke took an MCC side to the Argentine. Hawke described the tour as 'a holiday sort of country house trip'. His team included luminaries of the calibre of Archie MacLaren, A.J.L. Hill, who had scored a century in a Test match against South Africa as long ago as 1896, and C.E. De Trafford, the former captain of

Leicestershire. The balance of the party was made up by E.R. Wilson (a Yorkshireman who had scored a hundred in the Varsity match of 1901), M.C. Bird (the Surrey batsman), C.E. Hatfield and L.H.W. Troughton (both of Kent), N.C. Tufnell (the Cambridge blue), H.H.C. Baird (who had hit a hundred at Lord's for the Army against the Navy in 1910), W. Findlay (the former Oxford blue) and E.J. Fulcher (a fine club cricketer who, alone among his fellow tourists, had yet to appear in a first-class game).

It was Hawke's third visit to the country. He had financial interests in the Republic, mainly in its railways, and so when the President of the Argentine invited him to bring out a team he was happy to accept the invitation. In purely cricketing terms the tourists were, against expectations, tested more than once. Many of the matches were played out in debilitating heat and the older members of the side – Hawke included – struggled. But it was a cheerful tour, a social triumph. So it was that Hawke played his 633rd and final first-class game at the Palermo ground in Buenos Aires for MCC against the Argentine at the end of February 1912. He batted at the foot of the order, scoring 16 not out and 5.

Perhaps it was because Hawke had carried on for so long that he did not miss playing when he finally laid down his bat. He organised cricket weeks at Wighill, now and then he carted the ball around the field in club matches, but otherwise he was content to leave the field to the younger generation.

Leeds was now the focus of Yorkshire cricket. The county club had erected a large shed for winter practice in 1911 at a cost of £600, a sum that Hawke and Toone assured the Committee was well spent. Time and again Hawke reminded the Committee that it should take the 'long view'. Yorkshire's success was founded on this 'long view' and any other approach was bound to result in failure.

Hawke became President of MCC in 1914, the year in which Lord's celebrated its centenary. It was an honour that filled him with unease, for although he had always hoped to hold the position one day he 'dreaded the responsibility of such an important year'. Hawke could hardly have suspected that he would hold the post of President of MCC for the next five years. In normal times a new President was selected each year but, as Hawke was to recall, 'the war was the cause of complete convulsion in cricket as well as in more important matters'. Tradition was inviolable and so 'no change in the post could be made on account of the rule that the retirement takes place at the annual dinner, which, of course, could not be held'. It fell to Hawke to guide MCC through the long years of the Great War. His responsibility was not simply to maintain Lord's in readiness for peace: 'Besides having to supervise all the affairs of the club under unparalleled conditions, there was a great deal of charitable work to be organized,' and in looking to the future of the English game MCC did its 'utmost to help to foster cricket in the public schools'.

In his work for MCC Hawke could always turn to Lord Harris, of whom he was, remarkably, somewhat in awe. He invariably relied on Harris' advice, followed his lead, walked in his shadow. Hawke and Harris represented MCC at the funeral of W.G. Grace, who died of a stroke in 1915. They were inseparable at Lord's, increasingly known as the 'two barons' of cricket. Harris was nine years Hawke's senior, a wiser man, and much the stronger personality. Harris held Kent in the palm of his hand like Hawke held Yorkshire and from the security of fiefdoms such as these, they were impregnable. Harris saw himself as the guardian of the laws and under his influence the last vestiges of Hawke's reforming zeal ebbed away. By the end of the war Hawke had had his fill of change; he, too, was convinced of the primacy of the status quo. It is ironic to consider that henceforward the man who had done so much to transform the lot of the professional cricketer, expand the Championship, update playing conditions, regulate the organisation of Test matches in England and modernise the laws of cricket would become entrenched in cricketing mythology as the arch enemy of experiment and development.

In Leeds the offices of the county club became the headquarters of the West Riding Volunteers; Hawke was appointed major and county adjutant, with Fred Toone as his secretary. In 1918, with the unit up to brigade strength – twenty infantry battalions, five motor sections and two ambulance corps – Hawke was promoted to colonel and Toone took over the duties of adjutant with the rank of captain. Aside from military duties they raised over £20,000 for charity during the war by arranging cricket matches in the county.

Yorkshire's fund-raising activities could not have been so successful had not the organisation of the county club been largely preserved throughout those years. This was accomplished by appealing to the membership for financial support, an appeal that realised some £5,560 between 1914 and 1918. This was ploughed back into the upkeep of grounds and the payment of players – war work and military duties permitting – who played together for charity fixtures.

In 1915 Hawke's mother died. For nearly thirty years she had ruled Wighill, the epitome of the Victorian matriach. She had wanted to see her son settled but while she lived Hawke had never comtemplated matrimony. Within a year of her death he was engaged to be married to Maud Cross, a widow of his own age. Maud was a keen golfer and she soon prevailed upon her fiance to take up the game. An early partner was Stanley Jackson, who like Hawke had only taken up the game after he retired from first-class cricket. Maud had a house at North Berwick and in April 1916 Hawke went out and tackled the nearby links. Unlike Jacker, Hawke never threatened scratch. Nevertheless, he soon became enthralled by the game, later writing that:

> I have been accused of playing it far more seriously than I ever played cricket. None of us see ourselves as we are seen, and so I do not attempt to refute the charge. I do think that golf needs more concentration than anything else I know. Like most cricketers, I began too late to achieve more than a respectable round, and perhaps I do not have the same enthusiasm for the big drive that is shown by those stalwart young hitters who want every course stretched out. To me the especial fascination is in the short game, and to putt well at least enables me to walk to the next tee without wishing I had not been born.

Hawke and Maud were married at St Paul's Church, Knightsbridge, on 1 June 1916. The best man was Christopher Heseltine, Hawke's companion on numerous tours and safaris. If marriage guaranteed domestic bliss, Hawke's public life was decidedly rocky. Public figures cannot afford to be accident-prone and Hawke had a talent for tripping himself up. His quick temper, his impulsiveness, his discomfort when addressing an audience and his tendency to speak his mind without a thought for the consequences gave his critics ample opportunity to shoot him down in flames. His friends marvelled at how it was that the tactful, hard-working, kindly man they knew and admired could behave like a complete ass in public. During the 1920s and 1930s Hawke seemed hell-bent on destroying his reputation. Nothing caused him more trouble than the question of amateur captaincy.

Hawke had strong views on the subject and indeed he had every right to have strong views on it; he was, after all, one of the most successful captains in the history of the game. Nor were his views based on mere prejudice. He believed that a professional captain was at a disadvantage; he could, for example, 'be nagged by his fellows in the dressing-room,' there was always the risk that he would 'be a butt for grumblers' and he doubted if any professional could 'exercise the same authority as an amateur'. However, when at the Yorkshire Annual General Meeting of 1924 he took it upon himself to defend A.E.R. Gilligan's much criticised captaincy of England in Australia, he abandoned reason and launched into his disastrous 'Pray God, no professioanl shall ever captain England' monologue. What Hawke had meant to say was that it would be a bad day for England if there was no amateur good enough to play for his country. Had he articulated his real opinion posterity might remember him rather more kindly. The furore that ensued was so great that Hawke practically went into hiding that winter.

By the standards of his age Hawke lived much of his life in the public eye. For a man in his position he was an appallingly bad speaker and he knew it. He regularly attended the House of Lords, but never rose to deliver his maiden speech. Had it not been for his many powerful friends in the Press his latter years might have been a nightmare. By the time of his death in 1938 Hawke had undone much of the goodwill he had built up in earlier days. Even in Yorkshire he aroused the fiercest emotions. The crusty old peer who ruled the county club with a rod of iron between the wars became the man the detractors loved to hate, not for what he was, for underneath he never really changed, but for what he seemed to be and what he seemed to represent; the dead hand of the past. His critics portrayed him as inflexible and obdurate; when contrary to expectation he was flexible he was attacked for being inconsisent and if he ever gave ground it was paraded as weakness. Gifted with an uncanny knack of saying the wrong thing at the wrong time, he courted controversy. In his playing days the cricket of his magnificent Yorkshire XIs did Hawke's talking for him, and the occasional *faux pas* was quickly forgotten. His teams were more than his pride and joy, they had been his sword and shield.

In the autumn of 1926 Hawke confounded both his friends and foes alike by offering the Yorkshire captaincy to a professional, Herbert Sutcliffe. Moreover, he accepted that Sutcliffe would retain his professional status. To many it seemed as if Hawke had made an abrupt volte-face on the subject of amateur captaincy.

In canvassing the mood of the first-class counties it soon became clear that several would openly voice their disquiet should a professional be appointed. Hawke also realised that there were faint hearts even on his own Committee. He vacillated. The man his critics damned for being a man of iron, hesitated. Wishing neither to be the cause of discord, nor the servant of Hawke's whim, Sutcliffe declined the captaincy. Significantly, he made his decision known not to the county Committee, but direct to Hawke.

Sutcliffe was too shrewd a man to believe that a professional captain, any professional captain, could be his own man in Yorkshire. He felt that a captain who was not free to lead as he thought fit was no captain at all. Besides, Sutcliffe was not alone among England's premier professionals in believing that the cause of professional captaincy had been set back a generation by Jack Hobbs's disinclination to accept the England captaincy. Bill Bowes explained Sutcliffe's rejection of the Yorkshire captaincy in his *Express Deliveries*:

> When Hobbs refused the captaincy of England Sutcliffe was deeply disappointed. 'Lord Hawke lifted professional cricket from here to there,' said Herbert, raising his hand from knee to shoulder level. 'Professional cricketers lifted it to there,' he continued, raising his hand above his head, 'and even Lord Hawke always wanted it back again. Jack Hobbs, for the sake of the professional cricketer, should have accepted.'

Sutcliffe's judgement was vindicated in the years that followed. Successive and, let it be said, successful Yorkshire captains had the galling experience of opening their morning paper to discover that they had displeased Hawke.

Frank Greenwood, under whose captaincy Yorkshire won the Championship in 1931 for the first time since 1925, fell foul of Hawke's wrath that year for being a party to a contrived finish of a county match against Gloucestershire. 'It cannot,' Hawke asserted, 'possibly be to the advantage of our game if the laws, written and unwritten, are tampered with. Ye Gods!' he exclaimed, 'is the game to be ruled by young men, some of whom are prepared to take the unwritten law into their own hands?'

Greenwood said nothing. Later that season against Northampton-shire at Bradford he repeated the crime. Gloucestershire had beaten the Tykes, Northamptonshire were roundly defeated. An amateur captain could afford to defy Hawke; it was a luxury that had been denied any Yorkshire professional for three decades.

In 1933 Brian Sellers took over the captaincy. His methods were reminiscent of Hawke's; if anything, Sellers was more of a disciplinarian, particularly in his early days in the captaincy. He was at least as good a batsman as Hawke, perhaps, a better player of fast bowling, and like Hawke he had a sense of the dramatic. A man of immense drive and determination, gifted with a rare talent for repartee, Sellers was the first Yorkshire captain since Hawke to be captain in more than name alone. Hawke and Sellers did not always see eye to eye, but their differences should not be overstated. Under Sellers's captaincy Yorkshire were almost invincible in the thirties and in his heart of hearts Hawke yearned for nothing more.

Away from Yorkshire Hawke remained a tireless servant of MCC. When Lord Harris died in 1932, Hawke succeeded him as Treasurer and almost immediately was caught up in the midst of the bodyline controversy. At the height of the crisis, which he was intent on defusing at any cost short of publicly undermining Jardine's captaincy, he told the cricket correspondent of the *Guardian* to remember the Tests of 1921. Understandably, the Australians were not at that time particularly receptive to a discussion of the rights and wrongs of the terrors that their own fast bowlers had visited on England in previous series. Hawke was not a defender of Jardine's bodyline tactics. He believed that if such theories were applied in the county game it would destroy cricket as a spectacle.

Hawke continued to hunt and shoot and to travel widely throughout his latter years. He visited Stanley Jackson in Calcutta when the latter was Governor of Bengal and spent many happy interludes as Ranji's guest in India. The grouse moors and golf links of the British Isles became safe havens from the Press, places far from the public eye, far from the controversy that he came to loathe. In 1924 the lease on Wighill had run out and the Hawkes had decamped to North Berwick, where Hawke continued to live after Maud's death in 1935.

From childhood Hawke had nurtured a morbid dread of illness. He had seen his elder brother's protracted suffering, witnessed so many of his friends succumb to crippling and eventually terminal diseases. In later years he was preoccupied with suffering the same fate. Death held few fears for him, but the thought of declining into a state of humiliating helplessness terrified him. It was a fate that he was fortunate enough to be spared. The end came quickly. He collapsed at his home in North Berwick and was rushed to Edinburgh. The surgeons operated but to no avail, for he died shortly afterwards, without regaining consciousness, on 10th October 1938.

Epilogue

When Percy Holmes was asked in a pub at Barkisland, near Halifax, why he thought he had never been to Australia he explained: 'It was that bugger, 'Awke. 'E said to me one day, "Olmes." And I said, "Yes, 'Awke. Wot?" And that's why I nivver went to Australia.'

Apocryphal, perhaps, but wholly indicative of the public perception (at the time of his death and since) of Hawke's high-handed ways.

In 1937 Herbert Sutcliffe dared to comment that he was confident that England had a team good enough to beat the Australians in England the following year, if only the selectors could be induced to select it. At Hawke's last Annual General Meeting of the Yorkshire County Cricket Club at Sheffield in January 1938 he took Sutcliffe – that most unimpeachable ambassador for Yorkshire and England cricket – to task for his temerity. His Lordship was surprised that 'a man of Herbert's standard should venture to discuss the selection at all'. Right to the end Hawke was indefatigably outspoken.

Yet the same man who felt duty bound to rebuke publicly Herbert Sutcliffe had, forty years before, demanded that the Yorkshire Committee should pay a 'winter allowance' to John Thewlis. A.W. Pullin had discovered Thewlis – then 70 years old – carrying laundry from his home in Failsworth four miles to Manchester for a few coppers. Thewlis had been a stalwart of Yorkshire cricket in the 1860s: Pullin found him in rags, toothless, going blind, destitute. Hawke had already taken up the cause of the professional cricketer but in the wake of the Thewlis affair the welfare of his professionals became his primary concern. It was a concern that never waned. As Patrick Morrah concluded in *The Golden Age Of Cricket* 'in the entire history of cricket no man ever did more for the professional that he'.

Unfortunately, Hawke's own *Recollections and Reminiscences*, published in 1924, did little to enhance his reputation. Partly ghosted by Home Gordon, to the contemporary reader the book is full of unintentional humour. Hawke was not an egalitarian, he was a nineteenth-century man and his attitudes reflected it. *Recollections and Reminiscences* is an object lesson in how ridiculous Victorian values can seem in the light of a more enlightened age. Despite Home Gordon's obvious interventions and editing, a great deal of the real Hawke comes through. If *Recollections and Reminiscences* disappoints on a literary level and lacks coherence as a chronicle of Hawke's part in the rise of Yorkshire cricket, it is, nevertheless, very revealing. The book displays the strengths and weaknesses of the inner man, laying bare the contradictions that plague any understanding of Hawke.

Writing in *Wisden* after Hawke's death F.E. Lacey offered the thought that 'to him cricket was more than a game. It was a philosophy that coloured his dealings with people and things . . . ' Certainly, few men can have carried a sport abroad with such missionary zeal and still have achieved so much at home.

To answer those who dispute Hawke's rightful place among the first rank of captains one need look no further than the pages of *Wisden* for the years 1893 to 1908. The entries surely refute any argument. When he retired he was, without question, the most successful county captain in the history of the game. In the past eighty years only two men, Brian Sellers and Stuart Surridge have even come close to rivalling Hawke's feats.

On Hawke's death English cricket lost one of its great men; Yorkshire lost an institution. Stanley Jackson, who stepped into Hawke's shoes as President of the county club, said of him in *Wisden*, that he was 'a straightforward and honourable gentleman,' who had had 'a long innings, played it well and enjoyed it'.

Jacker's obituary of his old captain was a somewhat distant, unemotional remembrance of former years, its tone perhaps dictated by a desire to ensure unity within Yorkshire. However, he paid Hawke the one tribute that he would have valued above all others:

> A personal interest in each individual player and his welfare, which . . . lasted until the end, gained for 'His Lordship' a respect and loyalty from every member of the team which I think must have been unique.

If in Yorkshire Hawke's work fell to Jackson, Plum Warner was his spiritual heir. Warner had been Hawke's protégé. He shared Hawke's *philosophy* of cricket, believed that cricket was more than just a game, that it was a bridge across racial and social divides, a great power for good in the world. He recalled with sadness in *Lord's, 1789–1945* how Hawke's colours (light blue, dark blue and yellow, a combination of those of Eton and the Quidnuncs) seemed to have 'lost some of their lustre in the minds of many who held them in high regard' in his later years.

In The *Cricketer* Warner said of his old friend:

> He knew how to maintain discipline but he ruled by love and example and not by fear. There was seldom need to put anyone 'on the carpet', a word or a look was enough. Unselfish to a degree and with the kindest of hearts, sympathetic and understanding, he always thought of others and very seldom of himself.

It was also Warner who said of Hawke that 'He made Yorkshire cricket.' It was no less than the truth; a fitting epitaph for the great man of Yorkshire cricket.

Statistical Section

Batting in First-class Matches

(a) All matches

Season	M	I	NO	Runs	HS	Ave	100	50
1881	2	4	0	46	32	11.50	0	0
1882	18	33	2	570	66	18.38	0	2
1883	19	29	1	557	141	19.89	1	1
1884	9	16	0	108	22	6.75	0	0
1885	12	19	2	357	73	21.00	0	1
1886	19	36	1	831	144	23.74	1	4
1887	25	41	2	967	125	24.79	1	5
1887–8 (Australia)	3	5	0	76	48	15.20	0	0
1888	10	20	1	155	21*	8.15	0	0
1889	15	25	1	426	69	17.75	0	2
1890	18	33	3	658	74	21.93	0	3
1891	14	26	0	344	126	13.23	1	0
1891 (North America)	2	4	0	144	74	36.00	0	1
1892	17	32	1	532	74*	17.16	0	1
1892–3 (India)	3	5	0	100	79	20.00	0	1
1893	11	16	0	241	59	15.06	0	2

Season	M	I	NO	Runs	HS	Ave	100	50
1894	25	38	2	725	157	20.13	1	4
1894 (North America)	2	3	0	141	78	47.00	0	1
1895	32	51	6	1,078	79	23.95	0	7
1895–6 (South Africa)	4	6	1	46	30	9.20	0	0
1896	26	36	7	708	166	24.41	2	1
1897 (West Indies)	7	9	0	113	26	12.55	0	0
1897	21	30	7	642	91*	27.91	0	5
1898	31	38	7	950	134	30.64	2	4
1898/99 (South Africa)	5	8	2	69	31*	11.50	0	0
1899	29	41	6	923	127	26.37	1	4
1900	30	41	3	696	79	18.31	0	2
1901	32	42	5	902	89	24.37	0	7
1902	27	33	6	565	126	20.92	2	0
1903	28	38	7	766	79	24.70	0	4
1904	29	33	5	669	100*	23.89	1	4
1905	26	37	10	494	51	18.29	0	1
1906	19	29	3	302	36	11.61	0	0
1907	23	29	3	316	61*	12.15	0	1
1908	24	28	8	317	50*	15.85	0	1
1909	8	9	1	71	22*	8.87	0	0
1910	4	6	0	59	31	9.83	0	0
1911	2	3	1	30	20	15.00	0	0
1912 (Argentina)	2	4	1	55	27	18.33	0	0
TOTAL	633	936	105	16,749	166	20.15	13	69

(b) Matches in the British Isles

(i) For Yorkshire in the County Championship

Season	M	I	NO	Runs	HS	Ave	100	50
1881		did not appear						
1882	8	16	1	212	66	14.13	0	1
1883	9	11	0	171	60	15.54	0	1
1884	4	8	0	43	22	5.37	0	0
1885		did not appear						
1886	13	25	1	615	144	25.62	1	3
1887	16	24	2	636	125	28.90	1	4
1888	8	16	1	115	21*	7.66	0	0
1889	11	19	1	351	69	19.50	0	2
1890	10	18	2	444	74	27.75	0	3
1891	8	14	0	235	126	16.78	1	0
1892	12	22	1	343	74*	16.33	0	1
1893	6	7	0	82	25	11.71	0	0
1894	12	20	1	197	56	10.36	0	1
1895	25	38	4	847	79	24.91	0	6
1896	20	26	5	577	166	27.47	2	1
1897	13	19	5	436	91*	31.14	0	3
1898	25	30	6	797	134	33.20	2	4
1899	23	33	3	769	127	25.63	1	4
1900	25	32	2	513	79	17.10	0	1
1901	24	30	3	691	89	25.59	0	6
1902	18	20	2	316	126	17.55	1	0
1903	20	28	4	573	79	23.87	0	3
1904	21	25	3	510	100*	23.18	1	3
1905	22	30	8	460	51	20.90	0	1
1906	15	23	3	244	36	12.20	0	0
1907	20	25	3	251	61*	11.40	0	1
1908	19	22	7	274	50*	18.26	0	1
1909	8	9	1	71	22*	8.87	0	0
1910		did not appear						
1911		did not appear						
TOTAL	415	590	69	10,773	166	20.67	10	50

Statistical Section

(ii)   Other matches for Yorkshire (1881–1911)

	M	I	NO	Runs	HS	Ave	100	50
TOTAL	98	154	22	2,424	71	18.36	0	8

(iii)   All matches for Yorkshire (1881–1911)

	M	I	NO	Runs	HS	Ave	100	50
TOTAL	513	744	91	13,197	166	20.20	10	58

(c)   For teams other than Yorkshire

(i)   For the Gentlemen versus Players (1887–1908)

	M	I	NO	Runs	HS	Ave	100	50
TOTAL	10	15	0	236	38	15.73	0	0

(ii)   For the MCC (1884–1910)

	M	I	NO	Runs	HS	Ave	100	50
TOTAL	28	43	3	851	107*	21.27	1	5

(iii)   For Cambridge University (1881–5)

	M	I	NO	Runs	HS	Ave	100	50
TOTAL	20	34	2	657	141	20.53	1	2

(iv)   For the North versus the South (1883–1908)

	M	I	NO	Runs	HS	Ave	100	50
TOTAL	15	24	1	312	47	13.56	0	0

(v)   For I Zingari (1885–1904)

	M	I	NO	Runs	HS	Ave	100	50
TOTAL	5	9	1	173	47	21.62	0	0

(vi)   For the Gentlemen of England (1886–1910)

	M	I	NO	Runs	HS	Ave	100	50
TOTAL	3	6	0	126	56	21.00	0	1

(vii)   For an Eleven of England (1882–4)

	M	I	NO	Runs	HS	Ave	100	50
TOTAL	2	3	0	52	31	17.33	0	0

(viii)   For the rest of England (1903–4)

	M	I	NO	Runs	HS	Ave	100	50
TOTAL	2	2	1	8	5	8.00	0	0

(ix)   For C.I. Thornton's XI (1895–8)

	M	I	NO	Runs	HS	Ave	100	50
TOTAL	2	3	0	72	40	24.00	0	0

(x)   For the Honourable M.B. Hawke's XI (1885)

	M	I	NO	Runs	HS	Ave	100	50
TOTAL	1	2	1	68	42*	68.00	0	0

(xi)   For Lancashire and Yorkshire (1903)

	M	I	NO	Runs	HS	Ave	100	50
TOTAL	1	1	0	14	14	14.00	0	0

(xii)   For 'Over Thirty' (1901)

	M	I	NO	Runs	HS	Ave	100	50
TOTAL	1	2	0	49	32	24.50	0	0

(xiii)   For Oxford and Cambridge University past and present (1890)

	M	I	NO	Runs	HS	Ave	100	50
TOTAL	1	2	1	24	21*	24.00	0	0

(xiv)   For A.J. Webbe's team (1894)

	M	I	NO	Runs	HS	Ave	100	50
TOTAL	1	2	0	166	157	83.00	1	0

(xv)   All other matches (1881–1911)

	M	I	NO	Runs	HS	Ave	100	50
TOTAL	92	148	10	2,808	157	20.34	3	8

(d)   Overseas matches

(i)   In Australia for G.F. Vernon's team (1887–8)

	M	I	NO	Runs	HS	Ave	100	50
TOTAL	3	5	0	76	48	15.20	0	0

(ii)   In North America and Canada for Lord Hawke's team (1891, 1894)

Season	M	I	NO	Runs	HS	Ave	100	50
1891	2	4	0	144	74	36.00	0	1
1894	2	3	0	141	78	47.00	0	1
TOTAL	4	7	0	285	78	40.71	0	2

Lord Hawke

(iii) In India for Lord Hawke's team (1892–3)

	M	I	NO	Runs	HS	Ave	100	50
TOTAL	3	5	0	100	79	20.00	0	1

(iv) In South Africa for Lord Hawke's team (1895–6, 1898–9)

Season	M	I	NO	Runs	HS	Ave	100	50
1895–6	4	6	1	46	30	9.20	0	0
1898–9	5	8	2	69	31*	11.50	0	0
TOTAL	9	14	3	115	31*	10.45	0	0

(v) In the West Indies for Lord Hawke's team (1897)

	M	I	NO	Runs	HS	Ave	100	50
TOTAL	7	9	0	113	26	12.55	0	0

(vi) In the Argentine for MCC (1912)

	M	I	NO	Runs	HS	Ave	100	50
TOTAL	2	4	1	55	27	18.33	0	0

(vi) All overseas matches (1887–1912)

	M	I	NO	Runs	HS	Ave	100	50
TOTAL	28	44	4	744	79	18.60	0	3

Batting in Test Matches

England versus South Africa (in South Africa)

Season	M	I	NO	Runs	HS	Ave	100	50
1895–6	3	4	1	46	30	15.33	0	0
1898–9	2	4	0	9	5	2.25	0	0
TOTAL	5	8	1	55	30	7.85	0	0

Mode of Dismissal

Season	I	NO	B	C	C&B	St	LBW	HW	RO
1881	4	0	2	1	1	0	0	0	0
1882	33	2	15	9	3	1	0	0	3
1883	29	1	12	13	1	1	1	0	0
1884	16	0	8	7	1	0	0	0	0
1885	19	2	7	9	1	0	0	0	0
1886	36	1	19	13	2	0	1	0	0
1887	41	2	23	13	2	0	0	0	1
1887–8	5	0	2	3	0	0	0	0	0
1888	20	1	12	5	0	0	1	1	0
1889	25	1	10	11	0	1	2	0	0
1890	33	3	15	12	0	1	0	0	2
1891	26	0	9	11	0	2	3	0	1
1891 (North America)	4	0	1	3	0	0	0	0	0
1892	32	1	16	14	1	0	0	0	0
1892–3 (India)	5	0	4	1	0	0	0	0	0
1893	16	0	5	8	2	1	0	0	0
1894	38	2	16	16	0	1	2	0	1
1894 (North America)	3	0	0	3	0	0	0	0	0
1895	51	6	25	14	2	1	3	0	0
1895–6 (South Africa)	6	1	2	2	0	0	1	0	0
1896	36	7	9	15	3	0	1	1	0
1897	30	7	15	5	2	0	1	0	0
1897 (West Indies)	9	0	4	4	0	0	0	0	1
1898	38	7	15	15	0	1	0	0	0
1898–9 (South Africa)	8	2	3	1	2	0	0	0	0
1899	41	6	16	13	1	2	2	0	1
1900	41	3	19	15	2	1	1	0	0
1901	42	5	22	10	3	0	2	0	0
1902	33	6	14	10	0	1	2	0	0
1903	38	7	16	11	1	0	2	0	1
1904	33	5	13	10	1	1	1	0	2
1905	37	10	15	7	1	1	3	0	0
1906	29	3	9	16	1	0	0	0	0
1907	29	3	9	15	1	0	1	0	0
1908	28	8	8	8	1	1	1	0	1
1909	9	1	3	3	0	1	1	0	0
1910	6	0	2	3	1	0	0	0	0
1911	3	1	2	0	0	0	0	0	0
1912 (Argentina)	4	1	2	0	0	0	1	0	0
TOTAL	936	105	399	329	36	18	33	2	14
Percentage	—	—	48.0	39.6	4.3	2.2	4.0	0.2	1.7

Bowlers who Dismissed
Hawke Five Times or More

18 times: J.T.Hearne
16 times: W. Attewell, G.A. Lohmann
15 times: W. Mead
14 times: F.R. Spofforth
13 times: W. Barnes
12 times: F.W. Tate
11 times: F. Martin
10 times: J. Briggs, F.G. Roberts, T. Richardson, W. Wright
 9 times: E. Arnold, G. Cox, W.G. Grace, A. Hide, A. Mold, A.E. Trott, A. Watson
 8 times: B. Cranfield, W.A. Woof
 7 times: G. Burton, W. Flowers, J. Hulme, W.A. Humphreys, S. Hargreave, S.M.J. Woods
 6 times: W. Brearley, E. Barratt, W. Bestwick, A. Hallam, A. Hearne, J.T. Rawlin, A.E. Stoddart, F.J. Shacklock, C.L. Townsend, G.A. Wilson
 5 times: B.J.T. Bosanquet, G. Bean, T.W. Garrett, J. Gunn, W.C. Hedley, G.L. Jessop, C.J. Kortright, W. Lockwood, E.A. Nepean, G.G. Napier, A.D. Pougher, W. Rhodes, E. Robson, S. Santall, C.M. Wells, H. Young

Pattern of Scoring

Score	Innings	Per cent of innings
0	122	13.0
1–9	323	34.5
10–19	181	19.3
20–9	128	13.7
30–9	65	6.9
40–9	35	3.7
50–9	31	3.3
60–9	20	2.1
70–9	15	1.6
80–9	2	0.2
90–9	1	0.1
100–166	13	1.4

The Thirteen Centuries

Score	For	Against	Ground	Season
141	Cambridge University	C.I. Thornton's XI	Fenner's	1883
144	Yorkshire	Sussex	Hove	1886
125	Yorkshire	Lancashire	Old Trafford	1887
126	Yorkshire	Somerset	Taunton	1891
157	A.J. Webbe's team	Cambridge University	Fenner's	1894
166	Yorkshire	Warwickshire	Edgbaston	1896
110*	Yorkshire	Kent	Headingley	1896
107*	Yorkshire	Kent	Sheffield	1898
134	Yorkshire	Warwickshire	Edgbaston	1898
127	Yorkshire	Hampshire	Southampton	1899
107*	MCC	Oxford University	Lord's	1902
126	Yorkshire	Surrey	The Oval	1902
100*	Yorkshire	Leicestershire	Bradford	1904

Bibliography

Ainger, A.C., *Memories of Eton Sixty Years Ago* (John Murray, 1917)

Altham, H.S., *A History of Cricket* (Allen & Unwin, 1926)

Ashley-Cooper, F.S. *Eton v. Harrow at the Wicket* (St James's Press, 1922)

Bailey, P., Thorn, P. and Wynne-Thomas, P., *The Who's Who of Cricketers* (Newnes Books in association with The Association of Cricket Statisticians, 1984)

Beldam, G.W. and Fry, C.B., *Great Batsmen: Their Methods at a Glance* (Macmillan, 1905)
Great Bowlers and Fielders: Their Methods at a Glance (Macmillan, 1907)

Betham, J.D., *Oxford and Cambridge Cricket Scores and Biographies* (Simpkin, Marshall, 1905)

Bettesworth, W.A., *Chats on the Cricket Field* (Merritt and Hatcher 1910)

Bowes, W.E., *Express Deliveries* (Stanley Paul, 1949)

Brodribb, G., *The Croucher* (London Magazine Editions, 1974)

Coldham, James D., *Lord Harris* (Allen & Unwin, 1983)

Coldham, James P., *F.S. Jackson* (The Crowood Press, 1989)

'Country Vicar, A', *Cricket Memories* (Methuen, 1933);
The Happy Cricketer (Frederick Muller, 1946)

Darwin, Bernard, *W.G. Grace* (Duckworth, 1934)

Down, M., *Archie: A Biography of A.C. MacLaren* (Allen & Unwin, 1981)

Ellis, C., *C.B.: The Life of Charles Burgess Fry* (J.M. Dent and Sons Ltd, 1984)

Ford, W.J., *A History of the Cambridge University Cricket Club: 1820–1901* (William Blackwood, 1902)

Frindall, W., *The Wisden Book of Test Cricket : 1876–77 to 1977–78* (Macdonald and Janes, 1978)

Fry, C.B., *Life Worth Living* (Eyre & Spottiswoode, 1939)

Gibson, A., *Jackson's Year* (Cassell, 1965)
The Cricket Captains of England (Cassell, 1979)

Gordon, Sir Home (ed.), *Eton v. Harrow at Lord's* (Williams and Norgate, 1926)

Gordon, Sir Home, *Background of Cricket* (Arthur Barker, 1939)

Hawke, Lord, *Recollections and Reminiscences* (Williams and Norgate, 1924)

Haygarth, A., *Cricket Scores and Biographies, Volume XIV* (Longman and Co., 1895)

Hill, A., *A Chain of Spin Wizards* (Kennedy Brothers Publishing, 1983)

Holmes, Revd. R.S., *The History of Yorkshire County Cricket : 1833–1903* (Constable, 1904)

Jessop, G.L., *A Cricketer's Log* (Hodder & Stoughton, 1922)

Kilburn, J.M., *The Scarborough Cricket Festival* (The Yorkdale Press, 1948)

   History of Yorkshire County Cricket, 1924–1949 (Chorley and Pickersgill, 1950)

   A History of Yorkshire Cricket (Stanley Paul, 1970)

Leveson-Gower, H.D.G., *Cricket Personalities* (Williams and Norgate, 1925)

Lewis, A.R., *Double Century* (Hodder & Stoughton, 1987)

Lyttelton, Hon. R.H.L., *The Crisis in Cricket and the Leg Before Rule* (Longmans, Green & Co., 1928)

MacLaren, A.C., *Cricket Old and New* (Longmans, Green and Co., 1924)

Martin-Jenkins, C., *The Complete Who's Who of Test Cricketers* (Orbis, 1987)

Midwinter, E., *W.G. Grace: His Life and Times* (Allen & Unwin, 1981)

Morrah, P., *The Golden Age of Cricket* (Eyre and Spottiswoode, 1967)

Parkin, C.H., *Cricket Triumphs and Troubles* (C. Nicholls, 1936)

Pullin, A.W., *History of Yorkshire County Cricket: 1903–1923* (Chorley and Pickersgill, 1924)

Pollard, J., *Australian Cricket: The Game and its Players* (Hodder & Stoughton, 1982)

Ranjitsinhji, K.S., *The Jubilee Book of Cricket* (William Blackwood, 1897)

Robertson-Glasgow, R.C., *Rain Stopped Play* (Dobson, 1948)

   Cricket Prints (Laurie, 1948)

   All in the Game (Dobson, 1952)

Roberts, E.L., *Yorkshire's 22 Championships: 1893–1946* (Edward Arnold, 1949)

Rogerson, S., *Wilfred Rhodes* (Hollis and Carter, 1960)

Ross, A., *Ranji: Prince of Cricketers* (Collins, 1983)

Sewell, E.H.D., *Well Hit Sir!* (Stanley Paul, 1947)

Standing, P.C., *The Honourable F.S. Jackson* (Cassell, 1906)

Stevenson, M., *A History of County Cricket: Yorkshire* (Arthur Barker, 1972)

Thomas, P., *Yorkshire Cricketers: 1839–1939* (Derek Hodgson, 1973)

Thomson, A.A., *Odd Men In* (Museum Press, 1958)
  Rhodes and Hirst (Epworth Press, 1959)
  Cricket: The Golden Ages (Stanley Paul, 1961)
  Cricket: The Great Captains (Stanley Paul, 1965)
  Cricket: The Wars of the Roses (Pelham Books, 1967)

Warner, Sir Pelham, *Cricket in Many Climes* (Heinemann, 1900)
  Cricket Across the Seas (Longmans, Green and Co., 1903)
  Cricket Reminiscences (Grant Richards, 1920)
  My Cricketing Life (Hodder & Stoughton, 1921)
  The Book of Cricket (Dent, 1922)
  Lord's: 1787–1945 (Harrap, 1946)
  Gentlemen v. Players: 1806–1949 (Harrap, 1950)
  Long Innings (Harrap, 1951)

Webber, R., *The County Cricket Championship* (Phoenix Sports Books, 1957)

Wild, R., *The Biography of His Highness S.S. Ranjitsinhji* (Rich and Cowan, 1934)

Woods, S.M.J., *My Reminiscences* (Chapman and Hall, 1925)

Papers, Periodicals, Annuals

Ayres' Cricket Companion
Cricket: A Weekly Record of the Game
The Cricket Field
The Cricketer
James Lillywhite's Cricketers' Annual
James Lillywhite's Cricketers' Companion
The Sheffield Daily Telegraph
The Strand Magazine
Vanity Fair
Wisden's Cricketers' Almanack
The Yorkshire Post

Index